You *Can* Teach Your Child Successfully

Grades 4 to 8

Ruth Beechick

arrow press

Arrow Press—Pollock Pines CA 95726
Distributor: 8825 Blue Mountain Dr., Golden CO 80403

Library of Congress catalog card number: 88-20014

Cover art by: MDC Publishing Services, Brunswick, Ohio.

© 1988, 1993 by Arrow Press.

Printed in the United States of America.

ISBN 0-940319-05-5

Table of Contents

List of Charts

Letter to Teaching Parents

I meet teaching parents all around the country and find them to be intelligent, enthusiastic, creative people doing a marvelous job of teaching their children. But, sad to say, most of them do not know what a great job they are doing. Everyone thinks it goes smoothly in everyone else's house and theirs is the only place that has problems.

I'll let you in on a secret about teaching: there is no place in the world where it rolls along smoothly without problems. Only in articles and books can that happen.

You parents naturally know how to relate to each of your children and to help them learn. Your biggest problem is that so many of you are afraid that teachers or society or somebody out there will frown on your way of teaching. You feel safer if you stick closely to a book or series of books, because that is somebody else's plan, that is in print, that must be right.

For some children and for some of the time, certain books will happen to be just right. But if you find yourself struggling to mold your child to a book, try reversing priorities. It's the child you are teaching, not the book. Bend the book, or find another; make the studies fit the child.

Bend this book, also, to fit your needs of the moment. Take it in any order you like. The last chapter makes just as good a starting point as the first. And when you come to lists or other items you don't need very soon, skip them. You will know they are there for reference when the time comes.

For those of you who have not had college teacher courses, I hope this book will give you the confidence to talk "education" with anybody you need to. From information here you could set yearly goals for most of the traditional subjects. Teaching methods and ideas are scattered throughout, as I like to place a method right beside the content it can be used with. But many methods can be used elsewhere too. For instance in the history chapter you will find a way to begin a unit study, which your family could also use for a science unit. Or in the arithmetic section you will find some principles of review that work for any subject.

I hope that just reading or browsing through these chapters inspires you to let a wider variety of learning happen in your home. But I suggest that you make changes gradually. If you're going to try the individualized spelling system, for instance, you and your children need time to develop your plan and work out the bugs. So you probably shouldn't be trying a new system in too many other subjects at the same time.

Learning wasn't meant to be drudgery. Have fun!

Ruth Beechick

Part I: Reading

1. What Do You Do After Your Child Can Read?

The Information Stage of Reading

While children are learning to sound out words, we say they are in the **decoding stage** of reading. After they can use basic phonics, they need a year or two of easy reading which is called the **fluency stage.**

After decoding and after fluency comes a period of reading development that can be called the **information stage.** In this stage children need not concentrate so heavily on phonics and on reading a sentence smoothly. The mechanics of reading have become so easy that they now concentrate more on the content of reading. Children can use their reading skills to gain information from books, newspapers, labels, and other materials.

Some children breeze through phonics in a few weeks and become fluent readers with just a few months of practice. If your children learn like that, you may wonder what these stages are all about. You might want to name just two stages—1) learning to read and 2) reading. But many other children take more time in the early stages—so many children, in fact, that schools generally treat fourth grade as the beginning of the information stage. The content subjects of history, geography, and science are begun in earnest at fourth grade level, and these studies are more bookish than in primary grades.

In home tutoring, you don't need to worry much about grade levels; you just move along with your children. Permit a lot of overlap of fluency and information reading. In other words, don't say, "Now you're in the information stage, so you can't waste time anymore with those easy books." Let children continue to read easy books for both fun and information, and at the same time challenge them with more difficult books that stretch vocabulary and thinking.

The middle and junior high grades are years when many children read more than they ever have time to later in life. One homeschooling mother reports that her children read a book a day. Many report that they check out several library books every week and most of them get read. In "reading" families this takes little effort or push from parents. It just happens, like baseball or TV happens in other families

If yours is a reading family, you may want to push for a little more baseball or music or something else. If yours is not a reading family, you should push reading. In our society, reading is so important for a full and effective life that it must have a high priority in educating our children.

The information stage of reading is not yet the highest stage. It is well to keep in mind that at high school and college levels there are more advanced abilities, such as understanding others' points of view, reflecting upon complex issues, and evaluating writings according to well-thought-out standards. All our adult lives we grow in reading abilities, so don't fall into the trap of thinking that your children are through learning to read after they know enough phonics.

Your children will grow a lot during the information stage. You will see the growth by looking backward occasionally and thinking about what they can now read that they could not formerly read. Another way to get information about their progress is to use achievement tests.

What Can Test Scores Tell You?

If you understand just two statistical concepts, that will carry you a long way in a conference with testing people about your children's scores. The first of these is **grade level**. Grade levels are averages.

Thus if your child made a score of 8.2, that officially means he had as many right as the average student in grade 8, month 2 (10 months to a school year). Now if your child is beginning eighth grade, that's enough to know about the score. The official explanation is close to the picture of grade levels that most of us have. But if the child is starting fifth grade and scores that high, then you can't jump to the conclusion that he should be moved to the eighth grade. The child probably took a test for middle graders instead of a test for junior highers, and he scored high on it. Another way to state those results is to say that he scored on that test the same as the average of beginning eighth graders would score on that test. The junior high test has different content, and you don't really know what your child would score on it.

Why, then, is the score quoted as a grade level? Simply because that was chosen to be a unit of measure, something like inches on a ruler. Near the middle of a test range, the grade-level units work very well, and they are similar to our feeling of what grade levels should be, but on the low and high ends of the range, they don't work so well. They are simply statistical units of measure stretched out as far as anyone is able to score on the test. If your child happens to score very low or very high on a test, you could get a truer grade-level indication by retesting with another test on which he will come out closer to the middle.

Consider, also, that if your child is bright, you wouldn't want to move him into books where he could do only average level work. That's what would happen if the fifth grader in the example were moved into eighth grade books on the basis of his score. You might want to try moving him into sixth or seventh grade books, though, where he could continue to do above-average work, instead of confining him to fifth-grade books.

A second statistical concept to understand is **percentile rank**. This is not the same as percentages. If you see a score of 60, that does not mean the child got 60% of the items right, which is a rather low score according to our usual idea of percentage grades in school. Instead, it means that the child scored higher than 60% of other children in his grade. That puts him slightly above average, because average is 50. No one ever rates a percentile rank of 100, because you could not say a student scored higher than 100% of all students. The highest score on this kind of scale is 99.

Twenty percent, or one-fifth of all children in a grade, rank between the 40th and 59th percentiles. Half of all children rank between the 23rd and 76th percentiles. This large group can be lumped together and thought of as the average group of children. Those lower than 23 are below average and those higher than 76 are above average. This chart shows the normal distribution of percentile ranks. Notice how slightly over half of all children are in the large average group. And the number of children making certain scores thins out at both the low end and the high end of the scale. If this were plotted on a graph it would make the familiar bell-shaped curve—high in the middle and low on both ends.

Percentile Ranks	Percent of Children in Each Group
Below Average	
up to 4	4%
4 to 10	7%
11 to 22	12%

Average	
23 to 39	17%
40 to 59	20%
60 to 76	17%

Above Average	
77 to 88	12%
89 to 95	7%
above 95	4%

Once you have a grade-level score or percentile rank for your child, what do you do with it? If you are teaching at home because you want to avoid stress and competition with other children, then you must handle these scores carefully. By their very nature these scores compare your child with other children.

But you can let most children in on test scores and how they are interpreted. This is usually better than being secretive, as though test results are only for parents and teachers. On the profile page of your children's achievement tests they can easily see where their higher and lower scores are, and they can plan with you which scores they should try to raise before the next testing. The scores can be viewed something like golfing or bowling scores, and used for motivation.

In reading, study the subscores and see if there is one called "Vocabulary." On this section the tester usually reads aloud the words and the four answer choices. So your children's scores on this can be called their "reading capacity" score. If they understand words up to a certain level, they ought to be reading up to that level. See if a child's total reading score is as high as his vocabulary score. If it is not, that means he needs more phonics or other instruction on reading mechanics. If it is, then commend him for doing well on reading. With normal reading practice he will probably continue to advance at about the pace he is now moving.

If a subscore is not called "Vocabulary," try to find out which subsection was read orally during testing, and use that as the capacity score. This reading capacity idea is little known among teachers, being used mostly by a few reading specialists, so people may not understand what you are asking and you may have to figure it out on your own. But it is an extremely valuable piece of information to have.

Test companies obtain their scoring norms from all schools, public and private included. Some companies publish a separate set of norms for private schools only, and these are a bit higher, or tougher competition to meet. Private schools sometimes use these results to argue that they do a better job. But other educators argue that private schools have a more select group of students—those whose parents value academic success—and thus they should score higher. If a local private school uses achievement test results in their advertising, you have a truer picture if you understand that they are probably using the general norms unless they specifically say that they are using the private school norms.

What this all means for you as a homeschooler is that if your children are normally bright, and they score somewhat higher than grade level, that's what you should expect, because they too are in a select group. If any of your children have difficulty with academic work, then don't discourage them and pressure them to be average or anything that is beyond their capabilities. Tests should not be used as clubs in this way. Get from tests what information you can, use the information for planning and goal setting (We'd better do more science this year), but don't let anyone in your family get ulcers over them.

What Is Comprehension?

One subscore on reading tests is called "Comprehension," and that has caused so much confusion and so many questions from teaching parents, that it merits special attention here. Comprehension is a fuzzy that needs redefining in our time.

If you are thinking about leaving reading textbooks and using "real" books and other self-selected materials, it won't be long until someone says to you, "How will you teach comprehension?" This is not really a question; it's an accusation. "That's dangerous," your well-meaning friend implies. "The textbooks know how to teach comprehension, but all on your own, you don't." That thing called comprehension can intimidate you. If you can't answer your friends, you might retreat to textbooks again.

In the field of reading, it sometimes seemed that comprehension was a word in search of a meaning. Here was a word—a fine, upstanding, educational word. All it needed was a thing.

Educators valiantly attempted to describe this thing and break it down into teachable parts. Questions to see if children have these parts are in so many books that if you have ever been close to reading workbooks or reading tests, you have seen them. The questions determine whether the child can recognize facts or details in a paragraph, identify the main idea, understand cause and effect, know what is actually stated in a paragraph, know what may be inferred though not specifically stated, know whether it is real or fantasy, and other such skills.

Lesson plans were built around these parts of reading, tests were developed and, presumably, everybody was happy. Teachers could teach the thing called comprehension, publishers could make books, testers could test, parents could see numbers that prove their children know the thing, and legislators could feel that they spent money responsibly.

For several decades that industry rolled comfortably along, but then cracks began to appear in the system. Researcher Jeanne Chall in a very influential book of the sixties wrote that children spend so many years answering questions about the main idea, the details, and what caused what in short paragraphs that they come to believe that *is* reading. When such children are through with school, they are through with reading. (*Learning to Read: The Great Debate*, McGraw-Hill, 1967.)

An achievement test company took a close computerized look at its questions on detail, main idea, causality, and so forth and found that they do not look like separate skills should look. A child who scores high on one type of question scores high on them all. And a child who scores average on one scores average on them all. In other words, the scores are so closely related that we have to assume there is one factor behind them all.

Others thinking about this problem have come to see that the most important factor in reading comprehension is what the reader brings to the book or passage. What's in the reader's head? Does he know enough about this subject and its vocabulary to understand what the passage is saying? If he does, then all the so-called skills fall into place. If he doesn't, then they don't.

It is not useful, then, to think of comprehension as a *part* of reading. It is better to view it as another word for reading, better to take the wholistic view.

A Wholistic View of Reading

With this commonsense view of comprehension, you need not be intimidated when people talk about this fuzzy. If you have already guided your child through the decoding stage and the fluency stage, you found natural ways to assure yourself that the child understood. When your daughter first wrote her name and proudly showed it off to whoever was nearby, you had no doubt that she knew whose name it was. When she laughed or commented or remembered something the next day after reading it, you knew she understood. When you talked with her about a new idea, you helped her understand. There are no elusive pieces and parts to call comprehension that can't just as well be called reading.

As we have said, the single most important factor in understanding any particular reading selection is what a child brings to it. Is the child interested and attentive? Does he know enough vocabulary and concepts to enable him to understand the selection he is going to read? Is he mature enough mentally to think about ideas presented in the selection?

If all the above are not on "Go," the child is not likely to understand the selection well, and teaching him how to recognize causality, and other such skills, will not help him read it better. What will help is to give the child more to bring to the selection. If it is not way over his head but almost a Go, you can make it a Go by some comments or questions that raise interest in the topic if that is what is needed, or by preteaching some of the difficult vocabulary and ideas if that is needed.

Notice the not-so-subtle change of technique. In this wholistic view, your teaching, questions, and discussions with the student center upon the content of the reading, not on those elusive skills. Is the child reading about ancient Egypt? Then he needs to know how to pronounce Menes, Thebes, and Pharaoh. He needs to know that *Pharaoh* was the title for a ruler, and that *dynasty* refers to a succession of rulers in the same family. Is he reading the directions for doing long division? Then he needs to know which numbers are the divisor, the dividend, and the quotient.

This technique of focusing on content has the double effect of helping children learn the subject matter at hand and also helping them grow in reading ability. When children have good understanding of what a passage is saying, they can figure out the main idea, the supporting details, whether it is fact or fiction, and so on. Skills in these grow together, not separately.

Types of content can be grouped into three major categories, and your children should get experience in all three, because skills gained in one kind of reading do not necessarily carry over into the other kinds. Reading in nonfiction and textbooks, such as geography, science, or arithmetic, is one kind. Literature—both prose and poetry—is a second kind. And daily life reading of directions, signs, advertisements, labels, and so forth is the third kind. The three kinds can be called:

1. Textual reading
2. Imaginational reading
3. Functional reading.

A closer look at each of these categories follows in the next three chapters.

2. Textual Reading

The biology teacher complains, "Why doesn't the reading teacher teach these students to read?" The reading teacher responds, "Every teacher must be a reading teacher." "But I have enough of a job teaching biology," retorts the first. "I can't be bothered teaching reading too."

Though the subject specialists may at times have legitimate gripes, the reading teacher is closer to a good solution to the problems. To teach a student to read a biology book is to teach him biology. Is that the job of the biology teacher or the reading teacher?

Some reading teachers give teen-age students directions that go something like this: "When you sign up for a course, get the textbook as soon as you can and start learning all the words in the glossary or index. Put each word you don't know on one side of a card and put information about it on the reverse side. Write the page numbers where the word is found, look on those pages, figure out what the word means, and write the meaning. Carry the cards around with you and drill yourself until you know them."

Students who do this find that they not only learn how to read the textbook, they also complete half or more of their learning for the course—before the course even begins. Vocabulary and subject learning grow together.

Some Sunday school teachers have learned this principle. Instead of waiting for the fourth grade teacher or the seventh grade teacher or somebody out there to teach children how to read the Bible, they get busy themselves teaching the specialized vocabulary that children need.

Vocabulary

When the teen-age students make their vocabulary cards and review them, in which direction does their learning proceed? Are they learning words which will in turn help them learn the subject? Or are they learning something about the subject so they can learn the words? Both. The two processes are so intertwined that they cannot be separated. Learning expands vocabulary, and a wide vocabulary helps a person expand his learning.

How do you teach a new word to your child? First of all, you put enough context around it to make it memorable. Memorizing a definition is usually a poor way to do this. Let's say you are teaching the word *compass* in its meaning of "an instrument for showing direction by a swinging magnetic needle pointing north." A child who doesn't know what a compass is will still not know much about a compass after he learns the definition. Will he picture a needle like his mother sews with? Will he picture something swinging like a pendulum or like a baseball bat? He may have an inkling of the purpose of a compass, but no understanding of how or why it works or who it might be useful to. The bare, unadorned meaning he gets, whether more wrong or more right, certainly is not easy to remember, and especially so if this is just one in a list of words he is learning out of their natural context.

To enrich that meaning you could show the child a compass and let him play with it awhile, watching the swinging needle and observing what it does when he turns in different directions. You could also teach a little about the earth's magnetic pole, finding it on a globe, relating its location to the true north pole. You might stop with that, but if the topic of study happens to be magnetism, the child could go on to learn such things as magnetic forces and which metals can be magnetized, thus understanding still more about why the compass acts as it does. But if the topic is how to find your way in the woods, you probably won't be so scientific about it—at least now.

This rich context makes the word easier to remember. During that learning the child heard the word and spoke it several times. Perhaps he also read it and wrote it. If you talk about it later that day and again the next day, you reinforce the word with review. All in all, a child—or any of us—must meet a word fifteen times or so before it becomes a part of our speaking vocabulary.

Fewer meetings may make it part of the child's recognition vocabulary. That is, he may recognize the word *compass* when he meets it in a story, and he may remember that it is some kind of gadget for finding your way, but he is not yet friendly enough with the word to use it in his own conversation.

While you teach a few words in this manner, seeing that your child meets them at least fifteen times, your silent assistants—books—can be teaching hundreds of new words. This is one advantage of supplementing textbooks with library books. In a science textbook, your child may struggle with two or three pages of difficult, condensed information about magnetism, and meet some of the new words only a few times. But if he also reads easy books on the same topic, he reads many pages and thus meets the words more times. If you talk with him about the topic, you help him to meet the words even more times. And if he writes about it, that helps too.

Knowing the vocabulary and ideas helps children read better, and that reading, in turn, builds knowledge of vocabulary and ideas. It is a two-way street. Thus, to help your children be good readers in textbooks and other nonfiction books, you need to see that they understand enough of the vocabulary and ideas before they start. That's just another way of saying that the material should not be over their heads. And when it's not over their heads there's no big problem about comprehension. They will comprehend the material at hand and gradually move on to comprehending more and more difficult material.

No one has found a workable way to cram vocabulary and verbal knowledge. When students try to cram for college entrance exams, they have better success brushing up on math than on vocabulary. Vocabulary builds in the thorough ways hinted at in the compass example, and with each passing year your child grows a wider knowledge and vocabulary to bring to his reading of textual material.

Study Techniques

The preceding section on vocabulary reinforced the stated principle that "the single most important factor in understanding any particular reading selection is what children bring to it." Now, this section on study techniques will underscore the principle still more strongly.

Children must bring to their reading a mind-set of attention and inquiry. They must expect the selection to tell something and they must be ready to receive that something.

If a teacher says, "Read chapter 4," and children read chapter 4 with their minds on the next ball game or slumber party, they will get little or nothing from the reading. In fact, that probably shouldn't be called reading. But if a child has become curious about why the compass works, he may read a chapter about magnetism with his mind fully set to find answers.

Thus, as teacher, you can learn to take advantage of

children's interests as they show themselves, and by this means manage to get a lot of learning in science, history, and other content areas. Following up on interests works in varying degrees, and differently with different children, so that it's a nice trick to know, but few adults want to trust a child's whole education to this technique.

So what do you do when you must teach something and a child doesn't happen to be very interested? One approach is to teach children themselves about bringing the proper mind-set to their studies. Teachers through the ages have threatened with punishment and enticed with rewards to get children to study something, but these coercive means work only partially and only as long as there is a teacher to do such disciplining. Ultimately, children need an inner discipline if they are to become good learners.

Teach your children that it doesn't do much good to passively read a textbook or other study material. They must set their minds to learn something from the reading. They need to know ahead of time what a chapter or shorter passage is going to tell them. They should know what important ideas are in the passage or what questions it will answer.

When you began reading this section with its heading called "Study Techniques," you probably made a little turn in the setting of your mind. Perhaps you noticed that the "Vocabulary" topic was finished for now, and you were going to see what this author has to say about study techniques. If your level of interest in this topic happens to be high, you may have noticed the turning point more than some other readers. You may even have raised a question of your own. Perhaps, without putting it in words, you are looking for a concrete, clear formula for teaching study techniques to yourself or to your child, and you're still reading along looking for it. (Formulas are coming; hang on.) Or your question may have been along a different line. Some readers, no doubt, are thinking, "I do pretty well with my study techniques; I wonder whether this author agrees with me "

With such thoughts, you as reader are in a sense carrying on a conversation with the writer. In these conversations you can compare experiences and beliefs, you can disagree and argue, you can agree and rejoice that someone has put into print what seems right to you, and so on. Your mind reflects upon the reading from any and all angles you choose. This is called by some reading teachers *reflective reading*.

Your children in middle and junior high grades will experience some measure of reflective reading, but they probably are not ready for much of that yet. They are now in the information stage of reading. This means they must learn well how to gain information from study materials, and they must spend several years of their lives doing just that. They cannot compare, evaluate, make decisions, or do other kinds of reflective thinking at a very high level until they have a good background of information to use for reflections.

In teaching children to read actively and not passively, one simple technique is to have them read first any questions they must answer. In many study materials the reading selection comes first and the questions follow; so conscientious students proceed in exactly that order. They read with a vague idea that they must get it all because some questions are coming up. But it's not cheating, it is simply good technique, for students to read the questions first and see what the author thinks is important to learn from the passage. Then with a mind-set to look for those ideas or facts, they can read. If the author has formed the questions well, students will have in advance an "organizer" for their reading and thinking. That is, they know ahead of time what to do with details that they read. They can organize them in ways that will answer the questions. They can think, "Ah, when I'm finished I have to give reasons why food enters the blood from the intestines and not from the stomach." Then while they read they can select details and line them up— organize them —to be ready for answering.

If a selection has no questions, have your child read any

titles or headings and ask, "What do you expect to find out?" As the child answers your question, he is forming an organizer for himself. Sometimes an appropriate question is, "What do you want to find out?" If the student is making a poster or model of the solar system, he needs to know sizes, distances, and relative positions of the planets, and he can skip over material that tells who discovered a planet or other information that he doesn't need for this particular project.

From research it appears that bright students profit more from having organizers in advance. Slower students may need to understand various details first and then pull them together into a meaningful concept.

After the organizer and after the reading, a good student is not yet through. He now must see if he can answer the question or questions he set for himself. If he is working with you, you may want him to look up from the book and give you the best answer he can. Then you may have him look at the selection again to find some missed details and give a fuller answer. If he is working by himself, he may check the book quickly before writing his answer.

One formula sometimes taught for helping students to remember the above procedure is SQ3R. Read that: "S, Q, three R." The *S* is to remind students to survey the material before they read, to look it over and see how long it is, what the headings are, and so forth. The *Q* is to remind them to ask one or more questions. They either get these questions from the book or make them up themselves. The three *R*'s stand for read, recite, review; students read, they recite what they learned, and they review the material to check on their recitation and adjust it if necessary.

The full formula in exactly that form does not necessarily fit every textual reading task, but the general plan will work almost universally. For instance, sometimes the questions may already be asked even before the reading selection is located. A child making a solar system model already has questions about the positions and names of the planets, so he finds a book and surveys it to see if it is likely to have the information he needs. Thus the SQ is switched to QS; the question is asked first. But the general plan of setting a purpose for reading is still there. A child making a terrarium may review the directions many times during his work to see that he is not forgetting anything, but the general plan of checking on his learning is still there. The last two R's could be summed up in one R—reinforcement. When students use the information or review it in any way they strengthen their learning of it.

Review has a broader use than just a quick review after one reading selection. If the material is something a student must remember for a test or for studying future topics, then more reviews spaced out over time are needed to set the learning more permanently. One of the most effective ways for the students to reinforce their learning is to discuss things with you, or with other older people. Older students and adults think on higher levels; thus, such conversations stretch younger students' thinking.

This five-step formula is included here because many reading teachers know it and you may wish to know it too. But I prefer to condense this into a simpler three-step formula. The steps consist of the reading itself and what comes before it and after it. Before, students should get their minds ready by bringing their curiosity and attention to the task, by surveying and raising questions, and any other useful means. They should read with concentration. Then, to digest new learning, they should reinforce by some means, including: recite to themselves or to you, discuss, answer questions, review the pages. This simplified formula consists of three R's.

1. Get Ready
2. Read
3. Reinforce.

A subversive word about studying from textbooks:

When there are difficulties, the problem may not lie entirely with your child. It may, instead, lie with the book. Educators writing in their professional journals have lately taken to discussing the poorly written textbooks. Those of us who hated history books in school wonder why it has taken them so long to find this out. History books in the real world are fascinating to read, and some parents are learning to supplement and even to replace dull textbooks with the live kind of books.

Reading Speed

Another important study technique is to have varied reading speeds and to use the speed appropriate for each task. Thus the child making the solar system poster can skim through a book or encyclopedia article and stop to read carefully when he comes to figures that look like they might be sizes or distances that he needs. The child reading about the digestive system can adjust according to his purpose. Is he already quite familiar with digestion and does he just need additional information about absorption of nutrients into the blood? If so, he may read rapidly over parts of his selection and more carefully when he comes to what will provide the answer he must write down. Or is most of the material new to him so that he needs to think and make mental images and try to get everything learned as he reads along? If so, he should go slowly and allow himself thinking time.

Children who work hard on decoding for a long time become used to carefully pronouncing every word, and if they are continually pushed ahead to more difficult reading, they always carefully pronounce every word, if not aloud, then at least mentally, and rapid reading is an upstream struggle. These children need plenty of time in the fluency stage. That is, they should be allowed to read lots of easy material for a year or two until they can read well without even thinking about sounds and pronunciation. Children who easily learned to decode usually do not have much trouble with fast reading.

Why read fast? Many people have taken speed reading courses and then said, "I don't like to speedread. I like to savor my reading, enjoying it fully as I go along." That is a valid comment for recreational reading, but not so valid for textual reading. In reading text material all speeds are needed—the "savoring" kind, an even slower kind where the reader stops often to think things through in his own mind, and various fast kinds. The speed of reading should match its purpose.

To learn about speeds and where to use them, you don't need to spend $395 on a speed reading course. All you need is a few hints on how to practice and some motivation to do so. If your job requires you to skim down lists of names searching for one or two particular ones, you can learn to do that. One secretary used to read such lists name by name until she came to a name she needed, but when she heard about skim reading, she practiced moving her eyes down the lists rapidly, concentrating on the look of a particular name. After only a few practices she could find names quickly. One day she and her boss together looked at a list of names and while the boss was on about the third name, mentally pronouncing each one, the secretary said, "Here it is," and pointed halfway down the list. "How did you find it so fast?" he asked. "It's skim reading," she replied. And for a long time he believed she had a rare, magic skill that ordinary people do not have.

Children of school age who are good readers can catch on to speed reading more easily than most adults, because children have fewer years of word-by-word reading behind them to form slow habits which are hard to overcome. Your children can develop their own techniques for fast reading if you just think up a way to push them.

A grandfather tells how he learned to speedread. As a child he had the job of bringing in the evening paper for his father. The paper in those days ran a story in serial form and the boy became interested in the story, but he had to see what happened in each day's installment during the short time it took to walk from the road to the house, because dawdling would have upset his father. To this day he can read rapidly because of the skills he learned while walking along the path to his house.

Reading at the speed of speech means 200 to 300 words per minute. Most people can easily double that speed for silent reading, and some can double again for a speed in the range of 800 to 1200. Speeds beyond that are sometimes advertised as attainable, and a few people find them useful in their work. For instance, a person who has to read mountains of reports each day learns to go over the material at high speed and see what the reports say without reading in the sense of moving word-by-word or phrase-by-phrase along the lines of print. Instead, their eyes roam the pages picking up ideas from whole paragraphs and pages.

It is important not to equate speed reading with speed learning, as advertisements sometimes imply. The plodder who reflects while he reads is just as likely to invent or discover or make some other important contribution to society as is the speeder who takes in information rapidly. What goes on in the brain and what the reader does with information are important considerations too. Speed of reading the information is only one facet of learning.

So, although it's not the route to genius, students will find their lives easier if they can learn to read easy material at a speed of 500 to 900 words per minute. A simple way to raise the child's awareness of this skill is to have two or three (separate) minutes of timed reading each day for a while. Have the child mark his place in a book of his choice, and when you say "Go," he begins reading. You time an exact minute and then say "Stop," and the child counts how many words he read. Give him a second and a third try and have him date and save his scores. A few days, or a few weeks, of this practice allows the child time to experiment with his techniques, and probably he will increase his speed considerably just because he is writing his scores and trying to beat them. After his speeds are higher, you can add the feature of asking a question or two about what he reads during the minute. Emphasize this just enough so he won't speed unreasonably fast without getting the content.

After some success with the one-minute practices, move on to longer passages. It's handy if you find a book of reading selections that have the words already counted and questions already made at the end. But if you don't have one, you can improvise. Find a textbook or reading workbook that has selections followed by questions. The length should be what your child can read in less than five minutes at first and less than ten minutes later. Remember that speed reading takes high concentration and should be practiced in short spurts. The book should be about two grade levels below where your child is reading in his other study materials. For example, an average fifth grader should practice speed reading with third grade books. A fifth grader who scores at sixth grade on reading tests should practice from fourth grade books.

To find the number of words in each selection, count the words on one page of the book and assume that other full pages have the same number. For partial pages, divide that number by the number of lines to get an average word-per-line figure. With your line figure and your page figure you can save time counting the total words in any selection in the book.

If you are unable to find a book with handy questions, you can improvise even further by using any book. After the child reads the chapter or section and records his time, he hands you the book and you ask questions about the material he just read. (While skimming it and thinking up questions on the spot, you will be increasing your own speed.) The child should strive for about 80% accuracy on the questions. That is, he shouldn't feel badly if he doesn't get a perfect score on questions, but he should not miss much. On five questions, 80% is four right. On ten questions, 80% is eight right.

While trying to get most of the content, the child should also strive to increase his speed. To calculate the words per minute, divide the total words by the time. That is easy to do if the time is 4 minutes or 5 minutes or any full number, but it gets tricky when you have fractional parts of a minute. With older children you may use this as a learning activity for practicing decimal fractions, or you may forget about being exact, and round off the time to the nearest quarter minute as in the table below.

15 seconds = .25 of a minute
30 seconds = .50 of a minute
45 seconds = .75 of a minute

For simplicity, you may dispense with fractions and divide by the number of full minutes that pass while the child reads. Give him the extra seconds "free." On two- or three-minute selections this method may occasionally give too high a speed, but when the child advances to longer selections, it is accurate enough for your teaching purposes.

Have each child keep a chart which shows both his speed and his accuracy. The speed is the number of words per minute and the accuracy is the percent of questions correct. It may only take a few weeks for the chart to show that he improved at first quite rapidly and then leveled off. At that point you may suspend the practice sessions, and plan to repeat them again next semester or next year. The next time, improvement probably won't be so dramatic, but the practice will help the children keep their skills sharpened.

Teach your children that fast reading is for easy material. When textbooks describe something new and complex, and when the facts and ideas are jammed close together, they need to read slowly and carefully in order to understand. While people can read at any and all speeds, depending upon purpose, your children may think of using these three kinds of speeds:

1. Slow: to read difficult study material
2. Fast: to read easy factual material
3. Skim: to find something specific in any material.

When students can tackle textbooks with a variety of techniques, they also are well prepared to meet achievement tests and college entrance exams. Explain that in tests they can take more shortcuts than in daily study, because the only purpose in a test is to get the questions answered. Thus they can read the questions first, as in study, then use fast reading to find the answers in the reading selection. As soon as they find the answers, they should move on to the next item, even if they haven't finished reading that one. If they finish before time is up, they should spend the remaining time reading some of the items more carefully to check their answers.

Graphic Materials

You should spend some time now and then teaching your children how to read graphs, diagrams, charts, lists, and maps found in textbooks and elsewhere. Take advantage of these when they happen to be in materials children are studying, and look for other situations too. You can find graphs in newspapers and magazines, and if you use those to teach graph reading, you will at the same time be teaching a little current events or economics or other content.

To read **graphs**, students need to understand what is on the horizontal axis, usually labeled at the bottom, and what is on the vertical axis, usually labeled at the left side. Then they need to know how to read the bars or lines or pictures in relation to those axes. After your children become familiar with graphs, teach how they can be skewed to make a trend look more shocking or more mild. Simply spacing the lines differently can make a trend look more or less steep, as in the examples on the following page.

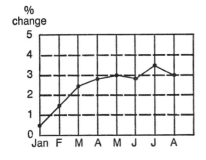
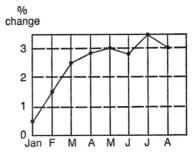

Changing the unit on either axis also would change the look of the graphs. For instance, if units at the bottom of these graphs were 1 year instead of 1 month, the rise might look more steep.

Still other means can be used by a writer or propagandist who wants to sway people's minds toward a particular opinion. Tricky maneuvers can be made with percents. Good graph readers must ask questions like: Percent of *what*? In the above graph, where does the March figure of 2½% come from? Is this 2½ % higher than February's total sales or inflation or whatever? If so, this is a way of making a large rise look small. Is it 2½% of the 1% rise during February? If so, this is a way of making a small rise appear large.

When you hear percentage figures in the news, often the base is missing or misleading. Recent figures showed that auto sales were up this year by a significant percentage, and some news reports indicated that was a sign of a strengthening economy. But one analyst said, no, you can't interpret it that way, because last year's sales were down drastically. You get a better picture of the trend, he said, by comparing this year's sales with those of two years ago.

Readers get more out of graphs and other statistics if they have more knowledge to put into them. This principle may be easier to see with graphs, but it is just as true with all of reading.

It is important that children have experience making graphs as well as reading them, and your arithmetic textbooks probably provide for that. When you teach about graphs you may feel you are teaching arithmetic or science or something else, and you are. All subjects overlap with reading. That is the essence of the wholistic approach to reading.

Diagrams and **pictures** are usually easier to understand than graphs. When you bump into one in a science book or wherever, teach your child how to read it. Try sitting with your child, closely scrutinizing it and asking questions to get him to notice more details. Stretch his thinking so that he can draw more meaning and make appropriate inferences. A few such sessions will greatly increase his awareness of, and his ability to learn from, diagrams and pictures.

Charts and **lists** also are not very difficult to understand, and often children catch on to them with no special help. But some lists, such as tables of contents, are so important that you should make sure your children know how to use them. Some books have lists of illustrations on one of the front pages that children can learn to read as easily as a table of contents. Glossaries and indexes in the back of books take a bit more teaching. Help your children toward the habit of using these routinely in their studies and their reading of nonfiction books.

Maps are perhaps the most complex of the graphic reading materials. Science, geography, math, and reading all are involved. You will need to work on map reading a number of times each year of a child's school life. He will gain more advanced understanding each year.

At first children must begin learning that a map represents some portion of reality. This understanding grows slowly. In primary grades children may have drawn and learned to read maps of their own houses or neighborhoods. Then they may have had some practice in locating places on a globe or flat map.

When your child has a few such skills, don't be fooled into thinking that his understanding of these places or distances are anything like yours, because those understandings grow slowly too. It takes a lot of driving or flying or mountain climbing and a lot of crossing of deserts, rivers, plains, and lakes to build the mental images and space relations that help us understand a physical map of the United States. The political features of states, counties, and capitals take a lot more learning. And the mathematical features of longitude, latitude, and scale of miles take still more.

Pictures and explanations in books must substitute for much of the traveling and first-hand experience, but use experience whenever you can in your teaching. Use maps on your highway trips and camping and fishing trips. Use maps when planning a vacation or reviewing it afterward.

Also use maps frequently in studies of history, missionaries, and current events. Maps are sometimes thought of as visual aids that help to make a Bible story or other learning "come alive," but the reverse is more probably true: the story helps to make a spot on the map come alive. In any case, map reading is complex and children need repeated practice with maps during their school years.

Hang maps on a north wall if at all possible. Spend time helping your children get the "feel" of directions, first near the map, and later in various locations outside. Have them face the map (on a north wall) and ask which direction is behind them, which is on their left, and which is on their right. Ask in which direction the Pacific Ocean is, the Atlantic Ocean, and other places they know, including some near places such as the shopping mall or a friend's house. Later, extend this learning from other locations: Those are the Rocky Mountains west of us; can you figure out north and all the other directions? When you are by a local river or on the shore of a Great Lake or any such landmark, do the same. Help each child get a map in his head.

Also, work on telling directions by the sun. Though it rises generally in the east and sets generally in the west, it also is somewhat south (if you live in the northern hemisphere), more so the farther north you live. Getting the feel of the sun in relation to the earth will help children to understand better the equator, the Tropics of Cancer and Capricorn, and the Arctic and Antarctic Circles. These are confusing even for many adults who memorized these terms in school. Some people tend to think of them concretely, for instance believing that above the Arctic Circle there are six months of darkness, instead of understanding how the length of the dark winter increases gradually as you go farther north from the Arctic Circle.

These difficult concepts provide a good example of why memorizing definitions is not enough. If you want your children to be thinkers, you must spend time helping them think about matters like these. Reading and thinking are inseparable.

Summary of Textual Reading

In this chapter on textual reading we have noted that the single most important factor in comprehending a reading passage is what children bring to it, their attitude as well as knowledge of the subject and its vocabulary. Students can improve their learning by: 1) getting ready to read, 2) reading with concentration, and 3) reinforcing. They can be more efficient by learning to use various speeds according to their reading purposes. And they can gain more reading power by studying a variety of content. This power consists of the added knowledge and thinking ability children gain to take to their next reading.

It helps if you are aware of the complexity of thinking and of the time it takes to understand concepts such as those needed for map reading. Don't expect instant learning. Have patience and think along with your children.

You can teach textual reading best by actually *doing* it in textbooks and other nonfiction books of science, history, and so on, not by teaching *about* it in reading books. You must use a variety of content, because vocabulary and concepts which help children read easily in biology, for example, are not what they need for reading about music. There is limited carryover of reading ability from one kind of content to another.

From the academic standpoint, learning to read textual material is more important than anything else for our children. Without this ability students lack the means for getting an education; and with this ability they can become more educated every day.

3. Imaginational Reading

Imaginational literature includes fiction, poetry, and humor, and it takes a different set of skills than does textual reading or functional reading. We are not using the term *imaginational* to mean frivolous and fanciful. But with this word we refer to products of human imagination, imagination being the power of the mind to form images and ideas which are not actually present.

Why Include Fiction?

Every study that mankind undertakes, he wants to carry as far as his mind enables him. Thus, in the study of our English language, we are ultimately led to the study of its literature— and the literature of preceding cultures which nourished ours.

In the language of music, children begin with listening to and singing simple tunes, and playing tunes on easy instruments. Then they advance to more complex music, to harmony as well as melody, and ultimately to familiarity with the greatest music our culture possesses and to performing and creating music on as high a level as their imagination and skill allow them to. No one could either play music or create it without the power of imagination—the power to image in the mind that which does not yet exist.

In the language of mathematics, there are ideas which do not describe or match anything in the objective world (the world outside the human observer), but which exist only in the mind of man. These ideas may be written in a book, but that is only to communicate them to the minds of other men; they do not become part of the objective world by being put into a book.

In music, in mathematics, and in every other field of knowledge, our studies carry us into the subjective world of the human mind. And language is no exception. If we looked only at spelling and sentence structure and other elemental aspects that are largely objective and ignore meaning behind the words and sentences, we would have an anemic education indeed. The human mind wants to explore the possibilities of language just as much as it wants to explore the possibilities of sound and rhythm in music or color and form in art.

The arts, including literature, are sometimes called the "subjective" world of the human mind, while the sciences are the "objective" world. This is not always a neat division, because sciences have a way of becoming creative and subjective so that good scientists use all the kinds of thinking that good artists do. And the arts incorporate the objective world and objective thinking. But even though objective thinking and subjective thinking overlap with each other, we nevertheless find these terms a useful means of describing two kinds of thinking. Literature studies make much use of subjective thinking.

Once we have named two kinds of thinking, an old American habit is to begin arguing about which kind is better, which kind leads to truth, and so on. But this wastes energy. Certainly all powers of the mind are God-given, and we should use them—

not only those powers we think we can describe but those we don't know how to describe.

Thus we shouldn't say that only objective knowledge is true or that only subjective knowledge is true. The first is what modern scientists who do not believe in God might say, and the second is what Eastern religionists might say. It confuses our thinking if we substitute the meanings *true* and *false* for the words *objective* and *subjective*. Here is a true-false item to illustrate.

The sun rises in the east.   **T   F**

Does it? Subjectively, as we see it, that is what happens. And at some times and places in history, scientists thought it was so objectively, as well. But according to modern science explanations, the earth is the moving body that makes it appear to us that the sun "rises." This is an example of how objective knowledge may change during history.

If your mind is full of thinking about objective and subjective knowledge, you can't even answer the above item on the true-false level. You think, "Well, subjectively it appears to me that the sun rises in the east, so I can answer *T*. But on the other hand, the sun doesn't actually 'rise' at all, so maybe I should answer *F*."

In this example, the test maker probably wants us to answer *T*, ignoring the subjectivity of "rises," and focusing on the word "east." The vast majority of true-false items call for us to equate true with objective, like this. Our Western culture has given us long training in this kind of thinking but objectivity provides an incomplete platform for determining what truth is.

Literary fiction, then, should not be taught to children as the class of writings which is "not true." Libraries have it right when they use the terms fiction and nonfiction. These do not mean false and true. They come closer to meaning subjective and objective writings, or imaginational and textual, as we are using those terms in this book.

Fiction and poetry, as products of the mind, and thus

subjective, should be seen as simply that. It is humankind exploring our God-given gift of language and imaginative thought.

Language, in fact, has a claim to being a more human field of studies than any other. Theologians have written of the logos (word) as the image of God within us, and even unbelievers see that a major difference between man and the animals is language. Some scientists would like to discover that dolphins or monkeys or something else have thoughts and communication systems akin to man's, but, instead, there seems to be an unbridgeable gulf between animal and man. And the gulf is language.

Human children begin easily, as with music—learning words and, more importantly, the meaning and thoughts behind words. They graduate to sentences and longer communications. They move on to books wherein are stored the products of man's high use of the logos within him—along with many mediocre and useless and downright trashy products, which we will not consider here. Now if we allow children to read only words and thoughts about the objective world because we have defined those as "true," and we deny them the subjective world, the world of language itself, because it comes from within and we define it as "not true," then we may be denying them familiarity with what is most godlike about humankind. So let's give our children stories—and poems—the literary products of man's image-making abilities.

Stories and Children

Many of our best children's writers say they do not write for children; they simply write stories, and if children happen to like them, well and good. Children do happen to like writings that are first of all stories. When writings are preachings or moralizings or other kinds of lessons embedded into stories because we adults think lessons are more palatable that way, "story" usually suffers, and children know it. Children may not be able to analyze and explain why such stories have less effect on their hearts and souls, but at some deep level they know this anyway.

I recently opened a primary reader and became engrossed in a story of the kind you cannot put down until you finish the last page. I didn't notice that the words and sentence structure were planned for young children; my mind was caught up into meaning and thoughts behinds the words—the story level. "Ah," I said to myself, "a real story. They used to have these only in the last section of readers, labeled 'Old Tales' or 'Stories from Everywhere,' and you only got to read them the last month of school."

But my happiness for the children of today was deflated when I examined the teacher's manual and the questions and study suggestions for the story. Tiny children were supposed to analyze plot and characters and other matters more suitable for a teen-age or adult class in story writing. "They're robbing children of their childhood!" I exclaimed to myself. The magician, or illusionist, might as well demonstrate his paraphernalia and techniques so his audience will be more educated when they watch his show. The artist may as well remind us, "Don't get carried away, folks; it's really only oils and colors and brush strokes."

In our American frenzy for teaching everything earlier and earlier, we sometimes hang learning up by its toes, and this is certainly such a case. A good story speaks directly to the heart. It is communication at a deep level. It is language at a high level. If a teacher has to do something after children read the story, she might let the children talk about how they admire the boy for his bravery. They might consider how they would act in a similar situation, tell who they felt angry at, and who they loved. These heart matters get closer to what the author was trying to say to her readers.

But heart matters are subjective, and when learning is

upside down only objective matters seem to count as an education. So, little children learn to identify the protagonist and
antagonist, to find the point at which the plot reaches a climax,
and in other ways display their knowledge of the craft of story.
They learn *about* story in their heads instead of experiencing
story in their hearts.

We carry this forward in the adult world, too, where scholars
pursue literary criticism and other scholars pursue a criticism of
literary criticism, and so on. One thinker has proposed that the
whole system must come tumbling down, so we can start at the
beginning again. But our children can now start at the
beginning.

Let them have their childhoods. Let them enjoy stories
without turning each into an academic exercise.

Let them read books, too, without the requirement of "book
reports." Book reports as usually carried out are basically a
management system wherein teachers have the children help
them keep track of whether everyone has read a required
minimum of books. Reports are "proof" to a classroom teacher
or a correspondence school office of the books read. Homeschooling parents need no such proof. Teachers who love books
the most require book reports the least. After reading a marvelous book, to write, "The book is about . . ." or "The part I like
best . . ." is a tragic waste, says one teacher. It is like going to a
beautiful garden and smelling only one flower.

How can you choose books for your children to read? One of
the best ways is to have good books available and then let your
children do the choosing themselves. You can hand them books
you loved as a child or books recommended on someone's list,
but in the end, if a book is not right for a child at a particular time
in his life, or if it is too difficult to read, or if it does not interest
him; he will lay it down.

With threat of punishment you can force children to read, or
with promise of reward you can entice them to read, but neither
is necessary if the books are right to begin with. That is, if books

speak to children's hearts and emotions and stimulate their minds, and if they are not too hard to read, the best reward is the books themselves, and time to read them. Sometimes simple rewards can entice reluctant readers to get started and discover the better rewards inside books. Reading books or parts of books aloud as a family also helps. Reading to children should not stop suddenly when children complete the primary grades.

Some parents, with good intentions of teaching character, unwittingly cause children to be wary of reading. At a library they might say, "Now remember, if you take it you have to read it," or "You only read two books last week so you only get to take out two this week." Or at home they don't let a child quit on a book: "You have to learn to finish what you start."

If you tend to think like that, try seeing the character qualities in decisions like these: "This book is a waste of my time; I'd better try the next one," or "I'll take books by five different authors and see which I'd rather read; then next time I can get more books by that author."

We adults do not read thoroughly everything we start, but we make judgment calls at any time, deciding to quit or skim or whatever fits our purpose with a book. Rather than learning to finish whatever they start, children would be better off learning the principles which Francis Bacon wrote long ago.

> Some books are to be tasted, others to be swallowed, and some few to be chewed and digested; that is, some books are to be read only in parts; others to be read but not curiously; and some few to be read wholly, and with diligence and attention. Some books also may be read by deputy, and extracts made of them by others.

What about book lists? In my office I have lists of Newbery medal winners, of junior discussion books for the Great Books Foundation, literature professors' lists, school districts' recommended reading lists, a university list of "Children's Books Too Good to Miss," librarians' lists of books of the year selected by children in this state, and lists by Christian authors for Christian children. But I think it will serve no good purpose to reproduce a list here for you. Every list differs, and the choices depend upon who made the list.

Anthologies collected into literature books present somewhat the same problem, in that every editor or committee chooses differently than every other editor or committee. One aggressive editor wanted to publish a book-length manuscript by F. Scott Fitzgerald, but his company was afraid they couldn't sell it profitably enough, since Fitzgerald had previously published only short stories. The editor, through his connections, managed to have a Fitzgerald story included in a college literature anthology. Then when college students by the thousands were familiar with the Fitzgerald name, the editor was able to bring out the book. Such business politics aren't always behind the scene, but at least anthologies and lists have a good chance of being made by people who hold differing values than you.

Lists have more limited use than we tend to think. They cannot be followed as a reading plan or reading curriculum, and the list makers do not intend them to be used that way. When you see one of these lists you and your child can look it over and find a few suggestions that seem right for this time and this child, and try them. This may lead to follow-up reading of more books by an author, or more books of a particular kind that the child was introduced to because of books on the list. In other words, you soon find yourself off on another path, developing your own list as you go. And this is the best way.

To a great extent you are guided by what you have and what your public library or church library has available. And new books are appearing at a rapid rate; lists are not able to keep up with these. Books that adults choose for children are not the same as children choose for themselves, so Books of the Year selected by children hold special interest. If your state or your library has such a program, you can obtain lists of recent selections from a librarian. You may even be able to get your children in on the voting process, and that would be a memorable experience. Remember that reading poetry and fiction is every bit as educational as reading nonfiction.

Sharing Book Experiences with the Family

While reading itself is the best reward of reading, there are times when you may want to expand the learning and sharing. Probably the most effective activity is **conversation**.

Family members can read the same book and talk about it as they go or after they finish. Or one family member who reads a book can tell others about it. There is no "right" way to talk about a book. Sometimes you may happen to do the book report thing by telling why you liked a book or what you liked in it. Other times you may find yourselves discussing, not the book itself, but a topic that your family happens to be interested in. For instance, after a sports story, you might discuss what you think about competition and the intense effort or the stress that goes with it.

Through these conversations, you will pass on your values to your children, some of them consciously and others unconsciously. Also through the conversations, your adult levels of thinking will guide and stretch your children to higher levels of thinking themselves. This one-on-one interaction of child with adult is a major advantage of teaching at home. In a classroom of thirty age-mates, your child never has this much interaction with the teacher. You need not necessarily be homeschooling to talk about books with your children. Conversations are a good way for parents of school children to help guide their learning, too.

Other ideas you may try from time to time are suggested

below. These activities are selected because they emphasize enjoying together the content and thoughts in books. They help you treat books wholistically.

1. **Ads.** Children may prepare written or oral ads for books they especially like, and see if they can talk other family members into reading them.

2. **Personal Reactions.** As an alternative to over-structured book reports, children may write personal thoughts about a book either when they finish it or at some time while reading it—at any time they have something to say. Have children write each reaction on a card or in a notebook, add the title and author, date if you wish, and keep them. Over time, these reactions provide a good picture of a child's reading—the variety or lack of it—and the development of thinking. There are no rules about what should be included in these writings; since they are personal reactions, children can say anything they want.

3. **Sharing Sack.** When a family member comes across something he would like to read to others, but they are all busy or not at home, he can either copy the passage or note the book title and page number and place it in the sharing sack. At dinner or whenever there is time, someone can draw one or more papers from the sharing sack. Make your own rules about whether the person who draws or the person who wrote the original does the reading. Periodically you can ask for specific items for the sharing sack. Have children look for good descriptive passages, funny passages, or whatever you wish.

4. **Drama.** Encourage children to present episodes from their books in puppet form, skit form, as radio or TV programs, or by any similar means they can work out.

5. **Maps.** Post a map on a bulletin board or wall and let children show where stories took place. Use a pin to

mark a location, and an attached string or ribbon running to the side, where the book title and information
about it are given. Instead of pins and ribbons, children
may prepare blank outline maps and put book information directly on the locations: "Johnny Tremain lived
here." For books like the Narnia series which have
imaginary locations, children may create maps.
6. **Timeline.** Help your children prepare a simple timeline
showing just the American period or a longer period of
history, depending on what books they read, and place
book information in their proper places along the
timeline.
7. **Art.** Using any art technique you or the children know or
want to try, depict scenes from favorite books. Display
these on a wall or collect them in a book.

Poetry

You are not alone if you feel intimidated by poetry. When
you have learned about meters and rhyme, is that poetry? When
you have learned about odes and sonnets, is that poetry? When
you have learned about images and symbols, is that poetry? No,
even all put together these do not add up to poetry.

One trouble with poetry is that there is no easy way to define
it. There is no simple list of skills and facts which you can teach
and then call the job done. The truth is, the job can never be
done. All you can hope to do is to give your child a happy start
toward a lifetime of enjoying poetry.

The best way to start is to share poems with your child—the
wholistic approach. Read something you like, and let the child
read to you something he likes. Such brief moments scattered
through a school year will accomplish more than you know.

Sometimes you can concentrate on the meaning of a poem
or one of its lines.

O Thou of God and man the Son

Can your child figure out that this means "O Thou Son of God and Son of man"? This usual sentence pattern is reversed in the poem in order to make a rhyme. Poets try not to do that, and it isn't nearly as common now as it used to be. Since this hymn was translated from German, the translator had both the problem of saying what the German said and of making it rhyme in English, so we can excuse him for his twisted line.

Robed in the blooming garb of spring

Can your child make sense of this? What is garb? *(Clothing.)* What is this particular garb? *(Spring.)* Who or what is clothed (robed) in spring? *(The meadows and woodlands.)* So the meadows and woodlands are wearing their colorful springtime clothes. That is called imagery, and poetry is hardly poetry without it. Who but a poet would have thought of giving us a picture like this? It is called an image because the meadows and woodlands are made to be like something they are not—people, who wear clothes. This helps us see them in a startling new way. It excites our intellect and our emotions.

Images are wonderful, but you don't need to turn your poetry teaching into simply a search for images. Let each poem speak in its own way, and help your children grow in understanding and love of poetry.

Poetry takes effort and thinking; it is not a frill that could be dropped from education without any loss to students. It is a highly intellectual pursuit for those who write it and those who read it. It is a way of exploring God's gifts of language and thought and trying to use them fully and powerfully.

Though most of a poem's power comes from the thoughts it expresses, some comes from its sounds and rhythm. In case you need a brief refresher, here are some of the elementary aspects of sound and rhythm as found in English poems.

Rhythm. Units of rhythm which we inherit from the Greeks are called feet. Four major feet are shown below, the *DUM* being an accented syllable and the *de* being an unaccented syllable.

> DUM de, DUM de, DUM de.
> (Holy, Holy, Holy.)
>
> De DUM, de DUM, de DUM.
> (O day of rest and glad . . .)
>
> DUM de de, DUM de de.
> (Wonderful, wonderful.)
>
> De de DUM, de de DUM.
> (I'm a child of the King.)

These feet each have names which are, in order: trochee, iambic, dactyl, and anapest. You may use these words in teaching about rhythm, but there certainly is no need for children to memorize these and write them for you on a test. There are other kinds of feet, too, which your child might discover. If you wrote a poem with absolutely regular feet it would sound too sing-songy. It would sound amateurish instead of artful. In other words, these are not rules to follow; they are simply helps for writing and reading poetry.

Lines of poetry usually contain from two to six feet. Your child can count the feet by counting beats or accents in some lines of poetry.

Sound. The best known sound feature of poems are end rhymes. When writing these, you have to watch accents as well as vowel sounds, so you would not rhyme *free* with *company*, if you could help it. Sometimes rhymes come in two successive lines and sometimes they come in alternate lines or in some other pattern. Many children enjoy writing a poem using the same rhythm and rhyme pattern of an existing poem. This is good practice for children, and it sharpens writing skills of everyone, including students who become news reporters instead of poets.

You can find rhymes within lines and within words, too, as in these phrases: beneath the trees; like the night. Or find various kinds of alliteration in which consonant sounds are repeated. Notice the words beginning with *b* and *s* in these lines.

> My boat is on the shore,
> And my bark is on the sea;

Poets are skillful in using hissing sounds, soft sounds, exploding sounds, and any variation that adds to the effect they want to make. Your children need not learn technical names for these, but they should be aware that there is more to making a poem sound good than just getting a rhyme at the end of a line.

Learning Activities. Such mechanics—sound, rhythm, and form—are not the main matters children should learn. Those are matters for you to know and to sprinkle into conversations about poems whenever they are helpful. What counts more is that poems begin to speak to your children's hearts and minds.

Here is a variety of assignments and teaching ideas, and at least one among them should appeal to even poetry-shy children. Once you find that one, several others become interesting too, and you will have opened up a new way for the mind to grow.

1. Browse freely through poems to find one you would like to read to your parents.
2. Listen to your mother read her favorite poem. Listen to recorded poems, possibly a poet reading his own poetry.
3. Rewrite a poem so that it sounds like regular sentences of prose. Then talk with your mother or other

family members about the differences. Does the rewrite say as much to your mind? To your feelings? Ask people what they think is lost or gained by the rewrite.

4. Try rewriting a poem (or part of one), using the same words but changing their order. Switch words or phrases or both, but have it still make sense. Then talk about the differences. Is the rewrite better? Worse? Do you have any ideas why?

5. Choose some important words in a poem and put in the place of each another word which means the same thing (synonym). Do your words change the meaning of the poem? Do they change the feeling? Can you explain how?

6. Try adding a nice word or two to some lines of a poem. Words that describe are easiest to add: *little* child, *green* valley, and so forth. Read aloud the poem and the rewrite. What happened? Is the rewrite better? Can you explain why they sound so different?

7. Change the words or change the order in a rhyming poem so it doesn't rhyme anymore. Do you think it still sounds as good?

8. Choose a poem you like and notice which lines rhyme with each other and notice how many toe taps you would make on each line. Then try to write a poem of your own using that same rhyme and rhythm pattern. This is hard work. You might have to think about your lines for several days or even longer. You may want to change words and fix things until you are satisfied with the way it sounds.

9. Choose a poem that you like and try to write a poem about the same subject. You could use the pattern from a different poem if you want, or just make up your own pattern. This is hard work, too. Every poet has to work hard like that.

10. Repeat 8 or 9, starting with a different pattern or a different topic. Repeat some of the other activities, too, when you find a new poem that will be interesting to play with.

If you have always disliked poetry, it just may be because of the way you met poems in your own school days. Maybe you had to memorize something you didn't understand or like very well. Maybe you had to write in order to receive a grade, instead of for the mental challenge of exploring thought and language. Maybe someone tried to push poems on you as though they were medicine you should have, because they were "great" or "beautiful."

If your experiences did not inspire a love of poetry, you now have a double challenge in teaching your children. Don't repeat the negative experiences, but aim to enjoy together a few poems along the way. Your life and the children's will be richer for it.

Summary of Imaginational Reading

In this chapter on imaginational reading, we have noted that reading of fiction and poetry takes a different set of skills than is needed for reading nonfiction. For a broad education, for all kinds of thinking, for educating the heart along with the head, imaginational reading should be included in children's education. In fiction and poetry, children encounter uses of thought and language that they would not meet in nonfiction.

In using imaginational reading with your children, it is best to take a wholistic approach. This helps children enjoy literature, and thus gain more from it, and it helps motivate children who need motivating.

4. Functional Reading

Functional reading is all around us in modern life. It includes signs, directions, rules, directories, advertisements, and, startling as it may seem, the skills you teach for textbook reading do not carry over adequately to these daily functional reading tasks. Research shows this to be a different kind of reading, requiring its own set of skills, and, as with textual reading, the skills come along naturally when you focus on the content, meaning, and use of the reading material itself. It is ineffective to try to focus on isolated reading skills.

Signs

We adults are so accustomed to many of these functional tasks that we fail to realize that children don't take naturally to some of them. For instance, consider the ever-present STOP sign. It may have been one of your child's early phonics lessons, and you and he were both proud that day in the car when he first sounded it out. Was that the end of learning to "read" it? No, that was the beginning. Does your child know the several important meanings we give to that one little word? If the sign is at the corner of a feeder street and an arterial street, it means we stop and wait until all arterial traffic clears enough for us to enter. Even if there is no traffic, we are supposed to stop and look for traffic. If the sign is at a four-way stop, it means we stop until it is our turn to cross the intersection. Other traffic signs have multiple meanings that must be learned.

The railroad crossing sign—is it simply giving information that a railroad crosses the street? No, it also infers a warning of possible danger. HIGH VOLTAGE also infers danger, and even an innocent looking KEEP OUT may mean more than that someone wants privacy on his own land. It may infer danger of electric shock or of drowning or something else.

NO LIFEGUARD ON DUTY, again, is more than just information. It is different from NO SWIMMING, inferring that swimming may take place at the swimmer's own risk, that no one should swim there alone, and children should be accompanied by an adult.

Signs in grocery store aisles have developed a system of their own. Categories like BAKING NEEDS mix with specifics like PEANUT BUTTER. But specifics in this context become categories. Does your child know that he might find jam in an aisle labeled PEANUT BUTTER, SYRUPS? Or in another store he might find peanut butter in an aisle that says CATSUP, DRESSINGS. These are floating categories and each store seems to make its own.

Food Labels

Learning about food labels today is a full consumer course or nutrition course. Differences such as among fruit juices, drinks, and punches we all know for a while after a new regulation is passed, but how many people are "functionally literate" in this area after the publicity dies down? Cereals and bakery items tell whether they are made with whole wheat flour, enriched wheat flour or bleached wheat flour. Products tell what kind of sweetenings are used. Meat and eggs are graded. For several generations, milk has not come in Guernsey or Holstein varieties of richness; it has stated percentages of fat, instead. The flavorings, colorings, and preservatives listed on packages make us all feel we need another chemistry course.

Children in the information stage of reading should begin learning about food labels. Choose matters that are most important to your family's nutrition and teach those first. That will help your child understand others as the need arises.

Rules and Directions

Directions for assembling a new toy and rules for playing a new game are usually condensed, with few extra words, and they must be read closely, with attention to every phrase. Some manufacturers are beginning to change this style, writing directions in more chatty, everyday language (Jiggle this around until it fits; then tighten the screw), but directions still must be followed in an orderly, careful manner.

Swimming pool rules, park rules, library rules, and such all have their distinctive flavors—often negative, usually succinct, with an abbreviated sound to the sentences. Children must learn to get the information and also the inferences that will keep them out of trouble.

Newspapers

A wide variety of reading is found in a newspaper— headlines, news, announcements, want ads, cartoons, features, and on and on. Large papers have an index on the front page, and each section of the paper has an additional index of its own. Even if you're the kind of family that doesn't spend regular time with a daily paper (and there is a lot to be said for that way of life), you can teach your children many valuable skills by occasionally having a newspaper lesson. Begin with the parts of the paper you use the most and branch out from there.

Schools used to teach that news articles were "objective" and unbiased, while editorials expressed opinions. But journalists do not believe anymore that it is possible, or even desirable, to be completely objective. The reporter, by his choice of what to include and what to omit, has already shown his bias, and his choice of words shows it even further. (Was the citizen "slammed" into jail, or "led off" to jail?) Nevertheless, it is useful for the student to understand the different purposes of news articles and editorials.

Does a writer upset you by the way he treats an issue or candidate that you care about? If so, analyze with your children how the story is slanted for or against the issue. Does the headline say that your congressman voted "against the consumer" when he opposed a bill that would have set up a new government bureaucracy of consumer affairs? It could just as well have said that he voted "for the taxpayer."

Unfortunately, many unthinking readers come away from slanted articles believing what the writer wants them to believe. To see through such tactics and do one's own thinking is often called critical reading. Your children in the information stage of reading have a long way to go toward this kind of reading, and newspapers are a good source of practice material by which you can help them along the road. Talk about articles or headlines with your children. You don't need a formal lesson plan or questions or worksheets. Simple conversation is a powerful lesson. Your adult level of thinking interacts with the children's level, and their thinking is stretched thereby.

Here are additional ideas for teaching from newspapers. Some of these, such as 4, 5, and 6 should be used repeatedly for best results.

1. Use a globe and maps to locate where major current events are happening. Stick with one war or one royalty tour long enough to become familiar with both the story and the locations. Each day your child can update you on the chosen news story by using the map instead of the news article.
2. Have your child collect in a scrapbook one of the newspaper features that he or she likes—children's puzzles, places to vacation in your state, favorite cartoons, etc.
3. Explain one or more political cartoons to your children. Who is each person caricatured in it? Are some of the persons not real, such as Uncle Sam? What recent event is the cartoon about? What is the funny point of the cartoon, or what message is the cartoonist trying to give? Do you agree with the cartoonist? After some experience, let your children see how much they can explain to you about cartoons.
4. Cut out some articles without their headlines and let your children write heads for them. Afterward, let them look at the originals and see if they like their own heads better than those in the paper.
5. From the sports page select a headline about a game of your town's team and rewrite the headline as it might appear in the town of the other team.
6. From a local newspaper you and your child together can choose articles which are interesting news for the neighborhood. When you have a bit more than will fit on one sheet of typing or notebook paper, let your child be editor to paste up the page of newspaper. He must shorten articles or headlines or omit articles or whatever it takes to make a nice-looking page. Afterward, let him explain to you why he chose to cut the parts that he did.
7. Have your child make a scrapbook called "The Fourteenth Year of My Life" or "The Year I was in Eighth Grade" or whatever title he would like to write.

The idea is to keep a history of the year that will be meaningful someday when he is an adult and looks through the book to recall what the world was like "way back then." Headlines, articles, pictures, ads for new products and any other newspaper parts may be selected for inclusion in the yearbook.

Ads

To be good functional readers, your children must learn about ads. They should understand that ad writers have only the goal of selling them something; they have no obligation to tell about problems with a product or about competitors with lower prices. Truth-in-advertising laws restrain them from outright falsehoods, but that doesn't mean we can read advertisements in the same way we read textbooks for information.

Here are some samples from a city paper, followed by questions you may ask your children.

1

Black cat silhouette with marble eyes catch the light and stare convincingly at you. So realistic it is sure to scare off uninvited rabbits, birds or other garden pests.

Can we be quite sure this will keep rabbits out of our garden? Why or why not? Who says "It is sure to scare"? Is that good enough proof for you? Can you think of better information the ad writer could have given you? *(Tests show 95% fewer pests, etc.)* Do you think he would have given you more convincing proof if he had it? Do you think we should buy this cat? Why or why not?

2

Now! 3.9% annual percentage rate financing or $500 cash back! On every new Taurus!

cash back on this car	500.
special value package savings	700.
total savings	$1200.

Does this tell how much you will pay for the car? *(No, and nowhere in the whole ad is the price given.)* If you choose to take cash back, what do you think happens to your interest rate? Could that cost you as much as $500? Where do you think they got the $700 savings figure? Does this ad convince you that you will get a better price here than at this dealer's competitors?

3

Low down cruiser. At just $99 down and $99 per month, you're not going to find terms much better than these. Especially for a bike like this: one of the hottest machines on the road. With our new easy financing, all you need is $99 and you'll be able to rumble off on the bike of your dreams.

What parts of the financing does this writer fail to mention? *(The interest rate and the total amount of interest payments, the number of months you have to pay $99, the total price of the bike.)* Why do you think the writer gives part of the financial information, but not all of it? Besides financial, what other appeal does the writer use? *(People's desire to rumble off on a bike.)*

4

We won't be undersold. We'll match any advertised price for the Michelin and Goodrich tires we sell. (Details in store.)

We believe these are the lowest prices in town for a steel belted radial with a 50,000 mile limited warranty. One week only! All-Star tires $45 for 14″, $50 for 15″.

If you found an All-Star 15″ tire for less than $50, would this store have to come down on their price for you? *(No, because it is not Michelin or Goodrich.)* If you found a Goodrich 15″ tire in another store's ad for $60, would it get you a discount at this store? *(It might. Can't tell, because we don't know the prices of their Goodrich tires.)* If your own friendly garage sells Goodrich tires for less than this store, would the store have to come down on their price for you? *(Maybe not, because the friendly garage may not have advertised their price.)* What do you need to do to get a lower price at this store? *(Get details in the store and follow them. Probably they ask you to bring in an ad which shows a Michelin or Goodrich tire price lower than this store has for the same size and same mileage warranty.)*

Ads require thinking. These samples show some of the matters you can discuss when you talk about ads with your children. Help them to see through enticing words and determine what an ad really tells them. If they want to take advantage of a special sale, they need to read other fine print on the page about how long it lasts, where the store is located, and what hours it is open. For better or for worse, this is part of functioning in our modern society.

Everyday Miscellaneous

You can hardly go through a day without having print thrust at you from numerous sources. Flyers are left on your lawn, Cancer Fund information is handed to you at the door, cashiers' tapes are dropped into your sack of purchases, bills and letters come in the mail, and storm warnings flash across the TV screen. Questionnaires must be filled out, contest entries followed to the letter, and warranty information saved. Dealing with much of this print does not come naturally to children, and most of it is not found in reading textbooks, so it is yours to teach.

Your children may need a bit of guidance to read bus schedules, tide tables, or weather almanacs, if those are used in your area. And you may (or may not) want to help them with radio and TV schedules.

Phone books are especially important. Your children may know how to look up names as a carryover from using a dictionary, but several other features are specific to phone books. In one town the schools are not listed in the white section by their names, they are not under "Schools" in the yellow business section, and there is no blue section for government entities, so where would you find schools? If you search long enough and ask people who know, you can locate them right up front where they were put so as to be easy to find. Acquaint your children with the idiosyncrasies of your local phone book and with features that they will find in most phone books.

Because these everyday items are so prevalant in our lives, we tend not to be aware of how much teaching children need. We expect them to pick up these skills by osmosis, and they do in some cases, but not all. In one high school, students using the office phone routinely bypassed the phone book and called information for the numbers they needed. Many of them could read their chemistry books well, but they were not at home with the phone book. English teachers drilled on irregular verbs and past perfect tense, they brought Shakespeare and Chaucer to class, but the phone book didn't seem to belong there. The office staff finally took the matter in hand by having the phone adjusted so it would not process information calls.

Summary of Functional Reading

Teaching functional reading is not difficult, but it does take an awareness that children need it and an alertness to the opportunities all around us. This chapter has shown some of the matters that should be taught concerning signs, food labels, rules and directions, newspapers, ads, and some other miscellaneous items. This is by no means a complete listing of what your child will meet and read, but this chapter will have served its purpose if it has raised your awareness of the very important area of functional reading.

Summary of the Information Stage of Reading

The preceding three chapters have covered three major kinds of reading which your children need to experience during the information stage, which lasts from approximately fourth through eighth grades. These areas are: 1) textual, 2) imaginational, and 3) functional reading.

Textual reading is the reading of nonfiction, including textbooks. To excel in this, children need to build their knowledge and vocabulary, have a variety of reading speeds, know some good study techniques and consciously apply them.

Imaginational reading is a highly intellectual activity involving the image-making powers of the mind. Included in this reading are both poetry and fictional prose. This reading helps to develop heart and character as well as mind, and is necessary to achieving a fully rounded education.

Functional reading includes everyday items like signs, labels, rules and directions, ads, tide tables, schedules, telephone directories, newspapers, questionnaires and other forms. These tend to be neglected in children's education simply because they are so everyday, and we assume children are as familiar with their uses as we are. But it takes a different set of skills to be good at functional reading. Skills from textual or imaginational reading do not carry over fully enough into this kind of reading, so you must make a point to teach functional reading.

By the end of eighth grade, students should be able to read a variety of materials up to ninth grade readability level and learn new information and ideas from them. Such materials include adult literature, popular fiction, science and social studies texts, newspapers and magazines, encyclopedias, dictionaries, and other reference books. Students should be able to use a library for enjoyment and for locating information for reports and for following up their own interests. They should have a good vocabulary of words in both general and technical use.

A reminder: these information-stage skills are not yet the end of reading advancement. In high school, students grow in analytical and critical reading and they learn from a broader range of books, both fiction and nonfiction, with many kinds of styles and content. They can understand other people's views better than in elementary grades, and can analyze issues from more than one viewpoint. They develop efficient study strategies, and their general and technical vocabularies continue to grow, as well.

At college level, students need to handle all kinds of difficult material—specialized, technical, and abstract. They need to analyze knowledge from many sources and synthesize it for their own beliefs and writings. They need the skills and attitudes that will carry them through a lifetime of learning.

Don't try to rush your children into advanced stages, but during the grades of about four through eight give them all kinds of reading experiences of the three types described in the preceding three chapters. Build a broad and solid base of reading and thinking, and they will grow toward an adulthood enriched by reading whether or not they choose formal education at the higher levels.

Part II: Writing

5. To Learn to Write, Write!

Writing is the other side of reading. Reading is receiving language and writing is producing it. While children grow in reading and writing abilities, they carry on a dialogue, like an extended conversation. Children write. Then they read and see the way books do it. Then they write again, influenced by what happened in their minds while reading. And so it goes, on and on for years. Children who read a lot are better writers.

Children are hardly aware of this process, and you have to watch closely to see it yourself, because it happens slowly. You have seen a similar process in your children when they learned to talk. The dialogue continued for three or four years. They listened and they spoke. They listened and they spoke. And by age five or so they emerged as competent little users of oral language. To do as well in written language, they need years of the same kind of dialogue. They must read, and write; read, and write.

The goal of this process is nothing less than a rich, quality education in all verbal areas. Except for math, arts, and other less verbal areas, this is the way that people have always become educated. By means of written words, humankind communicates with its own past, debates and enjoys its present, and looks toward its future.

When you read a book, you are in mind-to-mind encounter with its author, whether he lived 1000 years ago or lives today. This is the wonder of real books—all kinds of books, not only the serious and factual. Your mind grows through these encounters.

And while you read or after you finish a book, if you have a personal response of some kind, and write, your mind grows even more. You clarify your thoughts. You develop new ways of thinking. This is education, ongoing.

The read-write dialogue is of first importance. So keep your children reading and keep them writing.

Helpful Books

A few reference books are useful tools to help your family in the writing part of the dialogue. If you don't have a good dictionary, get one or more. A children's dictionary works well for a child in third or fourth grade who is learning to look up words and is not ready to read the fine print and confusing abbreviations in adult dictionaries. A college dictionary gives information about prefixes and root origins that some dictionaries omit. Drugstore or supermarket dictionaries (and encyclopedias) usually are inferior products. You will know such a one when you use it. A definition might just lead you to another word, which leads in a circle back to the original word. Or you can't find the words you need. A church secretary complained of hers, "Every time I want to look up a word, this dictionary doesn't seem to have it." Merriam-Webster has been in the dictionary business for a long time, and that is their only business, so you can trust their dictionaries. Several other companies also publish fine ones. Houghton Mifflin's *American Heritage Dictionary*, a desk size book, gives added information about usage by a panel of one hundred major literary experts. This usage information will answer many questions that arise during the course of writing, rewriting, and proofing.

An English handbook alongside the dictionary can serve as a reference on grammar, usage, mechanics (capitalization, abbreviation, etc.), syntax of sentences, effective paragraphs, and letter forms. Helpful features to look for in such a book are: simple organization, complete index, concise explanations, examples, and convenient lists (as of irregular verbs). You do not need practice exercises and assignments to clutter such a reference book. But children can sometimes study items directly from it, anyway, writing practice sentences of their own. Over time, they can become familiar enough with the book that they could use it to settle an argument about whether to say *I swum* or *I swam*. Using such a reference book is far better than having the grammar and usage information scattered through a pile of used workbooks. Also, it costs less than the pile of grammar books for grades 4 to 12.

If you have a high school or college textbook of your own, get that out again. Though the book is too advanced for your children, you, at least, will be able to find your way around in it and locate information as needed, and you can explain to your children. If you don't have one, buy an advanced English handbook when your family outgrows the elementary one. Brushing up again on matters that you forgot you ever learned is one of the bonuses of teaching your children. Many professional teachers admit to the same bonus. After teaching, they know some things better than they did during preparation for teaching.

Don't worry about trying to afford encyclopedias. They are not the route to a good education for your children. If you have that much money to spend on books, think what a library you would have if you used the money, instead, for family members to select books on subjects they are interested in, books they intend to read from cover to cover! Compare that use of book money with the shelves of encyclopedias that your children will use only occasionally, and in which they will read only a tiny fraction of the pages. Rewording encyclopedia articles is not an especially good way to learn to write, and it is a poor way to learn what research is.

If you really want encyclopedias, find out when the good used book sales happen in your area and buy an old set or a set with a volume missing, for less than one-tenth of the original price. That's about what it is worth to be able to look up a fact now and then. Old sets work fine for looking up most historical and literary information, but not so well for science.

When you go to a book sale, take your children and spend half a day. Everyone can find treasures to last for months and years and even a lifetime. If you decide later that you don't want to keep some of the books, donate them to the sale next year. This prevents books from pushing you out of house and home. In many areas, public library systems or hospital auxiliaries have huge annual fund-raising book sales. If no one is doing this in your area, perhaps your organization should.

When you use real books and real writing, you won't have much need for textbooks, and particularly workbooks. Your children should spend more time writing than learning *about* writing. But many good books have been written about writing. My favorite on the adult level is a government publication written many years ago to help IRS employees write clearly. Don't you wish they would read it? Volume 2 of *Effective Revenue Writing* now costs $5.50 and is item number 048-004-00037-7. It can be ordered from: Superintendent of Documents, U.S. Government Printing Office, Washington DC 20402-9325. You can read this just to entertain your friends with hilarious examples of bureaucratic writing. But it is a serious writing course. My favorite chapter is on linkage— connecting thoughts smoothly from sentence to sentence. If you are interested in writing, and study these matters on an adult level, you will find numerous little ways to help your children write better. You can help them in the context of their own writing, something workbooks can't do.

Writing Activities

In this section, we offer a few ideas to help keep your children writing regularly. Find some that will work well in your family and pursue them seriously. You don't need exciting new ideas every day. I used to think that, as a young teacher, so my children hopped around from topic to topic, trying this and trying that. My goal was that they never be bored. I almost forgot the goal that they learn to write well. But when I reversed priorities, I didn't have to worry about boredom. Writing is complex and difficult, it is hard work, but it is not boring, because it engages the total mind.

Letters. Homeschooling parents have shared letter writing ideas, and here are some you can adopt for your family. Write individual Christmas letters to friends and relatives instead of sending store-bought cards. Write letters to order merchandise by mail. Send for pamphlets and other free information that is offered by mail. Write thank-you notes for gifts received. Write "bread and butter" thank you's after being a guest at someone's house. Write party invitations. The child prepares his own envelope for each letter.

One family tells of setting aside an evening each week for letter writing. The whole family participates, and letters are written to congressmen or other elected officials, judges, newspapers, school boards, radio and television stations and sponsors, local celebrities, or manufacturers. The letters may be of praise, criticism or suggestion. Little children not able to write on abortion or education or other topics you are interested in can join at the letter-writing table, anyway, and write a letter to a friend. They will learn much about the duties of citizens, and they will grow in ability to follow their parents' example. If a thousand families followed that practice, generating thousands of letters every week, who can calculate the effect it would have on our society?

Missionaries are also on this family's list. Even if you're the only family in your church which takes on this ministry, it would greatly encourage the missionaries to hear regular news from home. Although some missionaries were the original home-schoolers in this century's revival of the practice, many missionaries have little contact with the movement and have been trained to think that they must separate from their children in order to send them to school. Perhaps your children's happy letters about their homeschooling will help to spread this way of life around the world. Besides learning to write better, your children can learn geography as they mark maps to show where each missionary works. And when missionaries come home for a visit, your children's lives will be greatly enriched by meeting these wonderful people and hearing their stories from around the world.

A special etiquette applies in writing letters to government officials. Some commonly used forms are shown below. For state legislators, use the forms given here for congressmen.

When envelopes are typed these days, the Postal Service prefers that we use all capitals and omit all punctuation—the better to go through their scanners.

Address	Salutation	Closing
The President The White House Washington, DC 20005	Mr. President:	Very truly yours,
The Honorable James Lee United States Senate Washington, DC 20005	Sir: or Madam:	Very truly yours,
The Honorable James Lee House of Representatives Washington, DC 20005	Sir: or Madam:	Very truly yours,

When writing about a particular bill you want your representative to vote for or against, it is best to give the bill number at the beginning of your letter. The same bill will have different numbers in the house and in the senate, so be careful with this. After telling what bill you are writing about, give in your own words one or more reasons for your position on the bill politely. This is far better than signing petitions or using form letters that someone has photocopied by the dozen. Individual, personal letters are one of the most effective means we citizens have for influencing our government. Elected officials really do listen to them.

Children's Choice. Sometimes it works to simply tell children that they must turn in to you one piece of writing each day. (This is besides any specific assignments they have in other subjects.) Once that routine gets going, children develop the habit of grabbing a good idea when it comes along. Sometime during the day each child is likely to have strong feelings about something or other, and they learn to think, "Oh, I'll write about that." Or ideas come to them in bed at night and they begin their school day with writing.

Journals. Some parents are successful in getting their children to keep a journal. Probably about half the children like personal journals. The other half are less open about their private thoughts and resist putting them into permanent form in a journal. Journals can have specific focuses, such as devotional, where children write their prayers and thoughts about spiritual matters. Other journals are diaries of events. Still others are homeschool journals in which children write briefly about their school work for each day. This kind of journal, when carefully kept, can relieve much of your record-keeping load.

Writing to Learn. In any subject, you can use writing to help your children learn difficult concepts. The addition lesson in the next chapter, especially activity 5b, is an example of this use of writing. Many people quote a saying that writing *is* thinking, so many that it is impossible to trace who thought of it first. But it is true.

If you think you understand something or think you have an opinion about an issue, try writing it in essay form for someone else to read. You will discover a lot about your thinking that you didn't know was there, including, possibly, gaps in knowledge that you have to look up as you write. Nothing sharpens and clarifies thinking like writing does. So learn to use writing in all your children's subjects; don't reserve it for language class.

Audience for Writing. An important function of yours as teacher is to be audience for your children's writing—not with a red pencil, but with genuine appreciation and encouragement, and with gentle guidance toward improvement.

When you can, provide other audiences, too. When you get together with other homeschooling families, one of your activities could be to have reading sessions where children have opportunity to read essays, stories and poems that they have written. Some small groups meet regularly and discuss the papers. Children learn to be helpful and encouraging to each other, and all strive to do their best writing, knowing that the audience will be there. Use similar group plans for speaking practice. Children may recite memorized poems or give talks on topics they have studied and prepared.

Submit writings to children's magazines and newspapers. Publish your own neighborhood magazine.

Writing Closely Related to Reading. After reading a story or poem that they especially enjoy, children can often be stimulated to write something of their own. Here are a few ideas.

1. After reading an animal story, write your own animal story. Is yours true-to-life or fanciful? Analyze your

writing and explain what you did that helped to make the story either true-to-life or fanciful.

2. After a story with a surprise ending, see if you can make up a story with a surprise ending. Tell it or write it.

3. After a story you like, rewrite it in play form. Or after reading a play, rewrite it in story form.

4. After reading a good poem, rewrite the message in prose. You can leave it that way, or a few days later you can look at your prose and see if you can turn it back into a poem.

5. After reading a saying or proverb that you think should help people's lives, write a paragraph about it.

6. After reading or hearing a saying that you don't agree with, write a paragraph about it.

7. Choose a favorite Bible verse and write a short poem or a paragraph about it.

8. After reading something full of information that you want to remember, develop an outline. You don't have to do the outline in order. First you could get down the main points, then back up and put information under each main point. Your second or third time through, you may change your mind about what points are the main ones, but that's all right. When your information is all listed, ask your teacher to show you how people number and label the parts of an outline, and how the subpoints should be indented under the main ones.

9. After reading a good old tale, try writing it in ballad form. Before starting, find a ballad to use for a model. Don't expect to complete this project in one sitting. It may take a number of work sessions before you finish a ballad that you like.

10. Use a narrative paragraph that is written in past tense and rewrite it in present tense. Another time, use a narrative that is written in present tense and rewrite it in past tense.

11. After reading a news article about an auto accident, talk about whether you think the whole story was told. Could it be that alcohol was involved but the reporter omitted that information? (This sometimes happens in small towns where fatal teenage accidents affect many citizens. There are "cover-ups" for other reasons too.) Pretend your story has such a cover-up and rewrite it to include the missing information. Talk about how news can be manipulated.

12. During or after a sermon, write about something that the pastor preached. Say anything you want to say about it. This is your personal response to one part of the sermon. On another Sunday, try to outline the sermon as you listen.

More ideas are given in the detailed writing lessons of the next chapter. You can glean ideas there and use them on books which you or your children choose. Or you can actually use the lessons to gain experience in relating writing, grammar, and spelling to a passage of literature. After you feel somewhat experienced with these techniques, branch out and plan your own. Yours don't have to be planned ahead in such detail as these, because you won't be writing them in a book. Much of the conversation with your children and the items they learn from a passage of literature will naturally be worked out in tutoring sessions. Dictate a paragraph, see what the children miss, and teach that.

Some of your lessons can take the form of intense study of details, as most of these examples do, and other lessons can concentrate on the thoughts expressed, without so much attention to mechanical details.

In language teaching, learn to get along without daily fill-in-the-blank workbook assignments. Use real writing.

6. Writing Lessons

The following lessons integrate grammar, punctuation, spelling, writing, and thinking, for a well rounded approach to language learning. After each literary passage are five numbered activities, and you can consider these as five days' work. Thus each topic can be studied for a week. But if they don't work out that way with your students, adjust in any way you wish. Some activities could develop into long projects, such as writing a play, and if interest is high you should not cut the project short just to keep up with a schedule.

These lessons are more structured than the ideas given in the preceding chapter, and you may get some groans: "Oh, do we have to write again today?" If your children's writing needs improvement, you can just say "Yes" and go ahead. Dictation is difficult at first, but with persistence it gets easier. Keep it up for a few months and the better writing which results will last a lifetime.

Copying is a lower level activity than dictation, and can be used for children who have too much difficulty with dictation. Children can copy one day as preparation for dictation the next day. Or they can just copy and proofread if that is the level that works best for them. Both copying and dictation require close attention to details, and that is why they are effective.

Other assignments here are also intense: rewriting fiction as non-fiction, rewriting in another tense, rewriting sentences into different forms, writing definitions and rules. These accomplish more for children's thinking and writing ability than appears on the surface. They are hard to do, and it helps if you are available to talk with your children when they want that kind of support while they work on these assignments.

These lessons will have served you best if you get ideas from them to continue this kind of wholistic language teaching using literary models that you choose. Activity 4 of the "Valiant" lessons is a good example of a learning activity which students may repeat again and again with different topics. It was Benjamin Franklin's self-teaching method.

Answers and some teacher notes are given at the end of the chapter. If you wish to photocopy assignments from the book for your own children to work from, that is legal for home-schoolers using this book. Classroom teachers, for a one-time trial use, may also copy one or two of the lessons. But for using more lessons or for repeated use, teachers must contact the publisher and comply with provisions of the copyright law.

The Writing Lessons

How Language Began

Then God said, "Let us make man in our image, in our likeness, and let them rule over the fish of the sea and the birds of the air, over the cattle, over all the earth, and over all the creatures that move along the ground." So God created man in his own image, in the image of God he created him; male and female he created them. The Lord God took the man, and put him in the Garden of Eden to work it and take care of it. And Adam gave names to all the cattle, the birds of the air and all the beasts of the field.

From Genesis 1 and 2

1. Copy this paragraph or write it from dictation. Compare your copy with the model and fix all spelling and punctuation. Notice that *he* and other pronouns referring to God are not capitalized. That's the way it is in the Bible (KJV), but we capitalize these pronouns in our writing.

2. Memorize the second sentence. Practice until you can say it from memory and write it from memory without any mistakes. The semicolon means more pause than a comma, but less than a period.

3a. Review yesterday's memory sentence.
b. One way that people are different from animals is that people have language. At the very beginning Adam could listen to God, think of animal names, and say the names. He had language because he was made in the image of God.

Write a paragraph (or more) telling some things you can do that your dog or other animal friend cannot do. Edit your sentences to try to make them better. Rearrange them, reword them, add more ideas, check the spelling. When you think everything sounds good, make a neat copy to save.

4a. Find and list ten pronouns in the Genesis sentences that refer to persons. Personal pronouns are words like *us, he* and *his*.

Write 1 or 3 by each pronoun to show whether it is first

person or third person. First person refers to the one or ones who are speaking. Third person refers to ones they are speaking about.

b. If you have a grammar book or English textbook, look up personal pronouns in it by using either the table of contents or the index. What does the book teach about personal pronouns? Can you explain to your teacher what first, second, and third person pronouns are?

5a. Mark some words you are not sure you will spell right. Learn them.

b. Write the paragraph from dictation. Compare your copy with the model. If you had errors, fix them, and tell your teacher at least one thing you learned while fixing your errors.

Valiant, Dog of the Timberline

One morning, sniffing as usual at the base of the fence boards, the little dog felt a sudden cool breeze touch his nostrils. Interested, he stretched a paw toward the narrow crack which was opening between the wooden panel and the ground, and began to scratch. His claws sank into the soft earth and as he drew them back, a small depression appeared letting not only wind, but light, filter beneath the fence. Excited by this, he began digging wildly with both paws. The tunnel swiftly grew larger and the loosened dirt flew back between his legs.

Jack O'Brien

1. Write this paragraph from dictation. Compare your

copy with the model and circle every misspelled word. Make a spelling list with these words. Fix the spelling, punctuation, and other things. Did you indent at the beginning?

2a. Study the spelling list you made yesterday, and have someone give you a test. If you miss some words, take a second test with only the missed words.

b. Find three sentences which begin with a word or short phrase set off by a comma. Underline these phrases. Read each of those sentences aloud, pausing slightly at the commas.

c. What do you think could happen next in this story? Pretend you are the author and write the next sentence or the next paragraph of this story.

3. This paragraph tells, or narrates, part of a story, so it is called narrative writing. Make a list of things that happen in this story. You may start like this:

> dog sniffed by fence
> felt breeze

Use your list to tell the story, in order, to your teacher. Improve the list if you find it didn't help enough, and tell the story again. Save the list for activity 4.

4. Use your list of events, and write the story without looking at the model. Tell events in the order they happened.

After your first writing, proofread and edit your work until it is as good as you can make it. When you are proud of your work, show it to your teacher. You may also, then, look at the model and reread what Jack O'Brien wrote. Don't feel badly if his sounds better. Remember that he had many years of practice.

5a. The last sentence in the paragraph could be made into two sentences if you omit the *and* that connects them. Rewrite this compound sentence as two simple sentences. Read the sentences aloud both ways—from the book and from your paper. Which do you think sounds better? Why?

b. Write the paragraph from dictation again. Or if you prefer, you may write a story of your own about Valiant or about a dog you know. What you wrote in 2c may give you an idea for a story.

Black Beauty

The first place that I can well remember was a large pleasant meadow with a pond of clear water in it. Some shady trees leaned over it, and rushes and water lilies grew at the deep end. Over the hedge on one side we looked into a plowed field, and on the other we looked over a gate at our master's house, which stood by the roadside. At the top of the meadow was a grove of fir trees, and at the bottom a running brook overhung by a steep bank.

Anna Sewell

1. Write this descriptive paragraph from dictation, or copy it. Compare your copy with the model and fix any errors you find. When you think everything is correct, ask your teacher to check again.

2a. In your copy of the paragraph, find some words that describe (adjectives) and draw arrows to the nouns they describe, like this:

shady trees

b. Read the paragraph aloud, omitting the adjectives you marked. Read it again using all the adjectives. What do you think about the way it sounds?

3a. Draw or diagram the horse meadow and surroundings. Put everything in your picture that is named in the paragraph. Does your teacher imagine things in the same places you put them? Talk together about your picture.

    b. Have someone give you a spelling test using any five words she chooses from the paragraph. If you miss any words, find out their correct spelling, and then take the test again.

4a. The adjectives you marked in activity 2 tell *what kind*. Review your work from activity 2 to remind yourself about them. Some adjectives tell *which one*. Examples are: *a* brook, *the* roadside. Now see how many more adjectives you can find in the paragraph.

    b. If you have a grammar book or English textbook, use the index or table of contents to look up adjectives, and find a definition of *adjective*. Read it to your teacher.

5. Write the paragraph again from dictation, and see how much better you wrote it than the first time. Or pretend you are a horse or dog or other animal you know, and write a paragraph describing where you live now or where you used to live. Try to make such a good description that a friend will be able to draw a picture from it.

Addition

Addition is the process of uniting two or more numbers. Each number to be added is called an addend, and the total is called the sum. Adding is something like counting. For example, to add 14 and 3 you can start at 14 on a number line, count up 3 more, and arrive at the sum of 17. Or if you start at 3 and count up 14 more, you will arrive at the same sum of 17. It does not matter which order you use when you add numbers.

1. Copy this paragraph or write it from dictation. In most writing, numbers under ten are spelled out as words, but in special situations like recipes and arithmetic you get to use the numerals instead. Proofread your copy, record the number of errors you find, and save the number for activity 4. Correct all errors.

2a. To show that you understand the vocabulary in this paragraph, write a column of three numbers, add them, and label each number with its name.
b. Pretend you are making an arithmetic dictionary, and write definitions for these words: addition, addend, sum.

3a. Show that you understand this paragraph by making a line of numbers from 1 to 20 and counting out the two examples given.
b. Write a rule or "Law of Order" which tells something that is true about addition.
c. This paragraph does not describe or narrate; it explains. One way to explain is to give rules. Find the rule in your copy of the paragraph and label it "rule" in the margin beside it. Two other ways to explain are to give definitions and to give examples. Find and label all the definitions and examples you can find in the paragraph. Find a statement that has examples following it, and label it "statement."

4. Write the paragraph from dictation. Proofread, and see if you made fewer errors than on the first dictation.

5. Choose *a* or *b*.
a. Make a list of information in the addition paragraph. Then put the paragraph out of your sight and rewrite it the best you can with only the list to help you.

b. Select another subject and explain it, using as many of these as you need: definitions, statements, examples, rules.

One idea for a subject is subtraction. It could include these features:

1. Definitions of *subtraction* and of each number.
2. Statement that subtraction is counting backward.
3. Example.

History of English Language

The English we speak is a rich mixture from many roots. Long ago, some Germanic tribes called Angles and Saxons settled in England. Their languages blended together and came to be known as Anglo-Saxon. Later, French invaders brought new words, and Latin words were brought in too. Pronunciations gradually changed over the centuries. If those early Angles could hear us today, they would think we were foreigners.

1. Write the paragraph from dictation. Compare your paragraph with the model and mark things you will need to learn before writing it again. The word *pronunciation* comes from *pronounce*. What change is made in the way the root is spelled?

2. Try to find a book about the French (Norman) invasion of 1066 or any of the early invasions of England. Read some of this history and tell your teacher something that you learned.

3a. Write a short list of names, including your last name, some friends' names, the name of your town, and some other geographical names. Then see if adults you know can tell what language any of the names came from originally. Write down answers as they tell you.

b. Read more of the early English history if you have time.

4a. Find out something about the Bayeux Tapestry. Look in an encyclopedia, or ask a librarian to help you find a picture that shows part of the very long ancient tapestry depicting some of the events of the Norman invasion of England.

b. If you like to make things, figure out a way to show something about your family life so people a long time from now could see how you lived. Start work on the project and get others in the family to help.

5a. Write one or more paragraphs about events in history that caused English to have many French words in it.

b. Write the original paragraph from dictation and try to do it better than the first time.

The White Seal

The first time that Kotick went down to the sea a wave carried him out beyond his depth, and his big head sank and his little hind flippers flew up exactly as his mother had told him, and if the next wave had not thrown him back again he would have drowned. He was two weeks learning to use his flippers; and all that while he floundered in and out of the water, and coughed and grunted and crawled up the beach and took catnaps on the sand, and went back again, until at last he found that he truly belonged to the water.

Rudyard Kipling

1a. Copy this paragraph. Notice the semicolon which joins two parts of a sentence. A semicolon is almost like a period, but when you read this, you should pause not quite as long as for a period.

b. Did you indent? Did you spell all the words correctly? When you finish checking, ask your teacher to check again. Save your copy for activity 2.

2a. On your copy of the paragraph, underline all the action verbs you can find. If you know about helping verbs like *was* and *had*, you may underline those too.

b. Make a list of all the action verbs that end with *ed* and put a heading over them called regular verbs. List the other action verbs and call them irregular verbs.

c. See if your grammar book has a list of irregular verbs. If it does, see if Kipling's irregular verbs are on the list. Notice how the list tells you the forms for present, past (without *ed*), and past participle.

3. Rudyard Kipling wrote long sentences here, and it gives a particular storylike effect. Rewrite this paragraph into shorter sentences, changing a few words if you need to. Then read aloud the rewrite and the original, and notice how they sound different. Can you describe the difference?

4a. Find all the *ou* and *ow* words in this paragraph and put them in lists according to the sound. You should end up with one long list and three other "lists" with only one word each.

b. Ask your teacher to give you a spelling test with five or six words she thinks you might miss. Check and retest until you get all the words right.

c. This is a narrative paragraph. That is, it tells a story. But in the story you learn some information about baby seals learning to swim. Use the information to write a paragraph about baby seals as it might appear in an encyclopedia.

5. Reread Kipling's long sentences. Then write the paragraph from dictation.

Slithy Wabes

'Twas brillig, and the slithy toves
Did gyre and gimble in the wabe;
All mimsy were the borogoves,
And the mome raths outgrabe.

Lewis Carroll

1a. Most of these are nonsense words, but you can find one word in each line that is sure to be a noun. List them. Write after each whether it is singular (one) or plural (more than one). Explain to your teacher how you know each of these words is a noun.

  b. From your grammar book, read about articles (a, an, the) and about how to make plural forms of nouns. Write at least one new item that you learn.

2a. Find two actions which the toves did and one action which the raths did. List these three verbs.

  Write a sentence telling what the toves did and another sentence telling what the raths did, putting real verbs in place of the nonsense verbs.

  b. All three of these verbs are intransitive verbs because they do not transport or transfer their action onto an object. Learn more about transitive and intransitive verbs from your grammar book. Get your teacher to help you understand the differences if this is confusing.

3a. Two more verbs in the poem are *was* and *were*.

It *was* brillig.
The borogoves *were* all mimsy.

These are called linking verbs. They link either a noun or adjective to the subject. Rewrite the above sentences two ways—

once with a noun following the linking verb and once with an adjective following it.

   b. Learn more about linking verbs from your grammar book.

   4a. Find two nonsense words which have to be adjectives. Explain to your teacher how you know these words are adjectives.
   Those adjectives are called descriptive adjectives. The four *the*'s in this poem are also adjectives. Sometimes they are called *articles*, too. But that is a kind of adjective.
   b. Review adjectives in your grammar book.

   5a. Get ready to write the poem from dictation. It is good spelling practice to see if you can spell the nonsense words the way they sound. Notice the semicolon after line 2, which is almost the same as a period. Ask someone to dictate the poem to you.
   b. If you are not tired of this poem by now, try one of the activities below.

   1. Write a nonsense poem, making it sound like real sentences. You'll have no trouble getting rhymes.
   2. Try to rewrite Carroll's poem using real words. This is very hard to do.

Alice's Adventures in Wonderland

   It was much pleasanter at home, when one wasn't always growing larger and smaller, and being ordered about by mice and rabbits. I almost wish I hadn't gone down that rabbit hole—and yet—and yet—it's rather curious, you know, this sort of life. I do wonder what can have happened to me. When I used to read fairy tales, I fancied that kind of thing never happened, and now here I am in the middle of one. There ought to be a book written about me, that there ought! And when I grow up, I'll write one.

Lewis Carroll

1a. Look at the dashes before and after each *and yet* phrase. Dashes show a sudden break in the thought of a sentence. Read aloud the sentence with dashes, trying to make it sound as you think the author wanted it to sound.

b. Contractions are two words made into one. An apostrophe is put in place of missing letters.

EXAMPLE: I'm = I am

Find four contractions in the Alice paragraph, and write them as in the example above.

2a. Have someone give you a spelling test using any five words she chooses from the paragraph. If you miss any words, find out their correct spelling, and then take the test again.

b. Now ask your teacher to dictate the paragraph to you. Listen carefully for pauses that sound like commas. Compare your copy with the model. Fix it. Then let your teacher check again.

c. Read your copy aloud to someone.

3a. One sentence in the Alice paragraph could be made into two sentences if you omit the *and* that connects them. Find this compound sentence and rewrite it as two sentences.

Read the sentences aloud both ways—from the book and from your rewrite. Which do you think sounds better? Why?

b. Find in your grammar book what simple sentences and

compound sentences are. Explain them to your teacher. Or write either a definition or example of each kind of sentence.

4a. Mark the words you are not sure you will spell correctly and have someone give you a spelling test over and over until you get them all right.
b. Write the paragraph from dictation. Compare with the model, correct it, and have your teacher check again.

5a. If you did well on yesterday's dictation, select an activity from the list below for today. If you need more practice with the Alice paragraph, study it and write from dictation again.
Activities:
Read part of the book *Alice's Adventures in Wonderland.*
Read from a book of your choice.
Write a short story.
Write a letter or report or something else you've been needing time to do.

Alice's Adventures in Wonderland, 2

Alice had not gone much farther before she came in sight of the house of the March Hare. She thought it must be the right house, because the chimneys were shaped like ears and the roof was thatched with fur. It was so large a house that she did not like to go nearer till she had nibbled some more of the left-hand bit of mushroom, and raised herself to about two feet high. Even then she walked up towards it rather timidly, saying to herself, "Suppose it should be raving mad after all! I almost wish I'd gone to see the Hatter instead."

Lewis Carroll

1. See how well you can write this paragraph from dictation without looking at it first. But if you don't know how to put quotation marks around the words someone speaks, then peek at the last two sentences before you write.

Compare your copy with the model. Fix everything. Then tell your teacher what you learned and what questions you have, if any. Jot down the questions so you can be sure they get answered soon.

2a. Find the hyphenated word *left-hand*. Use a hyphen when you write about the left-hand side of the street or the left-hand bit of mushroom or left-hand something else. In other words, if it is an adjective (a describing word), hyphenate it. If it is just your left hand or my left hand, do not hyphenate it. Write in your own words this adjective rule for hyphenating.

b. Find a contraction and tell what two words it stands for. Write a rule about using an apostrophe in a contraction.

c. Study the quotation marks in the Alice paragraph. Notice the comma before and the capital letter after the opening quotation marks. Notice the period inside the closing quotation marks. And notice how the marks curve in different directions. Try writing some rules about quotation marks. Save your paper for tomorrow.

3a. In your grammar book, look up a section about quotation marks. See if your rules from activity 2c are there. Find another useful rule and add it to your paper.

b. Read the Alice paragraph aloud, and try to give proper expression to the quotations.

4a. Have someone give you a spelling test with five or six of the most difficult words. Repeat the test until you get all the words right.

b. List five words which end with *ed*. After each, write the word as it would be without the *ed*.

An *ed* ending often signals that the word is a verb, an action word. The *ed* shows that action happened in the past. You nibble today; you nibbled yesterday.

c. See if you can find a section of your grammar book that tells about the past tense of verbs.

5. Write the Alice paragraph from dictation and try to have no errors. How close to perfect did you get? How was your penmanship? Think of a way to reward yourself for good work. (A little recess now, a snack, etc.)

Winnie-the-Pooh

"Where should we dig the Very Deep Pit?" asked Pooh.

Piglet said that the best place would be somewhere where a Heffalump was, just before he fell into it, only about a foot farther on.

"But then he would see us digging it," said Pooh.

"Not if he was looking at the sky."

"He would Suspect," said Pooh, "if he happened to look down." He thought for a long time and then added sadly, "It isn't as easy as I thought. I suppose that's why Heffalumps hardly *ever* get caught."

"That must be it," said Piglet.

A. A. Milne

1a. First, read these paragraphs just to laugh at the way Pooh and Piglet's brains work. Then look carefully at how the quotation marks are used. Notice:

   1. A new paragraph is started when the speaker changes.
   2. A quoted sentence can be interrupted with a phrase like *said Pooh*. Study the opening sentence of the fifth paragraph to see how this is done.

Notice, also, that Pooh capitalizes some words that we don't capitalize. This shows that Pooh thinks the words are important.

   b. Copy the paragraphs or write them from dictation. If you want more practice with the quotation marks and other details, choose to copy today. If you think you can do it well, choose to write from dictation. Proofread and correct your work. Then ask your teacher to check it.

   2. Take a good look at the paragraphs and then write them from dictation. If you did this well yesterday, let your teacher dictate some conversation paragraphs from another book. Try writing them without any pre-study. You and your teacher can proofread together. Learn something from each mistake.

   3a. Find in your grammar book a section that tells about common and proper nouns. Read about them if you don't already know what they are.
   b. List the common nouns and the proper nouns you find in the Pooh paragraphs. (HINT: Most of the time, *pit* would be a common noun, but A. A. Milne made *Very Deep Pit* to be the name of a particular pit in Pooh's mind.)

   4a. Rewrite the paragraphs in dialogue form for a play. You can start it like this.

> POOH: Where should we dig the Very Deep Pit?
> PIGLET: The best place would be . . . .

b. Read your play with a partner. Trade parts and read it again. Use expression that you think Piglet and Pooh would use on these words.

Read the paragraphs from this book, using good expression as though you were a librarian reading this in a story hour for little children. (Little children wouldn't understand all the funny parts that you do, though.)

5. Write the Pooh paragraphs from dictation again. Or if you did it well before, ask your teacher to dictate a different conversation from *Winnie-the-Pooh* or another book. Proofread, fix, and ask your teacher to check.

6. If you want to make a play of the whole Heffalump chapter in the book, take another week or so for the work. You will need two main characters to be Piglet and Pooh and a minor character to be Christopher Robin, the boy who owns the stuffed animals. You can write the play, think of how to stage it, practice it, and then find an audience to watch it.

The Great Depression

In 1931, most people worked at coolie wages. Big department stores paid salesclerks as little as five to ten dollars a week. Factory workers got twenty-five cents an hour, sometimes even less. Topnotch secretaries who had once been paid fifty dollars and more a week were receiving ten dollars. Servants were clamoring for jobs at ten dollars a month including board.

Irving Werstein

1. Write this paragraph from dictation. Circle every word you are not sure is spelled correctly. Then compare with the model. If some words are wrong and you did not circle them, try this circling technique on more writing of yours until you get better at it. It is important to know which words might be wrong. That's the only way you can check on those words and write a paper with perfect spelling.

Fix the spelling and any other errors on your copy of the paragraph.

2a. Underline the first sentence on your copy, and in the margin label it *topic sentence*. Tell in your own words what the topic of this paragraph is. (You may have to look up the meaning of *coolie* to do this.) Examine each of the other sentences and tell your teacher which ones give more information about the topic.

b. Write three sentences that could be topic sentences for paragraphs. Use topics that you are interested in.

c. In your grammar book, try to find four purposes of sentences. One is asking a question. What are three others? Which kind are your topic sentences?

3a. Mark five or six words in the paragraph that you might misspell the next time you write from dictation. Study the words and then have someone give you a spelling test.

b. Read carefully. Can you tell from this paragraph whether salesclerks earned more than factory workers? Did servants want $10 a month *and* their meals (board)? Or did the cost of meals get subtracted from $10? Explain to your teacher what you think and why.

c. Choose one of the topic sentences you wrote yesterday and list some information that will help develop the topic. Use an encyclopedia or other information source if necessary.

4. Write as good a paragraph as you can, using the topic and information you gathered for activity 3.

5a. See if your teacher can think of a way to improve the paragraph you wrote in activity 4. Does it tell enough details to be interesting? Do the sentences read along smoothly? Choose **b** or **c** for today's writing.
   b. Rewrite your paragraph, making improvements.
   c. Write the depression paragraph from dictation and try to make fewer errors than before.

Answers for the Writing Lessons

HOW LANGUAGE BEGAN. 3b. Sample paragraph: I can do many things my dog can't do. For example, I can write a paragraph like this. Even if Marcella Vanilla could hold a pencil, she still couldn't think up a paragraph. I can talk and read and write. Vanilla can only whine and bark. (Other ideas: Humans learn of the past, plan for the future, think about God, invent, make art.)
   4a. Pronouns: us (1), our (1), our (1), them (3), his (3), he (3), him (3), he (3), them (3), him (3).

VALIANT. 3. Got interested, reached toward the crack, began to scratch up the soft earth, made a hole, light and air came through, got excited, scratched faster, made a tunnel, dirt flew out behind him.
   5a. The tunnel swiftly grew larger. The loosened dirt flew back between his legs. (The third sentence can also make two sentences, by putting a period after *earth*.)

BLACK BEAUTY. 2a. Some possibilities are: first place, large pleasant meadow, clear water, shady trees, deep end, plowed field, fir trees, running brook, steep bank (with arrow over each pair).
   3a. This exercise helps students learn to read carefully and to develop thinking skills by forming mental images of what they read. The arrangement may vary from one student to the next, but check to

see that these items are included: meadow with at least two horses (because of the word we); pond with rushes, water lilies, and nearby shade trees; hedge; plowed field; gate; house; road; grove of fir trees; brook with steep bank.

3b. Suggested spelling list: pleasant, meadow, lilies, hedge, fir (trees).

4a. Adjectives: The, first, a, large, pleasant, a, clear, some, shady, the, deep, the, one, a, plowed, the, other (its noun, *side*, is missing but is understood), a, our, master's, the, the, the, a, fir, the, a, running, a, steep.

5. Check to see that the paragraph is entirely in the past or entirely in the present, whichever the student chose to use. If possible, let someone actually draw from the child's description, and have the child improve his description if it is not clear enough to make a drawing from.

ADDITION. **2a.** Possible answer:

```
14 addend
32 addend
 7 addend
53 sum (total)
```

2b. Writing definitions requires good understanding and clear thinking. Judge each definition by these standards: 1) Does it explain clearly enough for a person who does not know the word? 2) Does it explain without using the word itself? Possible answers:

addition   the process of uniting two or more numbers.

addend   one of the numbers to be united by addition.

sum   the total of all addends in a problem.

3b. Posssible answers: 1) The order of the addends may be changed without changing the sum. 2) It does not matter which order you use when you add numbers.

5b. Sample paragraph: Subtraction is the process of finding the difference between two numbers. The larger number is called the minuend and the smaller number is called the subtrahend. The result is called the difference if you are comparing two amounts, and it is called a remainder if you are taking away. In subtraction you start with the largest number and count backward. For example, to subtract 3 from 17, you start at 17 on a number line, count backward 3, and arrive at the difference of 14.

HISTORY OF ENGLISH LANGUAGE. 1. An *o* and the final *e* are dropped.

2. William, king of Normandy, thought that England was promised to him after the death of its king. But the English king died and Harold came to the throne, lawfully. So William invaded and after about a year won decisively at the Battle of Hastings. Many Norman French then settled in England, and their ways and their language became absorbed into English culture and language. (Children writing about this may tell the more vivid parts of their reading—details of crossing the channel, details of battle, and so forth.)

THE WHITE SEAL. 2a. Verbs: went, carried, sank, flew, had told, had thrown, would have drowned, was learning, to use (an infinitive), floundered, coughed, grunted, crawled, took, went, found, belonged.)

2b. Regular verbs: carried, drowned, floundered, coughed, grunted, crawled, belonged. Irregular verbs: went, sank, flew, told, thrown, took, went, found. (*Learn* has an *ed* form, so it can be added to the list of regular verbs.)

3. Possible rewrite: The first time that Kotick went down to the sea a wave carried him out beyond his depth. His big head sank and his little hind flippers flew up exactly as his mother had told him. If the next wave had not thrown him back again he would have drowned. He was two weeks learning to use his flippers. All that while he floundered in and out of the water. He coughed and grunted and crawled up the beach and took catnaps on the sand, and went back again. At last he found that he truly belonged to the water.

4a. List 1: down, out, drowned, floundered, out, found. List 2: would. List 3: thrown. List 4: coughed.

4b. Suggested spelling test: depth, exactly, while, coughed, crawled.

4c. Possible answer: Baby seals have big heads and little flippers, so their heads sink in the water and they cannot swim at first. But they keep trying. After about two weeks they can use their flippers properly and swim as though they belong to the water.

SLITHY WABES. 1a. Nouns are: toves (pl.), wabe (sing.), borogroves (pl.), raths (pl.). Brillig could be a noun ('Twas evening), but it could also be an adjective ('Twas stormy). Possible reasoning: 1) the *s* ending for plural is one hint. 2) The word *the* before each noun is a dead giveaway. 3) The *y* ending on slithy and mimsy mark them as descriptive adjectives, so the words they describe must be nouns. 4) Nouns have a position as subject, performing an action, or as object of preposition (in the wabe). Students may not be able to explain these, especially number 4, but they will use these hints, nonetheless. They will appreciate your showing them how much grammar they know.

2a. gyre and gimble; outgrabe. Possible sentences: The toves did heave and tumble in the wabe. And the mome raths forgot.

3a. Possible answers: It was evening. It was chilly. The elephants were all females. The elephants were all hungry.

4a. Adjectives: slithy, mome. Their position before a noun is a clue. The *y* ending is another clue. (This clue, by the way, would show that *mimsy* is more likely to be an adjective than a noun. See activity 3a.)

ALICE'S ADVENTURES. 1b. Contractions: wasn't = was not; hadn't = had not; it's = it is; I'll = I will.

3a. When I used to read fairy tales, I fancied that kind of thing never happened. Now here I am in the middle of one. (The second sentence can also be split into two sentences by omitting extra words within the dashes.)

3b. Definitions: A simple sentence has only one subject and one predicate. A compound sentence is like two simple sentences joined by connecting words or punctuation. (Note: The one subject can be compound: *Bob and I.* Same with the predicate: *looked and found it.*)

ALICE'S ADVENTURES. 2. 4b. shaped, shape; thatched, thatch; nibbled, nibble; raised, raise; walked, walk.

WINNIE-THE-POOH. 3b. Proper nouns: Pooh, Piglet, Very Deep Pit, Heffalump. (You could argue that Heffalump is a class like rabbit or mole, but Milne made it to be a proper noun. His creative use of words is part of the charm of his stories. *Suspect* is a verb.) Common nouns: place, somewhere, foot, sky, time.

4a. Suggested ending:

somewhere where a Heffalump was, just before he fell into it, only about a foot farther on.

POOH: But then he would see us digging it.

PIGLET: Not if he was looking at the sky.

POOH: He would Suspect if he happened to look down. *(Pause, thinking.)* It isn't as easy as I thought. I suppose that's why Heffalumps hardly *ever* get caught.

PIGLET: That must be it.

6. NOTE: In this project your child will learn from the careful reading, writing, planning, thinking, and organizing that will be necessary, and he also will learn about interpreting humor and other meanings in the literature he reads.

THE GREAT DEPRESSION. 2a. Topic: in 1931 people earned low wages. (Coolie means native unskilled laborer in poor countries such as China and India were in the 1930s.) All sentences are about the topic.

2c. Four purposes of sentences: ask a question, make a statement, give a command or request, exclaim. Student's topic sentences probably make a statement.

3b. For a 40-hour week factory workers could make $10, and in those days they usually worked 48 hours or more. So some could make more than clerks. Meals were *included* in the servants' pay, so would be subtracted, not added on.

7. Scale of Writing Quality

How To Use the Scale

In this chapter we look at these four kinds of writing: describing, narrating, explaining, and reasoning. Typical examples are given for each of three levels: lower middle grades (fourth and fifth), upper middle grades (sixth), and junior high (seventh and eighth). The examples were written at the end of the school year, so you should adjust appropriately in comparing your own child's writings with these. For instance, if your child is just beginning seventh grade, the sixth grade sample here is closer to his grade level than is the seventh, end-of-year sample.

As with all development, children vary greatly. In any classroom, samples which are better than these and samples which are not as good could be obtained. Your child, too, may produce writing which is above or below the quality of the sample closest to his age or grade.

While it may be of some use for you to know roughly where your child stands on a grade-level scale, that is not the main purpose of this scale. The main purpose is to provide a means by which you can assess important learnings your child has already acquired, and by which you can see ahead and get ideas for his next learning.

I cannot stress strongly enough that progress toward more mature writing happens within the child's total thinking abilities. It does not happen in any easy manner by simply learning techniques, forms, or tricks of writing. It is all right at times to learn techniques, but they, alone, do not do the job. To illustrate, here is a sentence from the writing of a sixth grader:

> Although they lived in the cool state of Michigan, the weather was very hot on that particular day.

You may not agree that Michigan is cool in summer, but that is beside the point for now. This is a complex sentence with the subordinate clause coming before the main clause. The subtle meaning of the subordinating conjunction *although* is not grasped by most primary children, so they do not write sentences like this. If you want to raise your primary child's writing to this level, you can't do it simply by saying, "Now write some sentences that begin with *although*." That's only the technique. What the child really needs is the kind of thinking that can relate two ideas in this way. The child grows to that level of thinking by continued dialogue, as described in an earlier chapter, between reading and writing. Conversation with you about the reading and writing also helps immensely. When the child's thinking is sufficiently mature, he is then ready for a conjunction like *although*, and for writing sentences like the one above.

In the children's writing samples given in the following sections, all errors of indenting, punctuation, spelling, and so forth are retained. The commentary mentions them in some cases, but not all. Those mechanics of writing, while important, are not the essence of good writing. A child could write a paper that is error-free as far as mechanics go but which is poor writing, nevertheless. Sometimes we "back to basics" or "excellence in education" people tend to major on the lower-level skills such as mechanics.

In this chapter, we call attention to some qualities of writing which are beyond mechanics—the qualities which mature as the child's total thinking matures. Among the features considered are: 1) the number and richness of ideas, 2) the development and organization of the ideas, 3) appropriateness and vividness of the wording, and 4) maturity and variety of sentence structure.

If you wish to compare your child's writing with the samples given, decide which of the four types—describing, narrating, explaining, or reasoning—is closest to a piece of writing you wish to judge, and turn to that section of the scale. Then lay your child's writing alongside the samples given here and try to find the one that most closely matches it in quality. To do this you must read and reread not only your child's writing and the children's writings in the scale, but also the commentaries here. They point out some important features and qualities to look for.

This procedure is difficult and inexact, not at all like scoring a spelling test. But if you're interested in teaching more than the mechanics of writing, you will find this a profitable exercise. The insight you gain from such a close study of children's writings will help you guide your child to better writing.

The grade levels assigned in this scale match national averages as determined by the research of an achievement testing company. Homeschooled children may tend to write better than the averages because they often have more dialogue with books in their families.

At the beginning of each section you can find the assignment that the children were given. You, too, may use the assignments and obtain papers from your children on these topics to compare with those in the scale. Your child should edit, revise, check spelling, and so forth, and then hand you his best effort.

All work, of course, should be the student's own; he should receive no suggestions or help either in the original writing or in the revising, or in any part of the work. It is a good idea to write only one of these papers per day.

Describing

Writing Assignment. Describe "My Room." Use this title if you have a room to yourself or if you share a room with someone else. If you don't have such a room to describe, then choose another topic that is almost like this: for instance, "Our Kitchen" or "My Study Place." After your first writing, you should look it over and fix it up the best you can. Copy it again if it gets too messy.

Fourth and Fifth Grades. Writing paragraphs that describe something familiar is less complex than most other kinds of writing. Fourth and fifth graders are just becoming aware of an audience, or reader, for their writing. So they, more self-consciously than primary children, can describe a place or object as though giving information to another person. Few children of 9 or 10 give an introductory, overall picture of what they are going to describe, but most just list detail after detail. They may misspell simple words, even children who do well on spelling tests. Here is how a fourth-grade boy described his room.

> My room is very small. But it has three calanders, ten posters, and one computer and one printer and one bed and a closit and a radio and two dresser and one toy box and last but not lest toys.

Sixth Grade. By sixth grade, children have developed still more awareness of their audience, and their writing shows more of the formality that distinguishes written language from spoken language. In the following example by a sixth-grade girl, the formality consists of an introductory sentence, a closing or summary sentence, and the technique of listing the "main" item first.

> My room is a room that I share with my sister! The main color of our room is dusty rose. We have bunk beds that are light brown. The bedspreads are covered with pastel flowers and are hand-quilted. Our curtains are pink, ruffeled, and are mid-length. My mom stenciled the top of our walls with baskets and John 3:16. We have an oak cabinet with drawers. A bookcase with pink pots of flowers and a lamp stenciled to match the room makes a nice east-wall decoration. Our room is very cozy and I really like it!

Junior High. In seventh and eighth grades, the better writers show little improvement in description over middle grades, probably because they already could write complete and organized descriptions in the lower grades. The writing of most children continues to be rather pedestrian. Instead of richer vocabulary, many students add details of measurements: "On the left side of the room is an oak dresser about 4½ feet high and 1 to 2 feet wide. On the left top side corner is a 12 × 8 black and white picture of my parents and me when I was 3 yrs. old."

Junior high writers, if they aren't listing details such as colors and measurements, often give less complete descriptions than younger grade children, as they seem to become less mindful of their audience at this age. Students who have good ideas for their writing seldom develop them as fully as they might.

The following example from a seventh-grade girl shows a degree of imagination that many students this age can produce.

My room has yellow and white wallpaper with flowers on it. It has a green rug to go with it. It makes me feel comfortable when I don't feel right. I can tell my secrets in my room because the walls can't speak.

When I'm mad. I can come in here and tell my problems and troubles too. I listen to my radio where I can sing and I can make believe where no one can bother me.

My room is very cheerful. When I'm angry, the bright colors makes me forget my troubles and makes me happy that I have my own room. I have so much privacy and I'm *very thankful*!

Narrating

Assignment. Write one part of a story you know. If you use a story you saw on TV, tell only about as much as would be on one half-hour episode. If you use a book you read, tell just one event or series of events so that yours sounds like a story without becoming too long. Remember to check over your work, rewrite as needed, and make the best story you can.

Fourth and Fifth Grades. These pupils have progressed beyond simply stringing bits of story together with "and then," and beyond telling stories dominated by "he said" and "she said." Their sentences show more sophisticated construction. In this fourth-grade example, you can find compound and complex sentences mixed gracefully with simple sentences. Yet the story, as is typical, is strictly a reporting of events with little attention to cause and effect relationships among the events. The doves, the olive leaf, even the flood itself, are not connected with anything else in the story. They just come along, each in its proper order.

This example also shows typical ability in spelling, where

some difficult words such as *daughters* and *except* are spelled correctly, but *there* is used for its homonym *their*.

> Once upon a time in the Bible there was a man named Noah. One day there was a great big flood that killed all of the people except Noah and his family. They were safe in the ark. When the rain stopped Noah sent out a dove and it came back. The next day he sent out another dove and it came back with an olive leaf. Then one day the Lord opened the door of the ark and they all went out into the beautiful world. There daughters went a little ways away and picked some beautiful flowers. The sons of Noah helped the animals out of the ark. Then they had to clean up that stinky mess Pewee!!!!

Sixth Grade. By this age, narrators have usually progressed beyond reporting events in order. They have a better grasp of the wholeness of stories. Consequently they make better selections of what to include, and they indicate relationships between events. Relating two clauses with *although*, as in the second sentence, is a mature construction that indicates a maturing level of thinking. This sample opens with the setting and characters, and progresses with minor awkwardisms toward its ending. Sixth graders also show better handling of psychological motivations in a story. Here, for instance, we are told that Tom was afraid but acted unafraid, and we see the significant detail of Tom wiping the sweat from his head.

The mechanics of punctuation and capitalization are mostly correct, but not the paragraphing. Notice in the first sentence the two spellings of *their*. And compare the comma after *Today* in the first sentence with the semicolon after *Later* in the last sentence. This student probably has learned about commas in series and commas after introductory words, but in these sentences the two rules bump into each other and she struggles for a solution. If you were teaching punctuation in the context of this writing, you could explain that many comma rules are not strictly kept and that commas could be omitted after these introductory words. Then the girl could look at her *suddenly* and her *so*'s and decide if she really wants the reader to pause after them.

Today, Tom, Sarah, Jesse, their uncle Rick and thier father were out in the field picking blueberries. Although they lived in the cool state of Michigan, the weather was very hot on that particular day. It was even hotter being out on the field. "Sarah!" said the little girl's father wearily. "Would you please run back to the house and fetch us a pail of water from the pump?" Sarah agreed and decided to take Jesse with her. Off they went, through the tall thick grass. Suddenly, they heard a quiet growl and then a loud bark. They were afraid! When they looked under a tree, they saw a large black shadow. They quickly ran away. "We saw a big, scary bear!" Sarah and Jesse shouted at the same time, as soon as they returned. "A-And it growled at us!" Tom laughed hestoricly and continuously made fun of the girls. "Go get the water yourself now, Tom." Uncle Rick said. So, Tom went through the grass and heard the same growl. It was a wild dog! Tom was so afraid. So, he too ran back. Tom acted unafraid. "That was just a little d-dog." He wiped the sweat off his head. Uncle Rick stood up and grabbed the pail. By this time, everyone was very thirsty. Uncle Rick went towards the house and saw a poor dog laying on a tree stump growling and whining. It had a small sliver in his paw and couldn't get it out. Uncle Rick took it out and then got the water. Later; Tom, Sarah, Jesse and father were all happy to see Uncle Rick return, with a cool pail of water, a cute pup and a grin from ear to ear!

Junior High. Like good sixth-grade writers, junior highers have a grasp of the cohesiveness of stories. In addition, many of them try to pace the action of a story so as to give pleasure to their readers. The seventh-grade girl writing this sample opens with Tom hearing a noise. Then she tries to build intensity before the second paragraph, where Tom realizes it is his stallion in trouble. Through the rest of the story things happen just in time or just too late, with the writer pacing it for us. It is flawed mainly because of viewpoint problems. We readers know in the second sentence what Tom doesn't know yet, because we suddenly are in the barn instead of with Tom. Action happens simultaneously on two fronts in the rest of the story, too, and the writer attempts to keep it all going.

Paragraphing in this story seems carefully planned according to what is happening to the stallion. Notice that *too* is missed in the next to last sentence. This is one of the most troublesome words for children of all ages. The drove-driven error in the last sentence probably happened because the *had* is so far away from it. If someone pointed out to this writer that she really means "barn is" and should use an apostrophe for the missing letter, the same as in *he's*, she probably would remember always, because of learning it in this context. Most language book exercises do not include an example of this kind.

It was around one in the morning when Tom heard a noise in the barn. It was his stallion, Blacky. Blacky had heard someone come into the barn. It was a stranger, short and fat. He had a thick stick that was burning with fire. He set the stick on the ground after he started some hay and wood on fire. When the stranger left the barn was on fire and Blacky was kicking his stall, trying to get out.

The stallion was making more noises and they were getting louder and louder. Then Tom realized that it was his stallion who was making all the noise. So he got out of bed quickly to get dressed. He ran down the stairs and flew out the door. He ran to the barn seeing it was on fire. He then yelled as loud as he could to his mother "the barns on fire, the barns on fire." His mother woke up and saw the fire. She ran to the phone to call the fire department while Tom was trying to get Blacky out of the barn.

When Tom got the stallion out he tied him to the fence, away from the burning barn. While he was doing this the fire truck came and put out the blazing fire. The whole barn was burned.

As they were looking at the barn, the stranger who set it on fire came back to get the stallion. He untied the rope and walked quietly through the field. Tom turned around to look at the stallion but saw it was gone. He looked into the distance where he saw his stallion. He ran after it but it was to late. They had loaded up the stallion in a trailer and drove away.

Explaining

Assignment. Write on the topic "How To Make a Sandwich." If you wish, you may add a word or two to the title: for instance, "How To Make a Tuna Fish Sandwich" or "How To Make a Sloppy Joe Sandwich." Explain carefully so someone could follow your directions. You might want to make the sandwich before you write about it. Remember to check over your work, rewrite as needed, and make the best explanation you can.

Fourth and Fifth Grades. In explaining, the task is to write precisely and completely enough that there is no room for error if someone tries to follow the directions. This example by a fourth-grade girl is short, so there is little chance for the back-tracking and overlapping that writers of this age sometimes include. Word choices are adequate, but mundane. The signaling words, *first, then,* and *next,* help the sequence. But clarity is lost when both bread and cheese are referred to as "slices" and then the wording switches to "piece." The paragraph is shaped with introductory and closing sentences.

> Once I wanted to make a melted cheese sandwich. First I took two slices of bread and laid them on the counter. Then I put cheese slices on one piece and the other piece on top. Next I put the sandwich in the microwave for about three minutes then I had a very good sandwich.

Sixth Grade. The organization in this sample moves beyond the step-by-step organization of the preceding sample, in that it begins with a purposeful statement of all materials needed. Omissions, the most common flaw in directions at this level, include how you cook the beef and where the gravy comes from. Most of the wording is precise and not dull; the adjectives are appropriate and don't have an artificial, overdone sound, as sometimes happens when children try to color their writing with adjectives. We get the feeling that this writer really enjoys his tasty beef sandwiches.

> In order to make a tasty beef sandwich; you will need the following items: a short piece of Italian bread, six juicy pieces of shaved beef and some kosher dill pickles. First off, you need to cook the beef. Then put some gravy on the bread. After you put your beef on the bread, you top it of with cool juicy pickles. Eat and enjoy!

Junior High. The seventh-grade girl who wrote the following sample concentrated on precise words, rather than colorful words. She made sure that we won't confuse which slice of bread is which, and continued this effort until she relaxed somewhat in her courteous final sentence. One small problem, though, is referring to *the* mayonnaise in the second sentence. If we were reading about mixing unfamiliar chemicals, we would be in trouble at this point, since *the* indicates that a certain amount was earlier referred to, and it wasn't. This could say "spread some mayonnaise" or simply "spread mayonnaise." Imprecise use of the word *the* continues into adult writing of many people who have never had this little problem pointed out, so we can excuse a seventh grader. When this girl masters the precision that she worked so hard at here, she could get a job writing computer manuals.

Repetition of the verbs *put* and *take* contribute to the lack of vitality in these directions. And the commonly overused *things* doesn't help either.

Though we sometimes teach that one sentence does not make a paragraph, this writer appropriately paragraphed her directions in this way. The clear opening and the summary closing shape the paragraphs into a cohesive whole. The signal words *first, then, after that,* and *finally* show a sequential organization that carries from start to finish. And there are no significant omissions, as in the sixth-grade sample.

How to Make a Turkey Sandwich

You will need the following things: two slices of bread, a slice of turkey meat, lettuce, and mayonnaise.

First you take the two slices of bread and spread the mayonnaise on both slices. Then you put the slice of turkey on one of the slices of bread. After that you will take some lettuce that you tore off a lettuce head and put it on the slice of bread with the turkey. Finally, you will take the other slice of bread with only a spread of mayonnaise and put it over the half with the turkey and lettuce. Now you are ready to eat your delicious turkey sandwich!

Reasoning

Assignment. Some people think that homeschooled children should spend part of their time helping the family with chores or family business. Do you agree? Why or why not?

Fourth Grade. The reasoning task includes stating an opinion, giving reasons, supporting each reason, and signaling when a new one starts. Better writers also close with a summing or concluding statement.

The first of two fourth-grade samples given below is somewhat lower than average, but is included here to help show progression of skill in reasoning. It states an opinion, gives one reason, and then does not support it, unless in the child's mind the discipline is connected with teaching responsibility by chores. After writing one sentence about what godly parents should do, this child pursued that thought and told something else that godly parents should do. Other children who got off the reasoning track began narrating stories about work in their families, and failed to make the necessary connections with their opinions.

The second fourth-grade example shows a contrary opinion, which was rare in this particular assignment. This writer opened with a clear opinion statement. Then his word *Beside* seems to signal a reason for the opinion, but the reason doesn't actually appear clearly until near the end, where he compared with public schools and said, "you shouldn't expect so much more out of a home schooler." The earlier statement, "I already have six school subjects," was a start toward that reason, but it gets derailed in the list of other chores. Possibly this boy viewed his chores as reasons in themselves rather than as illustrations or support for the stated reason. This essay gives one reason, illustrated. The clear opening statement (in spite of the misuse of *intend*) and the strong summary statement at the close indicate a shape for his thinking and for the paragraph.

1

Yes, I agree that children should help out with the household chores. People that are Godly people need to teach their children responsibility. Children need to be disciplined every time they do somthing wrong. I believe that Godly parents should have daily family devotions.

2

No, I do not feel that we should have to particapate in doing extra work or chores we do not intend to do. Beside the fact that I already have six school subjects, I deliver meals-on-wheels. I have a paper-route, I go to the store for my mom at times, I help in garden work, and other things like that, I know public schools would not do so and I don't feel I should do so either, because you shouldn't expect so much more out of a home schooler.

Fifth Grade. The girl who wrote this sample marshaled several reasons for her opinion. The first reason (working together seems like play) is illustrated with two examples (talk and races). The second reason is well thought out, but the little brother example doesn't quite connect. Two more reasons follow. Only one is signaled—with the word *Besides*. The final sentence, though good in itself, cannot be characterized as a closing statement for the paragraph. Thus this writer would rate high on number of ideas, but lower on supporting them, and lower still on organization.

I think that home schoolers should help with the family jobs. When the whole family works together, it seems like play and not work. We talk to each other and have races to see who gets done first. We ought to help clean the house and wash the dishes because we help make the house dirty and we eat of the plates. Even my littlest brother helps clear the table and take the dirty napkins off. Besides, we would get tired of playing all the time. Sometimes the work is not fun but if we do it, it makes us feel good about our selves.

Sixth Grade. This typical sample opens with a clear statement of opinion and closes with an appropriate reiteration of that statement. We are eased into the delightful firewood story through "I made up a saying," with no signal that we are leaving one reason and moving on to another. Similarly, it is difficult to decide whether to count "Each child is a part of the family" as a new reason or to consider it a commentary on the preceding story.

This essay has, possibly, three reasons, compared with four in the fifth-grade sample, and rates adequate on ideas. It supports the "play" reason so well that it rates high on that feature. The opening and closing statements help to shape the paragraph. The "play" topic is well organized, but otherwise the interior of the paragraph is flawed by lack of turn signals, so that it rates only medium on organization.

I think home-schooled children should help out with family chores and bussinesses. I think it will help the child when he/she is older to be able to manage his own home or bussiness. I made up a saying, "The family that plays together, stays together." When a family does work together it seems like play and a lot of fun. Once we were unloading firewood from a big stack. We had a race to see who could unload the most. Mom made us milkshakes when we where done. It was fun to have a prize at the end and better yet, a fun time with the family! Each child is a part of the family and should do his/her share of the work!

Junior High. In this seventh-grade sample we see more ideas and better organization than in the lower grades. But we see little development of the ideas. This is typical of junior high students, and it is often disappointing to their teachers. Perhaps we should not expect junior highers to spurt forward in reasoning, but let them consolidate their skills during this rapid-growth stage, and then move forward in their later teen years.

Turn signals in this essay are indicated by paragraphing. The closing is a fast-paced pile-up of reasons. It would be difficult to add a standard closing sentence after the force of this. There are fewer errors than in the lower grades. In the second paragraph, *them* has no antecedent, and you might question whether you *do* a business, but this verb is used for almost everything these days. Sentences flow quite smoothly and are structured in a variety of ways, with more subordinated thoughts than in the lower-grade samples.

Yes I do think homeschoolers should help out with a family business. If you do a family business together you will get closer to everyone in your family and you can have fun together.

When you do your business you can ask questions and not be afraid to ask because you know them better than other people.

When you have a job in the family business you help your family by not having to pay someone else to work there. It can also help you get some more money to buy that special thing you've wanted for the longest time!

A family business can help take up your spare time. A family business can help you learn about the way a business works. A family business is something you can really look forward to doing after school.

7. The Mechanics of Writing

The mechanics of writing include capitalization, punctuation, spelling, and form. Spelling is discussed in a separate chapter, and sections describing each of the other topics follow here. A section on penmanship is also included.

Capitalization

Some simple rules of capitalization are easily learned. These include the following.

1. Capitalize the words *I* and *O*. Be careful not to confuse *O* with *oh*. *O* is used only in expressions like "O Lord" and "O king."

2. Capitalize the first word of each sentence.

3. Capitalize proper nouns. This will entail learning proper nouns: geographical names, including East, West,

etc. when they refer to regions, but not when they are directions; names of persons; names of organizations (schools, businesses, government bodies, political parties, etc.); names of races, religions, and nationalities.

4. Capitalize important words in titles of books, essays, etc. This usually means capitalizing the first word and all other words except articles and prepositions. Don't forget that *is* is important, even though short, because it is a verb.

5. Capitalize names of days of the week, months, holidays.

This brief list is not complete, but covers the vast majority of cases that elementary and junior high students use. When they write letters, they should learn to capitalize the "Dear Friend" greeting and the "Sincerely yours" closing. Headings, labels, poetry, and other special cases of capitalizing can be learned in context.

The first word of direct quotations is capitalized, but this should not be learned in isolation. Along with it, children should learn to use a comma between the quotation and the *she said*, and to use quotation marks and other punctuation properly, as well as to indent each time a new speaker is presented. It all should be a package when children learn to write conversation.

Names of school subjects, such as history, arithmetic and spelling are not capitalized in ordinary use. After students spend years capitalizing these words on the headings of their papers, some can hardly write the words *history* or *language* without capitalizing them. But these are common nouns, not proper nouns.

To have accurate capitalizing, you may need to give attention to penmanship. Do your children form letters carefully enough that you can tell which are capitalized and which are not? Review letter forms when necessary. (See penmanship section at the end of this chapter.)

Punctuation

Exclamation Point. Children should have learned in primary grades about "end marks" of periods and question marks. A third end mark is the exclamation point. Children's first need for these is usually after true exclamations beginning with *how* or *what*. Examples: How red the sky is! What a lot of snow! After that, use of these marks becomes more complex. Except in an old book like *Heidi*, an exclamation point often does not follow an interjection such as *oh*, as language books say, because the interjection usually is not the end of a sentence. Writers more often use this form: Oh, you scared me! This sentence looks like a statement that requires a period, but because of the opening interjection it gets an exclamation point instead. The main problem people have with exclamation points is overusing them. If your children begin using these points too often, hoping to make their stories more exciting, explain that they must build excitement by the way they tell stories, not by punctuation. Statements should have periods. But this rule, as all rules, is broken in special situations.

Period. Most children by middle grades are fairly adept at using periods as end marks. And they usually know that periods should be used after abbreviations, but they need to learn more about abbreviations themselves. Here is a list of common abbreviations children find useful:

1. Days of the week: Sun., Mon., Tue., Wed., Thurs., Fri., Sat. Use these abbreviations only in special instances such as in filling out forms. Spell out in full when the days are used in ordinary sentences.
2. Months of the year. Jan., Feb., Mar., Apr., Aug., Sept., Oct., Nov., Dec. Use in special instances only. May, June and July are always spelled out.
3. A.D. and B.C. in dates, a.m. and p.m. in times. (A.D., which stands for *anno Domini*, the year of our Lord, is

written before a date, thus: A.D. 1990. The abbreviation B.C. stands for *before Christ* and follows the date.)

4. Addresses. St., Ave. and similar designations; NW., SW., NE., and SE., when indicating sections of cities. Notice that only one period, not two, is used in these. North, South, East and West are spelled in full according to most style manuals.

5. Mr., Mrs., Dr., Rev., and other titles. Books published in England will have the British form, which is to use no period after a title which ends with its last letter. Thus: Mr Jones, Dr Doolittle.

6. United States. This is written as U.S. when used before the word Government or the name of a U.S. Government organization: U.S. Congress, U.S. Army.

7. Organizations and companies: Red Cross, First Baptist Church, Radio Corp., Standard Oil Co.

8. Two kinds of abbreviations do not use periods: 1) the relatively new two-letter state and province abbreviations in which both letters are capitalized—NY, CA, BC; 2) the shorthand abbreviations for governmental agencies and other organizations—IRS, IBM.

Other abbreviations can be learned in the context of chemistry, mathematics, history and wherever else your child has need for them.

Comma. Commas are probably the most troublesome of all punctuation marks. Some publishers and teachers advocate "close" punctuation in which many commas are used, and some advocate "open" punctuation in which fewer commas are used. Nineteenth-century writers used long, involved sentences and close-style punctuation. Today the trend is toward open style.

Usage experts disagree on comma rules, so teaching about commas is not as simple and neat as teaching the multiplication tables. Another complication is that two comma rules sometimes get in each other's way.

An example of two comma rules bumping into each other occurs in a sixth grader's writing in the scale, where we find this sentence.

> Today, Tom, Sarah, Jesse, their uncle Rick and their father were out in the field picking blueberries.

The series of names requires commas in any style of usage— closed or open or in between. The only variance is that some people teach that there should also be a comma before the *and* and some teach that it can be omitted, as this student did. The comma after *today* is probably because this student has learned to put commas after introductory adverbs—today, later, however, etc. The awkwardness of that comma alongside the others is apparent, and students should know that they can "break" rules when one comma rule interferes with another like this. To keep *Today* from looking like part of the series, that first comma should be omitted. But if that seems awkward, too, because of the unintended alliteration in the first two words, then maybe a rewording is the best way out of this dilemma. Changing *Today* to *This morning* would keep it from looking like part of the series.

The rule about commas after introductory words is an example of a disputed rule. Some would teach that these words (or short phrases) need a comma only when you want the reader to pause. Commas slow down a story. Many writers use no comma after *suddenly* and other introductory words, basing their decision on the pace of the sentences. If they don't want you to pause they don't use a comma.

Children, at first, must learn the more common uses of commas. They should put commas where most all readers will expect them. As their writing matures and as they are able to reason about commas, they should gradually understand that some comma "rules" cannot or need not be strictly followed. The main purpose of commas is to add clearness of meaning.

Here are the most common uses of commas:

1. Use commas in certain situations, as in dates, in greetings and closings of letters, and between city and state names. (This last is not universal. Some users omit the comma in addresses before the two-letter, all-capital abbreviations for states. In sentences, state names are spelled out and the comma is retained—both before and after a state name.)

2. Use commas to separate items in a series, except that the comma usually is omitted before the *and*. Example: Tom, Sarah, Jesse and their father were picking blueberries.

3. Use a comma after an opening *yes*, *no*, *well*, or *oh*. Example: Yes, I agree that children should help out with the household chores.

4. Use commas before and after the name of a person addressed. Example: Go get the water yourself now, Tom.

5. Use commas before and after appositives—words which immediately follow a noun or pronoun and explain or identify it. Example: It was his stallion, Blacky. The comma can be omitted when a one-word appositive is so close as to seem to be part of the noun. Example: It was his stallion Blacky.

6. Use a comma to separate a direct quote from its "tag." Example: "Go get the water yourself now, Tom," Uncle Rick said. When the quote ends with a question mark or exclamation mark, a comma is not used.

7. A comma may be used to set off introductory words, phrases or clauses. The more favored open style omits the comma unless a phrase or clause is at least five words long, but makes exceptions when the writer wants the reader to pause. Close style practically

always uses commas. Examples: When I'm angry, the bright colors make me forget my troubles. (Close style.) After that you will take some lettuce. (Open style.) Finally, you will take the other slice of bread. (Close style.) A top-level editor says, "When in doubt, leave it out."

8. Use commas where they are needed for clarity. For children (and for all of us) this rule can cover a number of situations, without us having to explain each one in complex grammatical terms. Examples: 1) The family that plays together, stays together. (Ordinarily we do not put a comma between the subject of a sentence and its verb, but in this case the student knew that a comma was needed for clarity.) 2) Blacky was kicking his stall, trying to get out. (You might want to call this a participial phrase, or something else—I won't argue—but how long would it take for the seventh grader who wrote it to understand a grammatical reason for this comma? By using the meaning approach, she punctuated this properly.)

You can gauge from your children's writing when they are ready for one or more of these rules. Teach the rules in context as much as possible. For instance, when they are writing letters and addressing envelopes is the best time to learn about commas in addresses and dates. When a child writes a series of items is the best time to point out that he needs a comma after each item. Or if your child naturally puts commas there because of the pauses, you might commend him for it and explain that that is what people are supposed to do.

Colon. Colons are probably easier to learn about than commas. Here are the uses children are likely to need.

1. In writing time—1:00 p.m. or 2:30 o'clock.
2. In Bible references—John 3:16.

3. After the greeting of a business letter—Dear Sir:
4. Before a list that is formally introduced—You will need the following items: a short piece of Italian bread, six juicy pieces of shaved beef and some kosher dill pickles.

Semicolon. The only time a semicolon appears in the writing scale samples it is misused. (Later; Tom, Sarah, Jesse and father were all happy to see Uncle Rick return.) This sixth grader seems to know that a semicolon denotes a pause longer than a comma pause and she tried to keep the word *later* from appearing to be part of the series of names. But a semicolon does not belong in this sentence.

There are two major uses for semicolons and both require rather sophisticated writing. So you can delay teaching semicolons until your children write sentences that need them. To teach semicolons earlier may invite misuse and greater difficulty in understanding their proper use. Here are the two uses.

1. Use a semicolon between items in a series if the items contain commas. Example: For this sandwich you will need two slices of homemade, whole wheat bread; a slice each of ham, cheese, and turkey; and some lettuce and mayonnaise.
2. Use a semicolon between main clauses of a compound sentence in these cases: 1) when no conjunction is used, 2) when certain words such as *for example* or *besides* are used, 3) when there are commas within the clauses.

It is tricky deciding whether to to link two clauses with a semicolon or to write them as two sentences. It takes a good ear for subtleties of meaning. Usually they should be two sentences, but if the ideas are so closely related that you don't want a period between them, you can use a semicolon.

Apostrophe.

1. Use an apostrophe to show omission of letters.

Examples: The barn's on fire. Buy that special thing you've wanted.
2. Use an apostrophe to form the possessive of nouns. Examples: my sister's room, our family's business. With plurals or nouns which end in *s*, usually just an apostrophe is used—*boys' room*. But sometimes two forms are allowed: either Burns'house or Burns's house.
3. Use an apostrophe with *s* to form plurals of letters, figures, and words referred to as words. Examples: *a*'s, *5*'s, *and*'s.

Rule 2 is complex after you get beyond singular nouns, so the singular form is all children should learn at first. Plurals are best learned case by case as children run into need for them in their writing. Most books add pronouns to this rule, but as you investigate further you find there are probably more pronouns that do not take an apostrophe than do. At least a number of the most common possessive pronouns do not use an apostrophe— *its,his,hers,ours,yours*, and *theirs*. Only a few do—*one's,other's*.

Quotation Marks. When children learn to use quotation marks for direct quotations as in written conversation, they should learn them in a package along with all the other mechanics needed, and there are numerous mechanics to learn. The sentence being quoted begins with a capital. The tag (he said, she answered, etc.) is separated from the quote by a comma if it comes before. At the end of the quote, punctuation is inside the quote marks, a comma substituting for a period, and question marks and exclamation points used if needed. A tag can follow any of these. A new paragraph is begun each time a new speaker appears in a conversation.

Quotation marks are also used around some titles—not book titles, which are italicized—and in other situations that children are seldom likely to use. Periods and commas go inside the close quotes, while colons and semicolons go outside. Question marks and exclamation points go inside if they belong with the quote and outside otherwise.

Children need only learn how to punctuate conversations, particularly if they write stories, and to put quotation marks around titles when they appear in sentences. Other complexities they can learn gradually as they have need either in their own writing or in noticing the use of quotation marks in books that they read.

Reference books cannot cover all the possibilities that arise, and students should develop an ability to learn punctuation usage from their general reading as well as from rule books. This same principle holds for practically all usage matters.

Others. Parentheses, dashes, hyphens and all other marks are best learned when a child develops need for them. None of these are used, or needed, in the children's samples in the writing scale, and time spent learning about them in language books probably is wasted time.

A little attention may be given to end-line hyphenation, but just enough so children know when and how to check a dictionary for correctness. Too many books spend too much time on this. Careful secretaries and editors in their adult lives still keep dictionaries or syllable books handy. There are better things to do in life than memorize all the ins and outs of syllabication for the English language.

For a child who misses more than an occasional punctuation mark, dictation exercises are extremely helpful. Dictate a paragraph, sentence by sentence, for the child to write. He should listen carefully to your expression and decide by that what kind of punctuation to use. After writing, spend time comparing the child's writing with the original and analyze differences in punctuation. For wholistic learning, you should also look for problems in spelling, capitalization, indenting and anything else. At first this is difficult for some children, but use the method consistently for a few weeks or months and most children not only find it gets easier, but they achieve dramatic improvement in their writing.

Add interest to this work by choosing paragraphs from the child's favorite books. The child can even help to choose the paragraphs. When he finds one he would like to write, put it away for a couple of days before using it. Then he will have to think as hard as if he had not seen it before. A young child could join the writing session by writing just the first sentence. Another child may prepare by copying the paragraph first, perhaps the day before. By such variations, you can have children of differing ages join in the same dictation lesson, and they can discuss together the punctuation and other mechanics of their writing.

Sample dictation lessons were given in an earlier chapter.

Form

Handwritten Papers. Forms are matters like indentation and margins. On full size paper it looks nice to indent about an inch for paragraph openings, and to leave a margin of approximately an inch all around the paper, with a bit more—an inch and a quarter—on the left side. The left margin should be even, while the right margin may be "ragged"—slightly uneven.

Pages can be numbered in the upper right margin. Teachers often request headings in either the upper right or upper left of the first page, giving the student's name, the subject, and date in that order one under the other. If this practice is followed, children need to be reminded occasionally that while they capitalize the subjects *history*, *reading*, or *arithmetic* in these headings, the words are common nouns and should not be capitalized when used in sentences. The only subject that is always capitalized is *English*.

An essay or story should have a title at the beginning, centered. Titles in this position do not have quotation marks, as they do when used in sentences. Often when a title is used, the school heading is omitted. Skip a line after the title before writing the first line of the composition.

Neatness is important on the final draft. During proofing and rewriting there will of course be much crossing out, erasing, inserting between lines, and so forth. But a final draft should be as neat as your child can make it.

Should every paper be handled with all this care? Probably not, if you aim to have your child do a lot of writing. Essays submitted for contests deserve the greatest care. Papers saved as part of schooling records, to show a student's progress, should receive a fair amount of care, as should any other papers which will have an audience besides you, the teacher. This includes papers that are part of a notebook or science display or project which other people will be reading.

As for other daily papers which will be seen only by the child and parents, you can decide what makes sense. Some children seem naturally neat and others labor hard over handwritten papers and still end up with sloppy products. While you want to encourage neatness, you have other goals, too, for your children's writing, most of them more important than neatness, and you have to strike whatever balance seems appropriate for each child.

Typewritten Papers. If you have a typewriter or word processor available, middle grade and junior high children who are interested in learning to use it should do so. There is no reason to wait until high school. This takes time, but many children have done it. You don't need to aim for much speed, but do require that your children start out using the keyboard properly, with fingers held in the correct positions.

If your children are typing, they should follow standard manuscript form. This means double spacing, with margins about as before. At the top of the first page more space is left—about two inches. Indenting is usually five spaces. The left margin is even and the right margin ragged.

Some people who begin word processing get excited that their programs will also make the right hand margins even, and they use this feature too much. When lines are spread to accomplish a justified right margin, a paper is less easy to read because people's eyes are not used to the uneven spacing between words. Also for professional work later on, there sometimes are problems in translating or transmitting information because of the extra spaces inserted between words. So save the right justification for special situations when you want that look. Ordinary manuscript form, which children should follow, does not use it.

Footnoting is a feature that we have often required students to waste a lot of time on. One eighth grader had the picture quite clearly when he said, "When I was little they told me I had to learn something because I would need it in older grades; now they tell me I have to learn footnoting because I will need it in high school. Why don't they just let me be an eighth grader?" And if the truth be told the story could go on all the way up to graduate school where people do research papers and their readers might really want to use the footnote information. But in graduate school you don't remember details you learned in eighth grade about footnoting. You have to use a form book and follow every colon and comma exactly. And, again, if the truth be told, many students leave this up to the typists they hire.

So if your child wants to be a typist, you can help her understand footnote forms. The trend today is to place them at the end of a paper instead of at the bottom of each page, partly because it's simpler to plan the pages and to operate word processing programs that way.

The general guideline in all these matters is to keep the dog wagging the tail instead of the other way around.

Penmanship

During third grade most, but not all, children have made the switch from manuscript writing (printing) to cursive writing. Remember, the switch should not be made until a child has achieved speed and fluency in manuscript. If you attempt the change too soon it will affect your child's writings negatively. His stories and compositions will be shorter and contain a poorer vocabulary than if you let him continue using his more comfortable mode of penmanship. When the optimum time arrives for your child, the changeover takes only about three weeks. During those weeks you may concentrate on handwriting and neglect composition.

After children know all the letter forms and can write fairly readably, then what? Must they practice fifteen minutes a day for the rest of their elementary school lives? No. Repetition in itself does not bring improvement. Concentration and thinking are needed. If your child makes a particular letter poorly, help him to get a good picture of that letter in his head. Does he know it should be closed at the top? Is he aware that he does not close it? If he has a hard time closing it, how can the problem be solved? Does he need to curve the line more, or slant it more? Converse with your child about such matters while comparing his writing with a model. After a goal is firmly in his head, he can practice writing the troublesome letter by itself and in words.

This practice with concentration is efficient. It need not be done on a regular basis but can be intermittent, as problems surface or come to your notice. A few children, particularly girls, have beautiful handwriting that may surpass their teachers'. These children seldom need special practice sessions. Other children have poor, unreadable handwriting either for physical reasons or mental reasons. These need more attention given to their problems. And in between are the majority who could also profit from some concentrated work on handwriting.

I have found that an intense three-week unit on handwriting works wonders for practically all children. Two such unit plans are described below—one which focuses on physical means of improvement and one which focuses on the mental. If you use one of these and obtain the remarkable results that I have, you can dispense with daily handwriting practice for the rest of the year. You and your children will have developed ways to talk with each other about penmanship, so when you see a child becoming sloppy about this or that feature of handwriting, you will have an effective way to remind him of what he knows.

The Head Method. To start, you need a model sentence for your children to copy. This could be taken from a penmanship copybook, but if you wish to choose the sentences, you must make your own model. The best penman in the family can make this—mother, father, or older child. When making models, try to use a plain, "schoolteacher" style. Omit flourishes and any distinctive, nonstandard features as much as possible.

Each child is to make a copy of the model and bring it to you for a conference. You may comment first on something good about a child's writing and then find something that can be improved. Show the child exactly what can be improved and be sure he understands. Some possible items are: slant all letters uniformly, close tops of *a*'s and *o*'s, cross *t*'s more neatly, make better loops in *l*'s or *e*'s, make letters a uniform height, make straighter downstrokes on *g*'s and other descenders, or correct the form of any particular letter. During this conference you can circle items you want the child to notice, or rewrite one or more words below his sentence so he can compare your forms with his. The original model also can be used for comparing.

Do not overwhelm a child with all the kinds of comments mentioned above. Instead, choose one or two items to talk about in this conference. Then give a small assignment in which the child can actually do better on the items you chose. Usually the assignment can be to rewrite the day's sentence, trying to make certain improvements over the first try. But if the child is a slow writer and that would be too discouraging, give a shorter assignment. For instance, if you want him to close the tops of *a*'s, mark three or four of his words with open *a*'s and tell him to write each word once or more until he has good copies that he will be proud to show you. This second assignment is done on the same paper. You can praise the child for the improvement; then the paper is dated and filed in a notebook or folder.

The next day start on a new sheet of paper and repeat the same procedure with another sentence (or the same one again, if the child feels a need to make a better copy of it). Hopefully, you can comment that the *a*'s look good today and move on to another point for improvement.

Continue this procedure for about three weeks. The collection of dated papers should show improvement, and if you work it properly, this is good for some powerful motivation. With these papers, the child himself can see how his writing has improved in just a few days, and he will be spurred to greater effort for the remaining time in this unit.

Below are some quotations you can use for models. There are more than enough for a three-week unit, and there is no particular order for using them. In the first group are sayings of Solomon about wisdom and learning. The second group contains quotations from famous people (Plato's sentence has been shortened). With younger children, you could use small portions—for instance, "All men are created equal" or "I discovered my faults and corrected them." Have your children copy the author's name or not, as you prefer. The third group adds humor to the unit. Use the last rhyme to provide practice on all the capital letters. And use the "brown fox" sentence to check the formation of all lower case letters. (Some children will enjoy trying to compose a sentence like this, which has all the letters of the alphabet.)

My son, hear the instruction of your father, and forsake not the law of your mother.

The fear of the Lord is the beginning of knowledge, but fools despise wisdom and instruction.

Incline your ear unto wisdom, and apply your heart to understanding.

Happy is the man that finds wisdom, and the man that gets understanding.

Wisdom is better than rubies; and all the things that may be desired are not to be compared to it.

A wise son makes a glad father, but a foolish son is the heaviness of his mother.

I can't tell a lie, Pa; you know I can't tell a lie. I did cut it with my hatchet. —*George Washington (quoted in 1800 by Weems)*

I believe this government cannot endure permanently, half slave and half free. —*Abraham Lincoln*

Some books are to be tasted, others to be swallowed, and some few to be chewed and digested. —*Francis Bacon*

Until philosophers are kings, or political greatness and wisdom meet in one, cities will never have rest from their evils. —*Plato*

We hold these truths to be self-evident—that all men are created equal; that they are endowed by their Creator with certain inalienable rights; that among these are life, liberty, and the pursuit of happiness. —*Thomas Jefferson in the Declaration of Independence*

By comparing my work with the original, I discovered many faults and corrected them. —*Benjamin Franklin*

I think about the elephant and flea,
For somewhere in between them there is me.
                                    David McCord

          Behold the duck.
          It does not cluck.
          A cluck it lacks.
          It quacks.
                    Ogden Nash

The thing about cats, as you may find,
Is that no one knows what they have in mind.
And I'll tell you something about that:
No one knows it less than my cat.
                                    John Ciardi

          This troubled world is sighing now;
            The flu is at the door;
          And many folks are dying now
            Who never died before.
                              Old Rhyme

     The quick, brown fox jumps over the lazy dog.

               Z, Y, X, and W, V,
               U, T, S, and R, Q, P,
               O, N, M, and L, K, J,
                    I, H, G,
                   F, E, D,
               And C, B, A.

The Rhythm Method. In physical skills rhythm plays an
important part, and a three-week emphasis on using rhythm in
handwriting can produce remarkable improvement. This is a
unit that all ages can work on together as long as each uses

cursive writing. A boy who participated in this unit while in third grade in a one-room rural school has now finished school. Recently he was asked what he remembered about that one-room school, and his first answer was the rhythm practice on handwriting. He feels it is helpful even today.

On the **first day** of this unit, practice only the letters *n* and *i*. *N* has two counts, which you say on the two downstrokes. So that all children in the group can anticipate the downstrokes and do them together, count this way: and-ONE, and-TWO, stressing the counts. On each *and* you swing up the hump and on each count you pull strongly down. Demonstrate this on a chalkboard or large sheet of paper with your back toward the children. After the children see you write or trace the letter while counting, have them join you, writing with their fingers in the air. They can count too. The reason your back is toward the children is so that they can imitate the motions of your writing, which is too confusing if you face each other.

To use this method successfully you must not be timid about it. Admit, if you have to, that it may be silly, but since it works you are all going to try it anyway. Count loudly, over-emphasize the strokes, and get everybody writing *n*'s together in rhythm. After air writing, when each child knows what to do, have them write on paper, still in concert while you count. And-ONE, and-TWO. And-ONE, and-TWO.

After enough *n*'s that everybody has the feel of this rhythm, stop and analyze the writing. Are the tops of the humps nice and rounded? Are the humps the same size? Are all vertical lines slanted similarly? The last downstroke should not slant out to the right but should be parallel with the first upstroke. (If someone has a backslant, take that into account, and see that all vertical lines are slanted backward the same degree.) One purpose of this detailed talk is to get the letter form into every child's head. Write some more single *n*'s, all together while you count. Then write two *n*'s joined. Write several pairs.

Next, tackle the letter *i*. Its count is: and-ONE DOT.

Demonstrate. Do air writing, then paper writing. Talk about the looks of the *i*'s, then write some more.

Now you are ready for the word *in*. You can count "and-ONE, and-ONE, and-TWO, DOT." Or you can try to keep everybody on target by saying letters instead of counts, thus: "and-I, and-N, and-N, DOT." Do air writing, then paper writing. Develop a smooth, swingy feel, not jerky. Let the children try tracing over the same copy for a while instead of writing a new word each time. You might speed up a bit now and begin omitting the *and*'s except for the first one. And-I, N, N, DOT. Keep the rhythm, though, allowing the same amount of time as when you used the *and*'s. This shorthand counting is all that's needed after a careful introduction to the letters.

Try the word *inn*. Now that's all for the first day.

The **second day** review. Get the feel again. Make the letters roll out smoothly. Try *m*. It has three counts. Try *u*, with two counts. Write the word *nun*. Make up some syllables to write: *im*, *min*, *num* and others. That's all for the second day.

The **remaining days** of your unit should proceed similarly. Take up new letters in approximately the order given below. Practice each new letter individually, then in pairs, then in words which use only letters already practiced.

The listing below does not contain diagrams or go into detail about each letter, because I don't want to set out a penmanship style here, but want to provide a method you can use with any style. You could use a sample alphabet from a Zaner-Bloser or Hayes or Palmer book, an italic style, the old Spencerian style, your own family style, or any other you choose.

If you develop your own family style it is a good idea to prepare a wall chart of letter forms that your children can use for reference. The process of making the chart will help you, as you will be forced to make decisions about details and to check on consistency. Do similar letters begin with similar strokes? Are descending loops handled alike? At what height should the *t* be crossed? Such details will never make or break a day in our adult lives, but when you're teaching penmanship that's the way the game is played. At some point in their education, children must become aware of these details.

The listing also does not give the rhythm and counts for each letter, as some of these may vary depending on the style. Also, the rhythms work better if you plan your own. Once you have a careful start as described in the first two days' lessons, you can work out rhythm patterns for other letters. It takes a little experimenting at times. Try to consistently accent the downstrokes, but if that is not possible, plan something workable and move ahead anyway.

Here is a suggested order for introducing letters during this unit. If in your style of writing a letter fits better in another group, move it.

1. This group uses only two kinds of strokes—an over curve and an under curve.

    n, m, i, u

2. Add a tall letter which uses no new strokes. Now you can write *tin*, *nut*, *mutt*, and *mitt*.

    t

3. These letters contain the strokes of group 1, but additional strokes too. Invent wording or counts to take care of these. For instance the ending stroke on the *v* can be labeled "end," and its count could proceed like this: "and-ONE, and-END"; or "and-V, and-END."

    u, v, w, x, y, z

4. Practice the *c* group—all the letters which begin like *c*, with an over curve.

    c, a, d, g, q

5. These letters begin with an under curve. Practice *e* and

l first and use them in words (*tell, till, well, will, mill, all, tall, call, wall, dull*). Then try the more difficult letters in the group. (Your style of *r* may belong in group 1 instead of here.)

e, l, o, p, r, s

6. These remaining letters combine strokes already practiced.

b, f, h, j, k

7. This group of capital letters can all begin alike. *Q* may not belong, depending on the style you use.

H, K, M, N, Q, U, V, W, X, Y, Z

8. These capitals, too, may begin alike.

B, P, R

9. Here is a pair of capitals.

F, T

10. And here are the "leftover" capitals.

A, C, D, E, G, I, J, L, O, S

A final word: if you try this unit, you can achieve good results even if you don't practice the rhythm down to every last *q* and *z*. A very meticulous beginning for the unit is important, and a strong middle. The ending is less important, because children by then can apply the rhythm principles for themselves. So if you run out of time and never get to some letters, don't let that worry you. But near the end of your unit, do celebrate what improvement the children's "before" and "after" writing samples show.

When you go back to normal life, your children need not count and write in the rhythm of their practice sessions, but let each child integrate the new skills in his own unique way.

9. Spelling

Good spelling should mean to a child, getting the words right in her letter to a friend, in her essay contest entry, in her history research, and on her advertisement for babysitting services. It should not mean making A's on weekly tests of twenty words. To achieve this result, spelling must be integrated with every writing assignment in every subject. And only part of the time does spelling need emphasis as a separate subject.

Here we will look at information about the phonics and common-word approaches to spelling, so you can select items to teach when your child seems to need them. We emphasize, again, that individualized spelling is the most efficient teaching plan. Ways to manage that are discussed after the other two approaches.

Phonics Approach

In a time of frustration, when you feel like calling your child a poor speller, you might try noticing how many sounds he spells correctly. Most likely he handles practically all single consonant sounds well, and the digraphs *th*, *sh*, and *ch*, too. Maybe not *wh*. Among vowels he may make more errors, but he has some sort of reasoning behind his choices. Many such errors would be correct spellings except that our dictionaries happen to say otherwise. In addition to all these spelling skills, your child probably knows a number of words that are not easy phonetically, such as *once, listen, the*, or *want*.

With your child's spelling problem thus cut down to size, you should feel encouraged. Your next move can be to analyze some of his misspelled words and try listing a few items to teach. Does the child write *thro* for *throw*? Then put *ow* on the teaching list. You and your child together can think of some more words in the same spelling family as throw—possibly low, blow, flow, mow, row.

Other *ow* words, such as *how* and *cow* do not belong in this family. This probably is a complete reversal from the kind of thinking you did when you first taught phonics to your child. Most phonics systems begin with a spelling such as *ow* and teach its various sounds, because that is the order in which your child thinks when he reads; the child sees letters and he decodes their sounds.

In writing, however, the child already has the sound in his head. What he needs is the spelling for it. This simple principle is the key to vastly improved phonics instruction for spelling. So shift gears when you teach phonics in connection with spelling. The charts given here are arranged by sound instead of by spelling.

In using the charts, you should feel free to personalize them. Omit items that seem not very useful as spelling helps. If you speak Bostonian, or for some other reason find the sample words not good examples, then change the words. Change even the groups in any way that makes sense to you. Phonics, like grammar, is not neat; it did not come from God; and each published system differs from every other published system. So you may as well help to form your own system for teaching. That way you will understand it better.

If you are the notebook type of family, your child can make notebook pages for problem sounds. The child who writes *thro*, for instance, can begin a page for long *o* sound. The page can be for future reference, for adding more long *o* words, for writing rules or problems about this sound, and for you to select words for spelling review tests. An alternative to a notebook is for the child to build up his own charts on which he will put some of the items from the charts given here. Items can be added as they become meaningful to the child. After he catches on to the system in these charts, he may use the full charts, as in this book, for reference.

A number of spellings are not included on the charts (*sch*ism, for instance, as a spelling of *s* sound), and a number that are on the chart could be omitted for still greater efficiency in teaching. When you personalize, you can decide how far to go with rare spellings. Often it helps a child just to see that there are several other spellings for a sound besides the familiar ones, and it is not necessary to memorize them all.

A law of diminishing returns applies with phonics. The first rules about common spellings help the most. Then other rules help less and less as they become more uncommon. Remember, too, that teaching sometimes by words instead of by rule, *is* teaching phonics, since the child can then use words to figure out other words.

The best way to use phonics in the middle grades is for you to be somewhat familiar with a phonics system and then know when to look up some item to help your child. Phonics is the tool—the means. Don't go overboard and make it an end in itself.

The commentaries add information that may be helpful as you personalize the charts for your use.

Spelling Chart of Vowel Sounds

A Sounds

short:	cat
long:	cave, play, they, eight, mail, straight, great
broad:	salt, jaw, cause, thought

E Sounds

short:	get, friend, heifer, head, said, says, any
long:	he, see, tea, receive, believe, ski, people, key

I Sounds

short:	fix, hymn, pretty, been, busy, build, sieve
long:	I, my, high, tie, eye, height, island, aisle

O Sounds

short:	on, John, honest, knowledge
long:	go, hoe, throw, boat, oh, though, beau

U Sounds

short:	run, done, does, flood, tough
long:	1) Preceded by *y* sound: use, few, feud, beauty
	2) No *y* sound: tune, to, you, food, fruit, blue, through
other:	put, foot

Schwa Sound

	about, telephone, visible, control, until
	(Also many vowel combinations.)

Vowel Blends

oi:	spoil, boy
ou:	found, cow,

Vowels with R

er:	her, sir, worm, fur, pearl
or:	for, four, warm
ar:	far, heart

Spelling Chart of Consonant Sounds

B Sound	bat, buy
D Sound	dad, called, could
F Sound	fast, phone, half, enough
G Sound	gas, guard, ghost
H Sound	hat, who
J Sound	jet, gem, education, edge
K Sound	kitten, cat, sack, chorus, walk, quit
L Sound	let, apple
M Sound	man, lamb, phlegm, hymn
N Sound	not, know, pneumatic, mnemonic, gnome
P Sound	pan
R Sound	ran, write, rhyme, colonel
S Sounds	1. sat, since, listen, science, psychology
	2. leisure, azure
T Sound	tap, tapped, yacht, indict, debt, receipt
V Sound	van, of, have, halve
W Sound	went, one, quit, where (In most areas this is pronounced *hw*.)
X Sounds	No distinctive sound of its own, but besides *z* sound, *x* also stands for these combinations:
	ks as in mix (also spelled *cc*: accept)
	gz as in exam
Z Sound	zebra, busy, clothes, Xerox, Joe's

Combinations

Ch Sound	chin, catch, nature
Ng Sound	sing, bank
Sh Sound	ship, chef, nation, pension, ocean, passion, schwa, conscience, special
Th Sounds	1. this
	2. thing

Commentary on the Vowel Sounds

A. Short *a* is one of the simplest groups on the vowel chart, which makes it an ideal beginning for phonics teaching. But even this has two other spellings as in *plaid* and *laugh* (if you are a westerner). Though these two words are quite common, the spellings are not. So these are cases where I decide it is not worth the trouble to teach the phonics or spelling rules. It is easier for children simply to learn the words plaid and laugh, and if they ever run across other words like them, these words themselves can provide a phonics precedent.

Long *a* has more spellings than most reading phonics systems ever point out to you all in one place. Seven are given on this chart, and some people would add an eighth—*ei* as in *their*. But in the word *eight*, you have a choice of saying *eigh* makes the long *a* sound or that *ei* makes the long *a* sound and the *gh* is silent. This is an example of the choices you have when you set out to organize a phonics stystem.

Broad *a* along with short *o* present more difficulties than almost any vowel group on the chart. Are these two sounds alike? If different, how different must a sound be to go into the *o* group rather than the *a* group? Some phonics systems include in broad *a* sound everything from *want* or *wash* to *was*. Maybe you pronounce those the same, but I don't. Yet I would rather have one group than several. On the chart are some of the most common spellings of this sound. You could also include *augh* as a spelling, and include *ou* by itself without *gh*.

E. Short *e* sound has a number of spellings, some of which your child may know as being a way to spell long *a* or long *e* or some other sound. A rare spelling that could be added is *u* as in *bury*. When you see this many ways to spell a sound, you realize that there is more to spelling than memorizing phonics rules. Good spellers read a lot and get used to seeing how the words look.

Comparing the two *e* lists, shows that *ie* and *ei* are on both lists, for the short sound and the long sound. So the rule, "*I* before *e* except after *c*," will only be useful part of the time. A rare spelling that could be added to the long *e* list is *ay* as in *quay*, but this is a case where it is better to learn the word when you meet it than to learn a rule to help you meet it.

I. More rare spellings could be given on both short and long sound lists, but some of those given are rare enough. However, *ui* is more important than you may think at first glance because it spells this sound far more often than it spells long *u* sound. In this list, again, you may decide whether to include *gh* in the spellings or whether to call them silent letters.

O. Difficulties with the short *o* sound were discussed along with broad *a* earlier. Some of the spellings listed there could be listed here if you prefer. A rare spelling for long *o* sound is *ew* as in *sew*.

U. Ordinary people don't have much difficulty with long *u* sound, but a group of phonics specialists can spend an afternoon arguing about whether a man wears a *sute* or a *syoote*. Does long *u* begin with a *y* sound, or not? Most of us solve that problem rather easily by pronouncing the *y* sound naturally after some letters and omitting it after others. Included here are sounds and spellings often taught as short and long *oo*. This will simplify your child's notebook or chart.

Schwa. On this one, the phonics specialists would stay up all night arguing. The sound they disagree about is *uh*. It happens only in unaccented syllables and we say it so quickly that it is impossible to tell what vowel it's supposed to be. The actual spelling might be any of the five single vowels and, in addition, almost any combination of vowels. Most standard dictionaries indicate this sound with an upside down *e* (ə). Objectors say there should be no such thing as a schwa sound; it only indicates how our speech is decaying. True objectors use reprints of nineteenth century Webster dictionaries. Middle-of-the-roaders say children should try to pronounce all vowels so they are at least thinking them; this will make them better spellers. Those are your choices.

Vowel Blends. Blends (diphthongs) are different from other vowel teams in that both vowel sounds can be heard. Helpful rules to teach these are: 1) *oy* is used to end a word or root of a word, while *oi* is used within a word; 2) *ow* is used to end a word or root, while *ou* is used within a word except when followed by final *l*,*n*, and sometimes *d* (fowl, town, crowd; loud).

Vowels with R. Unless you speak Bostonian, the sound in *far* is usually spelled *ar*. The sound in *for* is usually spelled *or*. So those two are easy. The *er* sound has five spellings. So once again, you can see the importance to spelling of much reading and seeing how words look.

Some phonics systems would add an *air* group with words like fair, fare, marry, and merry. And then there is sorry, which has still another sound. Phonics zealots can make lots of rules about when the *r* is doubled and other matters, but I think that mastering such rules is more work than it's worth. Sound-alikes such as fair and fare, and hair and hare, have to be learned individually anyway. Children can use what they know about long and short vowel sounds to work out the spelling of many *r* words.

Commentary on the Consonant Sounds
B and Other Single Consonants. To make the chart more complete, and more complicated, we could add the spellings *bb* and *be* as in robber and robe. Some phonics systems do that, but most people seem more comfortable thinking of the *e* as a silent

signal that the other vowel is long. Knowing the silent *e* rule also helps a child know that robing and rober come from robe and require only one *b*, while robbing and robber come from rob and require a double *b*.

These matters of final *e* and of doubled consonants are the same for most of the consonants, so they will not be repeated for each one.

G. *U* following *g* signals that the *g* has its hard sound.

J. If you want to see your child's eyes light up with new understanding, then wait until he is stuck on a word like soldier, education, or gradually, and then show him that *d* is in the *j* section of the chart. When we follow *d* with a *y* sound, as in these sample words, we can hardly help it coming out like *j*. Some phonics systems allow for this, and others decry our horrible pronunciation.

L. *Le* at the end of a word is a different case than other consonants with *e*. Children seldom have trouble with this after they learn a few words like apple, little and table. If your child ever does have a problem, just tell him to spell his word like little, or whatever familiar word is like the one he is trying to spell.

Many phonics systems have to worry about where the vowel sound in this syllable comes from, or whether this syllable has no vowel sound. Here, I choose to ignore that problem. Children never ask.

X. *X* is a maverick. Technically it should not be listed on a chart of sounds, but I list it anyway and note the three sounds it can spell.

Ch. Here is a final choice for you. Many phonics systems include *t* as one of the spellings for *ch* sound, and others say this is slovenly pronunciation. So you can let your child say NAY-chur or teach him to say NAIT-yur. In either case he must spell it with a *t*.

Common-Word Approach

Weekly prescribed lists are a simple way to manage spelling in a classroom so that everybody studies some spelling, and they are a way to see that spelling doesn't get overlooked in the bustle of other work. In home teaching, you won't need to prescribe lists very often, but for those times when you want to, you may find some usable study information in this section.

Spelling Lists. To make lists as useful as possible, spelling books often derive them from the most commonly used words. So here we give three such lists for you—one for grades 4–6, one for grades 7–8, and one for 8+, which advanced spellers may use. This grouping gives a general idea of the difficulty of the words, but does not tie children too closely to grade levels. In individualizing, of course, you can use any list that fits, no matter what its label is. You may teach the words by sound groups, if you wish, or scramble them.

Some children will benefit from reading the groups of words as well as writing them. This gives added experience with common spelling patterns.

Common-Word Spelling List
Grades 4 to 6
These 300 words are arranged according to vowel sounds, given in the same order as in the vowel chart.

tax	rate	train	spell	tree
act	page	lady	spent	each
fact	take	they	when	teach
dash	gave	air	them	east
pass	game	care	then	least
past	made	bear	tenth	lead
cast	name		seven	read
add	same	saw	better	reach
back	came	fall	letter	real
black	became	want	head	deal
track	age	what	dead	mean
than	case	water	said	clean
camp	face	was	any	speak
plan	race		very	easy
glad	place	end	every	even
band	state	yet	where	dear
grand	paper	set	there	near
grant	May	sent		clear
plant	pay	best	even	here
glass	stay	rest	these	
class	away	west	meet	Miss
stamp	delay	left	need	miss
thank	maybe	felt	keep	list
after	paid	help	deep	trip
happy	wait	held	week	sick
cannot	sail	cent	seem	wish
	mail	went	seen	ship
lake	fail	less	feet	bill
sale	jail	press	feel	fill
date	rain	fell	free	still

print	Friday	show	two	nor
with	behind	blow	new	born
wind	high	boat	few	more
fix	sight	soap		short
its	fight	road	put	form
give	right	only	full	forget
think	night	open	foot	report
thing	might		could	horse
spring	light	cut	would	north
sister	tonight	shut	should	story
winter	why	such	poor	door
river	try	much		
finish	eye	club	house	far
city		under	south	car
	got	Sunday	found	card
mile	God	Monday	pound	hard
file	cost	son	round	dark
fine	lost	from	around	part
line	stop	some	about	party
mine	block	come	without	start
ride	song	cover	outside	March
side	long	coming	our	large
slide	along	become	hour	
life	belong	other	down	Mr.
wife	across	mother	town	Mrs.
nice	upon			
price		rule	sir	
white	hope	June	girl	
tire	stone	July	first	
fire	told	blue	word	
alike	sold	true	work	
inside	gold	noon	hurt	
find	hold	soon	burn	
mind	post	room		
kind	most	afternoon	or	

Common-Word Spelling List
Grades 7 and 8

These 400 words are arranged in groups as shown by their labels. Further information about the groups is given in the accompanying text.

Compounds

another
anything
anyway
gentleman
itself
herself
himself
however
newspaper
everything
nothing
something
sometimes
themselves
understand
within
railroad

Prefixes

aboard
above
among
arrange
await

according

account
address
affair
amount
another
appear
appoint
arrest
arrive
assist
attempt
attend
attention

almost
alone
already
also
although
always

because
before
beside
between

comfort
command
company

complaint
complete

connection
contain
contract
convention
convict

debate
declare
degree
department

employ
enclose
engage
engine
enjoy

except
expect
expense
express

importance
important
imprison

include
income
indeed
inform
information
inspect
instead
intend

object
oblige
obtain
offer
omit

present
president

progress
property
provide

regard
remain
remember
repair
reply
represent
restrain
result
retire
return

subject

unable
unless
until

Suffixes

awful
beautiful
wonderful

action
addition
combination
direction
election
population
position
question
section
station
vacation

measure
pleasure
capture
picture
figure

Calendar

Tuesday
Wednesday
Thursday
Saturday
January
February
April
August
September
October
November
December

Christmas
calendar

Vowel Sounds

happen
catch
half
shall
matter
rather
travel
rapid
family
factory
strategy
grammar
answer
perhaps
began
carry
carried

able
table
navy
change
mayor
favor
famous
escape
estate
statement
great
straight
chain
claim

raise
afraid
fair
pair
their
eight
eighth

father
small
all right
talk
walk
watch
auto
automobile
cause
daughter

beg
shed
check
dress
spend
ledge
length
else
guess
guest
request
ever
lesson
second
event
elect
collect

select
direct
getting
next
extra
enter
center
member

special
several
terrible
relative
yesterday
death
ready
weather
friend
many
says
again
against

region
speech
leave
please
reason
teacher
steamer
hear
nearly
either
field
chief
police
people

drill
bridge
fifth
which
since
cities
visit
ticket
district
history
prison
written
driven
children
minute
nickel
liberty
begin
pretty
been
build
built
women

size
write
quite
while
final
private
primary
flight
died
wire
desire

empire	throw	used to	were
entire	own	usual	
buy	though	refuse	firm
		sure	third
off	thus	during	worth
loss	trust	who	world
gone	struck	whom	turn
sorry	judge	whose	church
body	justice	prove	during
copy	study	through	surprise
o'clock	uncle	news	learn
proper	number	knew	heard
property	suffer	view	early
prompt	summer	suit	
doctor	sudden		order
dollar	running	push	support
follow	husband	took	morning
office	public	stood	forward
bought	publish	woman	fortune
brought	once		forty
thought	done	ground	four
	does	mountain	fourth
both	none	crowd	court
don't	month	allow	board
broke	money	flower	war
clothing	front	power	warm
close	dozen		
suppose	young	point	army
goes	trouble	royal	farther
those	enough	destroy	charge
stole	country		heart
whole		term	
wrote	due	clerk	
vote	duty	person	
know	human	personal	
known	use	perfect	

Dictionary of Prefixes. Many prefixes began life centuries ago as parts of compound words. All children should have enough acquaintance with prefixes to at least be aware of what prefixes do in our language. This helps them unlock meanings of numerous words. Many useful prefixes associated with specialized or technical language, such as *micro*, *macro*, and *tele* do not appear in the first one thousand common words. Children who understand the prefix idea often work out those meanings for themselves. And you can occasionally explain one of them.

Prefixes which appear in the common words have meanings largely lost on today's children because they reach so far back in the history of our language. These prefixes also are often attached to roots with lost meanings. Later, your child may study some of the Latin, Greek, French and other ancestors of our language, and learn more about roots. For now, a study of prefixes is a start.

Here are the meanings of prefixes found in the list of common words.

a   **1.** Intensifier, as in await.   **2.** Of, off.   **3.** Reduced form of *ad*.

ad   To, towards. This prefix often loses its *d* and often gains another consonant according to the root it is attached to. On the chart only *address* has the prefix in its original form. In the other words you see the prefix in some of its assimilated forms.

al   All. (All + one equals *alone*—all one. This meaning is so lost or ignored that we sometimes say "all alone.")

be   By, over, upon. (*Begin* and its derivatives were not formed originally from a root and prefix, so they are not in this group.)

com and **con**   Together, with.

de   Away, down.

em and **en**   In, into, cause to be, to make.

ex Out, beyond.

im and **in**   **1.** In.   **2.** Not.

ob Against. *Ob* is the original form. *Of* and *o* are assimilated forms.

pre Before.

pro Forward, for.

re Back, again. (About one-third of the words that begin with *re* are not in this group, because these words, which usually came from the French, were not formed historically with a root and prefix.)

sub Under.

un Not.

Dictionary of Suffixes. Only three suffixes appear frequently on the list of common words for grades 7 and 8. Their meanings are given below.

ful Full of.

tion Denotes a noun form.

ure Denotes act, process, or being.

Vowel Sounds. Words in the vowel sound groupings are arranged in the same order as sounds on the vowel chart. You don't have to look at these long to notice that the spellings are not nearly as easy as those in the list for grades 4 to 6. Whereas, on the earlier list, only one or two spellings appeared for each sound, on this list several spellings appear for most sounds. In addition, there are more spellings for the consonant sounds. Thus, our children have a complex job to do when we say, "Just sound it out."

There is no group for the schwa sound, because these words are classified by their accented syllable, and schwa always appears in unaccented syllables.

For more information about the sounds and spellings, refer to the commentaries on the vowel and consonant charts.

Common-Word Spelling List
Grades 8+
These 200 words are arranged by syllable count.

aunt	decide	really
course	divide	receive
doubt	effect	recent
drown	entrance	receipt
folks	extreme	refer
height	feature	region
lose	foreign	relief
meant	forenoon	secure
mere	further	senate
ought	honor	service
piece	increase	session
scene	injure	success
search	issue	suggest
stopped	judgment	summon
too	license	supply
wear	local	system
weigh	machine	therefore
wreck	manner	total
	marriage	toward
absence	mention	treasure
adopt	minute	vessel
accept	motion	victim
allege	neighbor	volume
assure	neither	whether
believe	often	witness
business	pleasant	
busy	prefer	accident
career	prepare	agreement
certain	proceed	annual
common	promise	argument
concern	purpose	arrangement

article
athletic
avenue
beginning
century
character
circular
circumstance
citizen
colonies
committee
condition
conference
consider
cordially
decision
develop
diamond
difference
different
director
disappoint
discussion
distinguish
distribute
earliest
entertain
entitle
estimate
evidence
excellent
finally
general
government
illustrate
improvement

interest
national
objection
occupy
official
opinion
organize
period
popular
possible
practical
principal
principle
probably
provision
questionnaire
recommend
recover
reference
salary
separate
serious
sincerely
souvenir
theater
together
tomorrow
various
visitor
vitamin

accuracy
adolescent
application
appreciate
associate
automobile

celebration
convenient
difficulty
education
elaborate
eligible
emergency
environment
especially
experience
explanation
immediate
impossible
investigate
invitation
majority
material
necessary
particular
political
propaganda
psychology
publication
respectfully
responsible
secretary
temperature
testimony
unfortunate

accidentally
association
consideration
examination
organization
preliminary
representative

Individualized Approach

There are many degrees and kinds of individualizing. If you decide to skip some lessons in a spelling book because your child already knows what's in them, that is a small step of individualizing. If you don't follow a textbook at all, but have each child collect his own troublesome words for spelling study, that is a larger step of individualizing.

The main idea in individualizing is to hold at the center of your thinking the children, and not a preplanned curriculum. Instead of trying to squeeze children through a curriculum, you reverse the order and custom build a curriculum for each child.

This is not as difficult as it sounds, because it does not mean that you must lay out a detailed spelling curriculum for a semester or even for a month. Custom-made curriculum works itself out day by day or week by week as you go along. Most people find this process easy, and sometimes quite exciting. A good starting point is to choose or invent a system—not the content, not the words to learn, not the rules or prefixes or definitions to study—just a system for working. Here are three sample systems.

Custom Lists. From the child's daily writing (and there should be daily writing) find misspelled words and write the correct spelling for the child to copy into a spelling notebook. After a specified number of words, you should quit finding candidates, or let the child start another list on the next page.

When a list is complete, you can start some old-fashioned tutoring. Look at a word together. What is hard about it? What part did the child miss? Can you suggest an idea for remembering it? Did the child write *gril* for *girl*? Then he had all the letters, but in the wrong order. Why? Is it not knowing how to spell the *ir* sound, or is it careless transposing of letters?

Straighten out the child's thinking. Get the proper image

and information into his head. This is far better than making the child write the word ten times, as though it were his hand that needs the practice. Don't do all the talking in these tutoring sessions. Get the child to tell you why the word is hard or how he is going to remember it. If any words on the list are similar, then study them together. For instance, if *first* was spelled *frist*, notice its similarity to *girl*, and learn the two words together.

After a brief tutoring session, you may give a short test on the words just studied. Sometimes dictate a full sentence for the child to write—perhaps the original sentence in which he misspelled the word. The next day review those words and teach a few more.

Devise a full week's schedule for the spelling list. Learn a portion of the words each day, have a practice test on Wednesday or Thursday to see which ones still must be learned before Friday. And finally, have the test and move on to the next list which was being collected while you taught this one. Tests don't have to be on Fridays. You could let a child work on a list until he announces that he is ready for a test.

What to do if a child misses something on the final test? That, too, is up to you (and the child) in an individualized program. One idea is to add the word or words to next week's list and study them some more. Another idea is to make a page near the back of the spelling notebook to keep track of particularly troublesome words. Then when the child wants to use one in some writing, he can refer to his own private list, which is much quicker than looking it up in a dictionary. This procedure would help adults, as well. Many of us have had the experience of repeatedly looking up a word because of inability to remember what we learned the last time we thought we had learned it once and for all.

After your children learn from these tutoring sessions some good ways to conquer spelling words, you can let brothers and sisters pair off and help each other learn their daily quota of words. They can even give Friday tests to each other. This cooperation may roll along rather smoothly for a while, but it probably will help if every once in a while you tutor again so you can keep in close touch with the kinds of problems the children are having and so you can insert new study skills that they might not think of.

Plan some kind of review. For instance, after a month, say, "This week I will give you a test using any words I want to from your last four lists." Offer a reward for getting a perfect score (or 90% or whatever you think is appropriate) and then let the children help each other prepare to win the reward. They may take practice tests all week long, with high motivation and concentration—tests they might groan about taking if you assigned them. Another kind of review is to add to each week's Friday test two words from the preceding list. A natural review is built into the custom-list system, because if a child continues to misspell a word in his writing, you will select it for inclusion on a new spelling list.

In using this system, you should take care that the child's attitude toward writing doesn't suffer. You don't want him to view the lists as punishment for his spelling errors. You don't want him to limit his writing vocabulary to words he is sure he can spell. You must create a feeling that you are on his team. The day your child asks if he can add a word to the spelling list you will know you have succeeded.

Non-list Study. By integrating spelling with writing even more closely, you can help your child improve in spelling without a separate subject called spelling. This may resemble a system you, yourself, have used in the years since you attended school. The heart of the system is the ordinary process of correcting and polishing a piece of writing.

If your child is submitting an article to a children's newspaper or writing a letter, he should do the best job he can, and that includes trying to make the spelling error-free. Every day's writing can't be mailed off to somebody, so you must be inventive about thinking up writing tasks that merit rewriting and polishing. The child can select one paper each week to go into his permanent record file. Other papers can be added to notebooks of history or science. After you get a couple of projects going, there will be plenty of writing that needs a good spelling check.

Proofreading to catch spelling errors does not require a national spelling champion. All it requires is that a person know what he knows—and what he doesn't know. Imagine looking over a paragraph you have just written. Most words you will be absolutely sure of, not only because you spell them that way, but also because you see them in printed materials, and because you know some of the rules about such matters as doubling final consonants. That part of proofreading is easy. Now the real skill comes in knowing which words to question. If you're writing a letter of application, you will question every word you are not absolutely sure of, and you will check them out with a good speller who happens to be nearby, or, failing that, you will use a dictionary.

This is the proofreading skill your child must learn if he is to turn out polished writings. The dictionary part, anybody can do once they have learned to use dictionaries. The skillful part is deciding *when* to use one.

To learn this skill, then, the child doesn't need to look up a dozen words per day in a dictionary. He needs freedom from that drudgery to concentrate on the writing itself. You might let the child ask you or older children how to spell words. You might let him at some stages of the editing simply circle words he is not sure of. Since some of them may not survive to the final version, it is more efficient to wait and correct the spelling after other rewriting and editing is finished.

A second strength of this system is that words are in a context rich in meaning for the child. In books with prescribed spelling lists, there is often an attempt to put meaning around the words by such techniques as adding sentences or asking students to look up and write definitions. But in this non-list system, the background of meaning is already there. Words learned in context like this tend to be remembered better. A child may be writing about Bambi and spell *dear*. If you say, "A deer like Bambi is spelled with two *e*'s," the child may remember it all his life. He can look in the book again and see, sure enough, that's the way they spell it. All he needed was for you to call attention to a detail that had slipped by him.

With some words, you should make more than a quick comment. Occasionally take a minute or two to study a word with your child. Analyze it phonetically or see what the dictionary has to say about its root and prefix, or in some other way teach something that enlarges the child's view of language and will help on other words besides the one you are now examining.

In using this system, as with the preceding one, you must take care that the child's attitude toward writing does not suffer. You can't be a heavy-handed perfectionist taking the joy out of compositions the child is proud of. Be sure to notice many good qualities in his writing and spelling, and be on his team when you teach him to find spelling errors and correct them.

If there are many spelling errors, this system can be too discouraging. In such a case, good individualizing might mean that you should teach spelling by phonics for a while. Or perhaps it means you should let up on spelling for now, and let the child use "invented" spelling a bit longer. If a child is not yet a fluent reader, it is more important that he read a lot and, perhaps, learn to spell a few common words. You could try a few weeks or a few months of the copying technique described in the chapter of writing lessons.

This, or any system, does not have to continue all year long. Part of individualizing is the freedom to try out various ideas and to change and adjust anytime. This continual seeking for the best way is not a weakness. On the contrary, it adds energy and enthusiasm to your teaching enterprise.

Advanced Word Study. This system can take any form you invent. Let's say that you find a book or section of a book (even just one page) that seems to have valuable spelling information. Then sit down with your child and, together, plan how the child should study and learn the information. Plan, also, what test or other means will show that he has learned it. By using such self-made plans your child could learn a group of spelling rules or generalizations, a list of confusing homonyms, a full sixth-grade list of words, some common prefixes and suffixes, and anything else that is easy to test.

Advanced students could also look up information about origins and history of the English language. They can find and share such information as that our silent *k* in words like *knot* used to be pronounced. Thus our spelling sometimes reflects historical pronunciation and not current pronunciation. They can puzzle over whether spelling could ever be changed in our age of the printing press and electronic type. They can enjoy reading about such efforts of Benjamin Franklin, Noah Webster and others. There are fascinating areas to explore in etymology, linguistic history, phonetics and related topics, and some children's books have been written that avoid highly technical terminology. Unfortunately, the pickings here are not as plentiful as in science and history, but your library should have a few good books for children who show an interest in words.

10. Usage and Grammar

The often-used phrase "grammar and usage" makes it sound as if these topics are two different kinds of knowledge. But in reality they become quite intertwined. On a grammar page of a book you might learn about adverbs like *awhile*. On a usage page you might learn not to confuse this adverb with *a while*, which is an article and noun. In "read awhile," the adverb modifies the verb. But in "read for a while," the preposition *for* changes things. The preposition needs an object (the noun *while*). This kind of detail is meant when a book promises to teach about English usage.

Usage

The best resource for teaching English usage is a reference book where you can look up *awhile* in an alphabetical list to refresh your memory about it at the very moment you or your child need to use it in some writing. Often a section of a grammar book—up to half—is devoted to usage. Dictionaries have this information too. Bits of usage information scattered throughout a series of workbooks is not nearly as efficient for learning. You can study a good grammar book as a text, you can use it for reference when you are not following a text, and all the time your child will become more familiar with one good grammar book. If the book is well laid out and readable, browsing can be fun, too.

I am looking now at the word *bug* in a usage list. The book tells me that bug is used informally for *germ* or *defect*, as in "catching a bug" and "a bug in the engine"; and it is slang for *annoy*, as in "Don't bug me."

Writing is more formal than speaking, nevertheless in some writing the informal or even the slang use of *bug* might be appropriate. But in a letter to your senator, you would not want to say that his voting record bugs you. You would have to use words in their general or standard sense to write an effective letter to the senator.

Usage labels such as *formal, informal*, and *slang* are important in studying language, and grammar reference books usually include a chapter or section on these. The actual labels vary somewhat from book to book. But in general, there are two levels: 1) standard English and 2) nonstandard English.

Standard English is subdivided into types: 1) formal and 2) informal. Informal usage includes words and expressions widely used by educated speakers and writers—and everybody—but which are not appropriate in a formal context such as your letter to a senator. A label dictionaries use for informal words and expressions is *colloquial*. *Bug*, which was listed as informal for its "defect" meaning in my somewhat outdated list, has now been taken over by computer programmers, and subsequently by the general public, so that it has become standard usage. New dictionaries have added hundreds of words and new meanings for old words because of computers. The language lives and grows.

Some people, particularly among Christians, are deeply bothered (shall I say bugged?) by teachings about formal and informal English. Christians are used to thinking in terms of moral and spiritual absolutes where everything is either right or wrong. This kind of thinking in language looks for a line with black on one side and white on the other. And it looks for an authority—a bible somewhere that tells students what they can and can't say or write.

If this were pre-Galileo days and the subject were science, that authority would be Aristotle and his encyclopedia. For English language—at least American English—some have suggested that Webster and his dictionary should be the authority. In language, we may be living in Galileo-type times, except that today we don't physically excommunicate or behead; we only do it verbally in the press. Over the last few decades, scholars who study language as a science and educators who want to teach the science have received that kind of abuse. Webster himself would not approve. He was a scholar who spent many years looking scientifically at the language, and he understood about living languages, that they change over time. He would expect after 150 years that his dictionary would need revising to show today's standard usage.

Nonstandard English also includes several categories. One of these is *slang*, which refers to jargon, the meaning of which is understood by groups of people in certain occupations or sub-cultures, but which are not general enough to be considered standard English. Here is an example of jargon from the early days of space flight in our country.

Mr. Cooper: (From the spaceship.) Fuel is go. Oxygen is go. . . . Faith is go. She feels real pretty.
Mr. Schirra: (From ground control.) You look real go, Gordo. . . . You're smack dab in the middle of the go block.
Mr. Cooper: Boy-oh-boy!
Mr. Schirra: Have a good drive, Bub.
Mr. Cooper: Thank you, Buddy.

One news reporter quipped that he hoped someday America would successfully launch an English-speaking astronaut. Not many of us became astronauts, so their jargon remains jargon to us. If an astronaut wants to write an article for the general public to read he must translate into standard English or we will miss much of his meaning.

In computing, the story is different. At first we couldn't understand the jargon about cursers, menus, floppy disks and so forth. Even the industry had trouble finding employees who did. I was editor and writer at a publishing company, and a salesman had so little understanding of what word processing could do for such a person that he sat in my office one day and tried to talk me out of buying a computer.

Well, things have changed. Today so many of us and our children are into computers that the language is no longer jargon. Much of it has become standard English. And, as in the case of *bug*, some of it has even spawned a second generation of meanings outside the field of computing.

Another kind of nonstandard English is that which dictionaries label *archaic* or *obsolete*. Why retain such words in present-day dictionaries? Because certain of these words are still used in poetry or in biblical and legal expressions. *Ark*, as in ark of the covenant, is one of these.

Another label is *dialectal*. It refers to words or forms which differ from standard English but are used in some local areas. *Illiterate* or *substandard* usages are not often included in dictionaries, but some language courses teach these labels, too.

Your children do not have to memorize all these labels and definitions, but older children should be introduced to the idea that there are different kinds of usage appropriate for different contexts. And you need some awareness of this yourself in order to guide their learning and to understand dictionary entries and other reference aids. Some students have learned to see *colloq.* in a dictionary and say, "Oh, we're not supposed to use that word." This limits those students' views of literature and language.

Young children's writing is informal and conversational, similar to their speech. As children mature they become aware that writing differs from speech and they gradually use more formal language in their writing.

Your children should find it helpful to keep notebooks or files of usage and grammar items for quick reference. Or have a family notebook. Include only items meaningful to your family, items you are likely to use repeatedly. If after checking a couple of reference books you decide that it is better to use *all right* instead of *alright*, then add it to the notebook in its alphabetical position. The next time someone asks, "Now which way are we supposed to spell *all right*?" he can look in the notebook and not have to do all the research again.

It is extremely efficient to learn good English usage in the context of daily writing and reading. Your children will be far ahead if you work at this approach instead of having them fill in *is* and *are* blanks in workbooks. Remember the dialogue: read and write, read and write.

Usage Bears

Here is a reference list of some of the most common usage problems that children—and even adults—have. A few of these perhaps should end up in your children's notebooks along with sample sentences and other information they collect about the items.

accept, except   You accept gifts or invitations; and you may like all except one of them.

affect, effect   These cause lots of trouble, being both nouns and verbs. Laws affect you, but you may effect (bring about) a change by working with other citizens. Medicine has an effect on you. Psychologists and educators like to use *affect* as a noun referring to an emotion.

all right   Because you spell *already* as one word does not make *alright* one word. Most authorities frown on this.

a lot   People write *alot* a lot, but it is not a word.

among, between   Use *among* when you are talking about several and *between* when you are talking about two. Usually.

awhile, a while   When you use a preposition such as *for* or *in*, give it an object by saying "for a while." Otherwise, you need the adverb: "Sing awhile."

be sure to   "Be sure and wash the dishes" gives your daughter two things to do. She is supposed to be sure (about something) and she is to wash the dishes also. "Be sure to wash the dishes" is probably what you really mean.

its, it's   You can substitute *it is* for the one with an apostrophe, but not for the other one. Try this test when you are not sure which one to use.

lay, lie   You lie down, but you lay objects down. That takes care of present tense, but confusion comes in the fact that *lay* is the past tense of *lie*. So yesterday you lay down for a nap. If you have questions about *laid* or *lain*, get out the grammar book and study the two verbs thoroughly.

sit, set   You sit and your hen sets. But you can set other things, like the clock, the table, and the date for a meeting. Grammar books have lots more to say about these two verbs.

their, there, they're   *They're* means *they are*, and many children miss this on *their* papers. *There* is little confusion about *there* when it means a place, as in "over there," but plenty of confusion when it begins a sentence such as this one. These three words require some study.

to, too, two   These three words also require some straightening out—especially *too*. It means *also*, and it intensifies as in *too* heavy. Students miss this clear up into high school level.

try to Use this form and not *try and*.

used to, supposed to These are two words each, and they need a *d*. Don't write *useto* or *use to*.

would have This can be shortened to *would've* but not to *would of*.

Grammar as a Scholarly Discipline

One reason we teach grammar is simply that we like to teach everything that man has achieved. Grammar is a way to think about language, and analyze it. It is a result of human scholarship. So we pass on this cultural heritage and this way of thinking to each new generation. Seen in this light, grammar is a subject worthy of study in itself. It is not merely a set of rules by which students learn to use the langauge.

Interestingly this is how grammar teaching began with the Greeks. It was closely intertwined with study of the classic poets, and not a means for learning language. In primary school, Greek children had already learned to write fluently, and then in grammar school they studied the classic writers, and learned grammar in that context.

You would not want to imitate Greek teaching methods, since they were limited. For instance, because they had no printed books, a great deal of time was spent comparing the students' written copies with the teacher's in a critical examination of the text. As time went on, the Greeks lost all sense of why they were teaching the classics. Emphasis was on words and details rather than on meaning. Knowing details of the classics became an end in itself, and lost was the vision of heroism, morals, thinking and other higher purposes in literature.

Some would argue that we are suffering the same loss of vision about why we teach grammar. As a scholarly discipline, it is one of the highest uses of the human mind. But as an authoritarian system, it fails us. It doesn't help our children write, as we hoped it would.

Grammar as Related to Writing

For almost a century now, researchers have explored the question, Does grammar knowledge help produce good writers and speakers? And recent surveys of all the research have uncovered startling results.

While educational research usually is equivocal and you can find studies to support both sides of almost any question, that is not the case with this research. On the question of relationship of grammar knowledge to writing ability, the research is clear and overwhelming on one side of the issue. This is the finding:

> Knowledge of the definitions and rules of grammar does not, in itself, improve student writing.

This finding is probably startling to people who have been calling for more grammar to be included in our curriculum. But it does not surprise many conscientious English teachers who discovered this on their own.

English teachers have long realized that the best way to develop better writers, is to get students to write more. But in classrooms, especially at junior high and above, if teachers assigned more writing, they couldn't keep up with the work of reading and commenting on papers because of their large student load. Homeschooling, then, is a solution to this particular English teaching problem. Parents can require daily writing from their children and can usually manage to keep up with the job of being an audience for the writing whenever that is needed.

Where, then, does grammar fit in? Not before the writing. Not as a way to learn to write. Reverse this order; have your children write as a way to learn grammar. They learned a great deal of grammar as they learned to talk. Now as they write and read, they continue learning grammar.

When you treat writing wholistically, encouraging and helping your child to ever better writing, the grammar comes along too. This happens even if you aren't necessarily using technical grammatical terms. You don't have to say, "Use an adjective to make the sentence more colorful." You can just say, "What kind of tree is it?" and the child can add *evergreen* or *pine*. This attention to meaning rather than to grammar, results in better writing. When children consciously add adjectives because that is the assignment for the day, they write sentences about tall, green trees beside little, white houses in large, sunny valleys. Later, they have to unlearn this schoolgirl style of writing.

The Origins of Grammar

Did God's voice thunder from Mount Grammaticus, "These nouns and these verbs which I give unto you shall you use with all the inflections thereof which I declare unto you; and you shall teach them unto your children and your children's children unto all generations"?

No one I know believes that such an event occurred, but many people treat grammar as though it occurred. For over two centuries our schooling has conditioned whole generations to view grammar as an authoritarian system. Our textbooks contained all the pronouncements about "right" and "wrong." Maybe we, personally, didn't understand some of them, but that was our fault, we thought. Right was white and wrong was black; it was as clear as that—to somebody.

Where do they come from—these textbooks that we revere so much? A brief history will help our perspctive.

In ancient Athens in the fifth century B.C., study of Greek

poets was the most important part of education. While at times the teachers quibbled over a tiny point of language, they often attained their higher purposes of using literature as a mental exercise, a way of studying relationships between thought and language. Children entered grammar schools for this study after they could read and write fluently, which was often age 10 or so. (Parenthetically, we might observe that those early Greeks did not have large libraries of philosophy, history, science, and so on to choose study material from. The best way they had to build thinkers was to use the classic poets.)

Through studying this literature, the teachers and pupils came to study seriously the laws of language. For them, it was theoretical and not related to everyday use. Several teachers wrote on etymology, diction, sounds, syllables, and other aspects of language, and the science of grammar began.

In the first century B.C., Dionysius Thrax compiled in a little treatise the results of those scattered language researches. The treatise began with vowels and consonants (long, short, mixed, silent, etc.); it moved on to syllables and then to words and parts of speech. It did not go so far as to analyze sentence construction, which we call syntax and now include in grammar studies. Dionysius had eight parts of speech, but they are not the same as the eight parts in our books. For instance, adjectives were not a class; they were just part of the nouns. Articles were a class (a, an, the).

Grammar was now codified. One can't help wondering if Dionysius had any inkling of the 2000-year history his system would have.

The Romans quickly adopted this new science and remained so faithful to Dionysius's model that they continued to teach Greek items such as the article, even though Latin had no such thing. Feeling obliged to find a Latin equivalent, they substituted demonstrative adjectives, such as *this* and *that*. Spelling laws were added. Syntax was added late—about the fifth century—by a man who found it helpful in teaching Latin as a foreign language to Greeks.

With the Romans, grammar continued to be a theoretical study, suited to grammar school (also called secondary school). It was not related to the living language, but to the old poets, those considered "classics." Although for a time both Greeks and Romans included Virgil and other "modern" poets, Quintilian later led a move back to the classics. By then Virgil was no longer modern, he was a classic too. Homer had been one for a long time. The list of classic poets was fixed, and grammar was wedded to it. Historians, orators and other prose writers belonged to the subject of rhetoric rather than grammar, but some teachers crossed the boundaries between subjects and applied grammar to the study of prose as well as poetry.

With these beginnings, grammar continued for many centuries to be associated with the classics, and with the passage of time the language of these classics became "dead." Grammarians love dead languages. They can make rules to their hearts' content and nobody will write a new classic and break them. And when they find inconsistencies they can get jobs as publishers' consultants and quietly edit them out. Centuries of this treatment have brought the classics and their grammar to us in neat form. Their grammar doesn't leak.

The same centuries built up a strong belief in that Latin grammar. During that time Latin schools were for the elite, both in England and America. They taught the Greek and Roman classics, and their neat grammar. In the middle of the 1700's, the colonial period of American history, interest grew in offering schooling to the common people, and letting them study in English. But English grammars had to be written for the purpose, and English grammarians borrowed from Latin grammar, just as the Latins had borrowed from the Greeks so long before. And, in a case of history repeating itself, this time there were misfits too. But belief in Latin grammar outweighed that.

Something must be wrong with English if it doesn't fit, reasoned grammar teachers for over two hundred years. So they pounded into our heads that infinitives should not be split, that verbs have a future tense, and other misfits.

In Latin, infinitives are one word and cannot be split; in English they are two words (to hurry, to try, etc.). And if Shakespeare or King James' translators or any writers predating those early grammarians had split an infinitive, they were pronounced "wrong." They should have known enough to play by rules that were invented two centuries after their time. Some of these instances have been quietly re-edited to conform to the new rules.

Latin verbs are inflected for a number of tenses, while English verbs change form only for past tense. But grammarians were resourceful, and where English inflections were lacking, they substituted "helping verbs" and were able to compile conjugations of our verbs long enough to rival those of Latin verbs.

Though English language has many ways to indicate future time, it has no special verb form for future tense, as Latin does. Consider a situation in which friends are discussing a concert scheduled for this Friday evening. You might say, "I'm going." But future tense in your grammar books was "I shall go." ("I will go" was reserved for indicating special determination, even though practically all speakers of English say *I will* for simple future and orators sometimes use *we shall* to dramatize determination. See the Gettysburg Address and Winston Churchill's "We shall fight in France, we shall fight on the seas and oceans . . . ." All this, you might remember, was reversed for second and third person usages. The will-shall rules came from grammarians who felt it their duty to lay down rules for such matters.) Your comment, "I'm going," is found in the grammar books to be present tense, progressive form, indicative mode. If your remark really means what the grammarians said it means, you are on your way to the concert right now; the action is progressing. If it's only Tuesday, you will have a long wait for the musicians to arrive.

Benjamin Franklin and Noah Webster were two early spokesmen for developing a grammar that fits our language, but 2000 years of Latin grammar were too difficult for them to wipe out.

In our century, language scholars have worked on the same problem, looking at English with fresh eyes, so to speak, and not through the eyes of the Greeks and Romans. They have proposed new grammars—structural, transformational, and generational—and in the 1960's some English teachers began trying to use these in the schools. This experimenting continued for a couple of decades but by 1980 it all had come to "a screeching halt," in the words of a language arts specialist in a large school district.

A major reason the new grammars didn't go, was the difficulty of making a significant change in such a leviathon as schools are these days. Parents, teachers, students, and publishers must together change their thinking, and that couldn't happen. Also, some objectors felt as though morals were being attacked and decay ruining the schools. So for now, we are still teaching our children traditional grammar, although modified in comparison with the early grammar books.

Teaching Grammar and Writing

In helping your child with daily writing, you teach more grammar than you may be aware of. And you can sprinkle in technical terms when you want to. For instance, after your child makes a tree sentence more specific by adding an adjective, as in the "pine tree" example given earlier, you can point out that she used an adjective to do it. This is called "incidental teaching," in which grammar gets taught incident-by-incident along with writing, and is of secondary importance to the writing. In this manner, you can use terms like *noun, verb,* and *complete sentence* with your children and introduce them to the vocabulary of grammar and to some of its ideas.

But at some points in your children's education, they should study grammar in a more formal way so they can see it as an organized discipline—a branch of human knowledge. Some advanced fifth and sixth graders and most junior highers can profit from such a study. Those who profit most are those who already write well.

For teaching grammar, you only need one good grammar book. You don't have to buy a stack of textbooks and workbooks two feet high. Such series of schoolbooks which claim to take a child through all the grades in English are the result of an aberration in our current textbook adoption systems. They are a strange result of marketing. A salesman presents his books to a school faculty and the fifth grade teacher says, "Why doesn't it teach descriptive writing?" while the seventh grade teacher says, "Why doesn't it teach punctuation?" Publishers have responded by putting almost everything in almost every grade. Some have done this so shamelessly that they use practically the same wording for similar lessons in each grade from 7 to 12. One teacher suggests, "Why not buy a twelfth grade book for each student in seventh grade and let him study it for six years, marking it and keeping it as his own? The cost would be no more than with the existing system, and the learning result much better." For homeschoolers, the cost of this plan is only one-sixth the cost of buying a repetitious book each year for six years. At the same time, learning motivation may be higher.

Parents have discovered on their own that language textbooks teach a little dab of this and a little dab of that, and they have felt let down by the "experts" who were supposed to guide them through the years of English teaching. As you shop for texts, you may now and then find something truly helpful. And new books are appearing all the time; hopefully more good ones are on the way. Thousands of homeschool families shopping intelligently have the potential to influence what publishers offer in the future.

Some language books only get to the topic of writing by the last chapter—the chapter that many teachers never manage to reach, the chapter most likely to be omitted in the year-end effort to wind things up. This is another reason you should not depend on language books for your children's instruction in writing. There is no better curriculum area than writing to try getting along without daily textbook or workbook assignments. Your children can write for all their other subjects—even arithmetic. They can do real-life writing such as memos, letters, and journals. And you can assign writing from ideas you pick up in this book and elsewhere. It is easy to get along without a writing textbook.

If you feel insecure about teaching grammar with the writing, it may help to know that about 95% of other people do too. Probably the main reason people feel this way is the nature of grammar itself. The system leaks, it is not exact, and most people blame themselves rather than the system. People who spend all their time with language, such as professional writers, constantly find better ways to use language, so if you don't know everything yet, that is only to be expected. You certainly know more than your children. And as you continue teaching them, you will gain, as well as they. One of the rewards of teaching is the chance to review your own knowledge, to consolidate it and extend it. Adult learning on a higher level proceeds alongside the children's learning.

If you have more than the normal reasons for feeling insecure, such as getting failing grades in English courses, then you can look on this time of life as a second chance. You may wish to have your children use language textbooks, and take time to see that you, too, understand the lessons. But since most grammar and English usage is learned in real life rather than in schoolbooks, you may be surprised at how much you know about the lessons. In any case, learning along with your child will be rewarding.

When your family becomes aware of a particular grammar problem, you should all work together on it. Some families, for instance, say "I seen" instead of the standard "I saw." If parents say that, their children will say that, and filling in a few seen-saw blanks in a workbook will not change the children's usage. Only a total family attack on the problem will work. If you say "I seen," it probably is because your parents did, so long-standing habits must be broken. You can invent games and practice ideas so everyone gets used to hearing and saying "I saw." Award points or M&M's for each "I saw" so children will try to say it a lot.

Your family may have one or two such items to work on, or possibly several, but there are never very many. Unless English is your second language, you naturally speak 99% according to the books, and only now and then you have a troublesome item. If you want to find these, try listening more closely to good, educated speakers and see what they say differently than you. When you find a difference, you can ask about it or check in grammar reference books, and decide if you want to change your habit.

When I was growing up we spoke of "boughten" dresses, which were rare compared with homemade dresses. We also sometimes had boughten candy or other items. Then I went off to college and noticed that I was the only one using that word, so I began saying "store-bought" or wording my sentences in a way that avoided the word altogether. In dictionaries the word *boughten* is labeled "dialect" or "nonstandard," to indicate that it is commonly used in some areas or some strata of society, but it is not the standard usage of educated speakers and writers. When I wanted to fit into the educated stratum at college, I had to change my usage.

Nonstandard words sometimes are either on their way in

or on their way out of standard usage. The word *boughten* is probably on its way out. It was particularly American and was much earlier labeled dialect in Great Britain. Now times have changed so that there is nothing particularly significant about a boughten dress and the word is hardly needed. It is homemade dresses which are rare and worth talking about. This is an example of living language doing its living.

If one of your goals is that your children fit in with educated people, that they be effective in writing and speaking in our well educated society, they must know and be able to use language according to the standards of that society. Study of language—even its grammar—can be one of the most fascinating parts of your home teaching.

Part III:
Arithmetic

11. Arithmetic Is Not Dull

The "utility" purposes of arithmetic are largely met when children know basic arithmetic facts from memory and can calculate in the four basic operations. But you can aim beyond that. Mankind for long ages has reached out for principles and patterns and other higher understandings, and students today still find challenge and satisfaction when their minds grasp some of this intellectual heritage.

Leading your child toward the higher goal of an educated mind is stimulating for both you and the child. We might say this is "close encounter of the mind kind." Such encounter occurs at scattered times in daily lessons as you try to explain some of the why's and wherefore's along with the how's of computation.

This chapter reminds you of some principles, patterns, and other insights that can make arithmetic a more stimulating study. Perhaps this will serve as a brief refresher course for you, and if your mind becomes a little excited about some of the deeper meanings in our arithmetic system, the children you teach will gain in countless ways throughout the lessons ahead.

Meaning of Number

Number Property. When the word *property* is used, many people turn away in fright, thinking they lack initiation into new math or higher math or something else scary. But even if you were not brought up on the word itself, you know all about it, as the five parts of its definition given below will show you. Think now of a group of 11 eggs.

1. It doesn't matter how your group is arranged—whether random, or in a pattern or in this order or that order. The number 11 will still stand for the group. If you compare your group of 11 with a standard group of 11, you would have a one-to-one correspondence, each individual in your group corresponding with an individual in the standard group, with nothing left over in either group.

2. Your group of 11 could be arranged in subgroups of any size or any order and the number 11 will still stand for the whole group. You would still have a one-to-one correspondence with the standard group. Also, if you had two subgroups, such as 8 and 3, you could move 2 from the subgroup of 3 over to the 8 and the number 11 is still appropriate to your whole group.

3. You could remove one or more of the eggs from the group and replace them with the same kind of item on a one-to-one basis, and the number 11 will still stand for the group. Thus you could, in time, change every individual in the group. You could remove 1 egg as you replace it with 1 new egg, then remove 4 eggs replacing them with 4 new eggs, and so on, until none of your original eggs remain. The number property, 11, remains the same throughout.

4. The number property of your group *does* change if you decide to reclassify any individuals in the group. Let's say that some of your eggs are hard-boiled, and you

decide to count only eggs that are available for cake baking. Now the number 11 will no longer do.

5. The number property of a group *does* change if any individuals in it are merged or split without changing classification. Let's say that an author has completed 11 chapters, but then decides to split 1 long chapter into 2 or to merge 3 chapters into 1. The number 11 will no longer do.

The number 11, then, is generic and names the number property of any group of 11 even if the individuals in a group are ordered or arranged differently and even if substitutions are made. But the number property of a group does change if any of its individuals merge or split while retaining the same classification.

Now, any reader is free to say, "Of course I knew all that. I just wouldn't take so many words to say it." Mathematicians, though, insist on precision. If your child likes precision, get him the book, *Carry On, Mr. Bowditch*, by Jean Lee Latham. In it the boy Nat says, "I like arithmetic better than history. Two plus two is four. Always." This is an inspiring story about a real person who learned math all by himself and used it to improve people's lives.

Abstract and Concrete. When the number 11 refers to 11 eggs or 11 dollars, it is concrete. When it refers to the elevenness of groups, it is abstract—a pure number. It is 11 times whatever 1 is; it is 1 less than 12; it is the sum of 5 and 6, or of 4 and 4 and 3, and so on.

Series Meaning. Eleven has a position in the counting series, coming next after 10, and preceding 12. Sometimes we think young children are learning this series meaning when they first begin to chant numbers in order, but the series idea is so abstract that it is only in our heads and not theirs. Children are learning the number names, though, and the order. And later on they can grow to understand series.

Collection Meaning. Children more readily understand the collection meaning of a number—11 eggs in the refrigerator door or 11 men on a football team. Even when it is not concrete—when we just ask how many are four 11's—the 11 is used to denote a collection or a group.

Component Meaning. Eleven is the sum of its components 10 and 1, or of the components 5 and 6, or others we could name. When we analyze a number additively like this, we are thinking of its component meaning.

Ratio Meaning. To say that you have 11 eggs is to say that you have 11 times 1 egg. That is the ratio of 11 to 1, or 11/1. This indicates that 11 is divided by 1, and ratio is sometimes defined as being an *indicated* division. One may not always be a single unit; it may be a pair or a dozen or 1/4 of something. So, using the ratio meaning, you might have 11 dozen eggs or 11 quarters—$2.75. Whatever 1 is in a given case, 11 expresses the amount 11 times as large.

As in the component meaning we can analyze a number in terms of its subgroups, so in the ratio meaning we can analyze it in terms of its factors. Ratio is multiplicative. Ten is ten 1's, but it also may be analyzed as two 5's or five 2's.

Percents are ratios. The ratio meaning pervades mathematics so much more than the other meanings of number, that enthusiastic educators from time to time have decided to teach it more and earlier, usually with disastrous results. One set of books which overdid this was published in 1897. So if you make a mistake or two in teaching your child, accept that as natural; educators have a long history of experimenting and bungling.

The ratio meaning is extremely important in mathematics,

but the series, and collection, and component meanings all play their parts too. Together they provide a rich sense of the meaning of numbers.

Kinds of Numbers

From the word *ratio*, we get the term **rational number**. All whole numbers are rational. So are fractions. That is, all of these numbers can be expressed as ratios. For instance, 6 oranges is 6 times 1 orange, which can be expressed as 6:1, or 6/1, or simply 6. A ratio can be expressed as division, which means it can also be expressed as multiplication (6 × 1).

Negative numbers also can be rational numbers, and they usually are included somewhere in the study of arithmetic.

Some numbers cannot be expressed as ratios, and we call them **irrational numbers**. Pi is an irrational number, even though it is intended to be the ratio of the circumference of a circle to its diameter. Likewise, the square root of 2 is irrational.

When the early Greeks discovered that some numbers were not rational they were greatly troubled. They supposed that the Maker of the universe had blundered, and for a long time mathematicians kept this information secret; it was unlawful to mention such numbers.

Later, people thought up the label of **real** numbers and included in that category both rational and irrational numbers, as well as zero. This list summarizes the kinds of real numbers.

Real Numbers
Rational numbers:
   whole numbers, positive and negative
   fractions, positive and negative
Irrational numbers
Zero

Imaginary Numbers. Real numbers are the only ones we work with in arithmetic, but in higher mathematics students will run into numbers which are not real. Such a number is the square root of -1. This number cannot exist in the real world, but only in people's minds, the reason being that neither a negative nor a positive number produces a negative when multiplied by itself; thus no real-number root can produce a square of -1. When people first stumbled across the square root of -1, they knew better this time than to blame it on God. Instead they just made up a new label, calling it an imaginary number, and proceeded to make rules for operating with imaginary numbers. Children learning arithmetic will not meet these, but a few math buffs will look forward to learning about them in higher math studies.

Zero and the Decimal System. Children who think arithmetic is difficult should be thankful every day for zero. The ancient Greeks did not have zero, and only good mathematicians among them could calculate with large numbers. Such men had no idea that someday every child would be able to compute division problems. The Greeks used their entire alphabet of twenty-four letters plus three more signs to express numbers. In English, the twenty-seven symbols might look like this.

a	1	j	10	s	100
b	2	k	20	t	200
c	3	l	30	u	300
d	4	m	40	v	400
e	5	n	50	w	500
f	6	o	60	x	600
g	7	p	70	y	700
h	8	q	80	z	800
i	9	r	90	&	900

The Greeks thought in tens even though this notation system doesn't show it. Thus 13 would not be written *ib* (9 and

3) or fg (6 and 7). It was only written jc or cj (10 and 3, or 3 and 10). The order didn't matter. The position, or place, did not matter either. Consider how easily in our system we can think $10 \times 13 = 130$. Our notation works together with the tens idea, so we manage more easily than the Greeks. In a more difficult problem such as 74×13 or 13×627, we arrange the numbers in their places under each other, and practically any fifth grader can carefully write the partial products in their proper positions and obtain the answer. But how would he calculate $j \times jc$ to get sl?

Actually, the Greeks did not compute with these symbols. Neither did the Romans with theirs. They used the computers of their day, an abacus-like machine with pebbles to move along a groove in a board or other sundry inventions, and when they finished a calculation they wrote its result.

From somewhere deep in the lost history of India, the Hindu-Arabians came up with the idea of zero, and with this came the ability to get along with only ten symbols and the revolutionary idea of assigning value to the place or order of numbers—a true decimal system. Europe had a decimal (tens) system of thinking but not a decimal system of notation, or writing, so when a European merchant or professor saw this powerful new Hindu tool he switched over immediately, right? Absolutely wrong!

Zero and decimal notation seem to have been discovered in India about the year A.D. 600. After seven centuries it seems to have been known in Italy, and after three more centuries it finally became the dominant system. That adds up to a full millennium for people to argue about the corruption of old standards, the watering down of curriculum, what God would think, and what the world was coming to. The combined power of Roman law and language and state religion, though it fought mightily to preserve the Roman number system, at last gave way to the new math, and Roman numerals passed into history except for decorative use.

After discovering zero, the Hindu-Arabians went on to

develop negative numbers. Already in people's thinking was the number-line idea, wherein number units are seen to be in a counting progression along a line, and with zero in its place the Arabians counted backwards, too. We now call these numbers to the left of zero the negative numbers. After the millennium of arguing, when decimal notation was firmly established, at least in India and Europe, the last great development came. That was the idea of expressing decimal fractions by marking a point and extending number places to the right in a descending scale of value. Thus we have 12.5 for 12½.

(NOTE: The usual number history, such as given above, probably only refers to the rediscovery or redevelopment of number use after the Tower of Babel. It seems clear that early man understood numbers, along with language. The developed calendar, the detailed genealogies, the careful record of the flood year and many other indications reveal a good use of number by pre-flood civilization. After the flood, too, people had advanced architecture and likely a reading of the stars that exceeds our own. But men so misused their high knowledge that God had to take the drastic step of "confounding" their language, which evidently confounded their thinking as well. Thus the various post-Babel groups of people had to rethink and reinvent ways to write and to work with numbers.)

Principles of Notation

Place Value. Closely akin to the zero idea is the place-value idea. This is easy to see by following the number 3 across columns in the English-Greek chart. Three alone means 3 units, 3 with a zero means 30 units, and 3 with two zeros means 300 units.

Three units we can easily understand directly. That is, we don't need to count in order to picture three people in a car, three hamburgers on a tray, and so on. Ten is about our limit for direct understanding of numbers, and even with ten it helps if the items are arranged as on dominoes or fingers of the hands, or some other pattern. Beyond that, we think of ten as a unit, and thereby handle up to ten tens in our thinking, not so directly to be sure, but less strongly. For larger numbers—hundreds, thousands, and millions—we make what mental constructs we can, because the human mind cannot grasp such numbers directly.

Our notation system, inherited from the Hindu-Arabians, helps us handle large numbers which we cannot grasp directly. Place value is key. This means simply that the value of a number is determined by its place. The three basic places are ones, tens, and hundreds; and these three are repeated in groups called *periods*, as shown below. Units are the first period; thousands are the second period; millions are the third period; and so on.

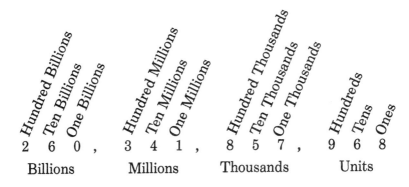

Few children actually understand place value very well as they use it in writing out problems, for instance in partial products in a multiplication problem. The brief explanations we give when teaching how to multiply by a two-place or a three-place number are not enough to build good understanding. It may be that good understanding can only come with maturing mental growth, continued work in arithmetic, and teaching that tries to emphasize the why as well as the how of each new process.

Here are some essentials of the decimal system of notation which all children can be expected to master.

1. Know the order of the places and the value given to each.
2. Be able to write numbers, putting commas and decimal points where they belong, and putting zeros as needed to keep other numbers in their proper places.
3. Be able to read numbers, naming each period, thus: two hundred sixty billion, three hundred forty-one million, eight hundred fifty-seven thousand, nine hundred sixty-eight.
4. Say numbers without using *and*, thus: "one hundred ten," not "one hundred and ten." "Threescore and ten" and "sixty and five years" are old and poetic ways of speaking.
5. Be able to write numbers as spelled out, placing commas after each period just as when digits are used, and using hyphens in the compound words from *twenty-one* to *ninety-nine*. We write sixty billion (no hyphen) in the above number, but forty-one million (hyphen).

Rounded Numbers. In real life, a number as large as billions is seldom written as shown in the example earlier, because of the limitations of the human mind already mentioned. No one can comprehend this number right down to the last 68 units, so this particular number may be rounded to 260 billion. Whether this is the national debt or a population figure or the distance of a star, it means something to us only by comparison with other figures. Is it twice the population of a previous century? Is it 60 billion more than last year? Or is it a small fraction of the distance of another star? We understand these comparisons—in some measure. One of the few places a number like this is printed is in a child's arithmetic book to demonstrate the order of places and periods.

Outside the Decimal System

Decem is the Latin word for *ten*, and that is where we get the word for our system which is built upon ten-ness. As mentioned earlier, we think in tens, and we write in tens using the Hindu-Arabic notation system.

Our notation does not have to be tied to a decimal system. It could work just as well in a system that has two or twelve or any other number for a base. People studying computers often learn about a base-two system of numbers, since computers read only whether a circuit is off or on. This takes only two digits—the digit 0 for off and the digit 1 for on. If you have never tried writing numbers this way, you might get a new insight into place value by trying to write base-two numbers up to ten or more. You won't have nine digits to write, so you very soon have to move over to the next place, and before you have counted very far your base-two number will look as large as a base-ten number in the billions. The second place is the twos (not tens), the third place is fours, the fifth is eights, and so on, increasing by powers of two—in other words, doubling each time. To get you started, the first few numbers look like this.

1
10
11
100
101
110
111
1000

Some people have proposed that we would be better off with a duodecimal (base twelve) system. They point out that 12 is divisible by more numbers than 10 is. Whereas 10 can only be divided by 2 and 5, 12 can be divided by 2, 3, 4, and 6. Thus there are many more fractions which would "come out even." Halves, fourths, fifths, and eighths come out even in our decimal system, but thirds never do. You can divide and divide until you run out of paper, but you will still have a remainder. In a duodecimal system you could express halves, fourths, and eights without a remainder, the same as in the decimal system; and you could also express thirds, sixths, ninths, and twelfths. Some people would gladly give up the fifths for that advantage. We do think in twelves when we use feet and inches and when we use dozens and gross.

In some matters we think in 60's. For instance, we mark out the circle of the earth into 360 degrees. To measure distance, navigators and others subdivide each degree into 60 minutes and each minute into 60 seconds. To measure time, we mark out an hour for each fifteen degrees of the earth's rotation so that there are 24 hours in all. These hours are subdivided into 60 minutes of 60 seconds each, the words having a somewhat different meaning than the space-minutes and space-seconds. Each 4 hours has been known as a "watch" on shipboard or other places where round-the-clock guarding is needed. A watch, then, lasts for 60 degrees of earth's rotation. And 6 watches make the full 24-hour day or the full 360 degrees of rotation.

For now the decimal system has conquered the world. Like music, the decimal system can be called a universal language; people in all countries understand us when we use this language. So every student should learn how to calculate in the decimal system, and those who want an educated mind should also learn to understand the system as well as they can.

One way to understand the decimal system better is to think sometimes of other possible systems such as a base-two or a base-twelve system. When students believe there is only one possible number system, they are like prisoners locked inside the walls. When you lead them outside the walls, you free their minds. They can glimpse other systems and can see the decimal system from a new angle; they look at it from the outside. And when they go back inside to use the decimal system, they have a better understanding than they used to have as prisoners.

This principle works in all of education. For example, knowledge of a foreign language increases students' understanding of their own language. Knowledge of earlier times in history increases their understanding of their own times. Knowing about your viewpoint frees them from the prison of their own viewpoint. Education releases minds from their little prisons of ignorance.

Exploring Numbers

Do people create mathematics, or do they discover it? This old, old, debate continues to the present time. In physics or chemistry or biology, it is easier to say that the stuff is there, along with the laws by which it all operates, and what scholars do is discover. In mathematics, the question is more debatable. "Look," someone can say, "we didn't discover a number system based on ten. Mankind made it up. We could have had base eight or something else, and probably would have if humans were born with eight fingers instead of ten."

Some mathematicians, though, are not convinced by the base-ten argument, which they feel is too superficial. One great mathematician has said, "We are up against the infinite." He believes it possible that men may discover everything in biology—a long, long time from now—but it will never be possible to discover everything in mathematics. Leaving the biology debate aside, those who believe in God can easily accept his statement about the infinity of mathematics.

What excites such men? They see mathematics as a beautiful jewel. It is order and beauty at its purest, beyond anything they could study in the physical world, and their job is to uncover facets of the jewel.

And what excites students? They can experience the thrill of thinking and of discovery as they uncover parts of the jewel for themselves. The infinity of mathematics holds excitement for everybody. Here are some topics in number theory for mathematicians of all ages.

Odd and Even Numbers. Your child can explore properties of odd and even numbers with some of the following questions and activities. These are arranged in order of difficulty, and you can likely find a level to challenge your child today.

1. Count to 100 by even numbers.
2. Count to 99 by odd numbers.
3. Notice that every even number, except 0, is an odd number plus 1, and every odd number is an even number plus 1. Is it also a property of even numbers that they each are an odd number minus 1?
4. Is every odd number an even number minus 1?
5. If you add two even numbers, will their sum be even or odd? Does your answer hold true in every case you try?
6. What happens if you add two odd numbers?
7. What if you add one odd and one even number?
8. When you multiply two even numbers, will their product be even or odd?
9. When you multiply two odd numbers, will their product be even or odd?
10. When you multiply an odd number by an even number is the product even or odd? Is it the same if you multiply an even number by an odd number?
11. Can you write a rule that tells which kinds of problems will result in an even product?
12. Which kinds of problems result in an odd product?
13. Square any number (multiply it by itself) and then add this product to the number itself. Your answer will always be an even number. Can you explain why?

Answers. **1.** *Begin with 0, 2, 4, etc.* **2.** *Begin 1, 3, 5, etc.* **3.** *Yes.* **4.** *Yes.* **5.** *Even, yes.* **6.** *The sum is even.* **7.** *The sum is odd.* **8.** *Even.* **9.** *Odd.* **10.** *Even, yes.* **11.** *If one or both of the factors are even, the product will be even.* **12.** *If both factors are odd, the product will be odd.* **13.** *If the original number is even, its square will be even and adding an even number produces an even sum. If the original number is odd, its square will be odd, but adding an odd number to it results in an even sum. (See questions 5 to 9 regarding adding and multiplying odd and even numbers.)*

Prime Numbers. A prime number is a number greater than 1 which can be divided only by itself and by 1. Two, 3, 5, and 7 are the lowest four prime numbers. Each can be divided only by itself and by 1. Four is not prime, but is the product of the primes 2 and 2. Six is not prime, but is the product of primes 2 and 3.

After your child understands why 3 is a prime and 4 is not, he may guess how many primes there are less than 100. Then he can find all the primes up to 100, using these steps which were invented by a Greek named Eratosthenes.

1. List numbers from 2 to 100.
2. Cross out all multiples of 2 (all even numbers).
3. Cross out all remaining multiples of the lowest number still showing, which is 3.
4. Cross out all remaining multiples of the lowest number still showing, which is 5.
5. Continue as in steps 3 and 4 until no more numbers can be crossed out.

The twenty-five numbers not crossed out are primes; they are divisible only by 1 and themselves. All numbers crossed out are composite numbers—the products of primes. Every number for as high as your child would like to test them is either a prime number or a composite number. (NOTE: Some books include 1 as a prime, and define a prime as a number that cannot be represented as the product of two or more smaller numbers.)

Does anyone want to guess how many primes there are less than 1000 and then show the answer by the same system as above?

Ask your children how many prime numbers are even. *(Only the number 2.)* If they solve that puzzle from their chart of prime and composite numbers, they already have made a discovery about the properties of prime numbers.

When you get to large numbers do you eventually run out of primes? That is, are larger numbers always divisible by something? Euclid, of ancient Greece, wrote that the supply of prime numbers is infinite, and no one to date has proved him wrong.

Familiarity with primes and composites can help your child to reduce fractions or to reduce long division problems to make them less long. But aside from such practical uses, mathematicians for centuries have been hooked on prime numbers because of their mysterious properties. Prime numbers are universal; the same primes appear in any number system, whether based on 10 or any other base. This universality has fascinated men. Science fiction writers, for instance, have imagined that extraterrestrials try to communicate with earth in codes or radio frequencies based on prime numbers.

Over two hundred years ago someone conjectured that every even number greater than 2 is the sum of two primes. For examples, 4 is the sum of 2 and 2, 6 is the sum of 3 and 3, 8 is the sum of 5 and 3, and so on. Let your child test this theory on some of the even numbers up to 100. For as high as anyone has tried this it still works, but that doesn't prove to mathematicians that it will always be true. They still need a proof that the theory is either true or false. Student minds and great, mature minds can play with prime numbers because of such unanswered questions.

Here's another puzzle. Twin primes are two consecutive odd numbers which are both prime. For example, 3 and 5, 5 and 7, 11 and 13, and 71 and 73. Does this pattern come to an end somewhere in the stratosphere? No one knows yet.

What can your children learn about prime numbers from studying a chart made by the five steps given above? Or what question can your children ask about prime numbers as they study the chart?

Perfect Numbers. The Greek Pythagoras proposed that any number which was the sum of all the numbers that divided evenly into it was a perfect number. Thus 6 is a perfect number because it is divisible by 1, 2, and 3 and it is the sum of 1, 2, and 3. Mystics, such as St. Augustine, believed that God created the world in six days because six was a perfect number. Other ancients said it was the other way around: six was a perfect number because God created the world in six days. Such debates give us an idea of the fascination that numbers have always held for mankind. People hoped that by numbers they could uncover the structure of the universe.

The next perfect number is 28. It is divisible by 1, 2, 4, 7, and 14, and it is the sum of those numbers. No one yet knows how many perfect numbers there are. And no one yet knows if any of them will turn out to be odd numbers. More problems for your children's generation to solve.

Let your children demonstrate that 6 and 28 are perfect numbers by doing the necessary adding and multiplying. Besides proving that the numbers are perfect, they will discover other patterns, such as that each divisor produces a quotient which is another of the divisors. Some students will enjoy playing with the larger perfect numbers, 496 and 8128. Mathematicians know of thirty perfect numbers, some extremely large.

Friendly Numbers. This idea is also from Pythagoras, as far as we know. A number, instead of being the sum of its own divisors, is the sum of the divisors of another number, which in turn is equal to the sum of the divisors of the first number. For instance, 220 can be divided by 1, 2, 4, 5, 10, 11, 20, 22, 44, 55, and 110; and these add up to 284. The number 284 can be divided by 1, 2, 4, 71, and 142; and these add up to 220. A friendly arrangement. Some writers have noted that Jacob in the Bible gave Esau 220 goats and 220 sheep to try to repair their friendship. Did these men have the concept of friendly numbers before Pythagoras? Did they play with numbers as youths so that Jacob could assume that Esau would understand a deeper meaning in his gift? They were no strangers to numbers. Somebody had to count up their father's considerable flocks and compute that his land yielded a hundredfold. Jacob had twenty years working for Laban in which to compute the sizes of flocks and herds and to connive ways to make his own flocks larger at Laban's expense, so he may well have become intrigued with numbers during this time and could have exercised his brain with them beyond what was needed in his daily work.

Let your children demonstrate that 220 and 284 are friendly numbers by doing the necessary adding and multiplying. The next smallest friendly numbers are 1184 and 1210.

Ramsey Theory. This theory builds on the idea of order. It says that disorder is impossible. A group may look disorderly so that you cannot find an orderly mathematical "object"—for instance, a pair—in it. But enlarge the group enough and you can find any object you want. Frank Ramsey was a mathematician of this century who died at the young age of twenty-six, yet left us with a whole new class of brain teasers. Not wanting to settle for overly large groups in which to find his objects, he posed problems asking what was the smallest group in which an object might be found.

Take the sock problem. There are blue socks and red socks mixed in a drawer. Without looking, you pick socks out of the drawer. What is the smallest number you can pick and still be sure you have a pair of socks—either red or blue? *(Three. If the first two do not match, then the third is sure to match with one of them.)*

Now assume a character with three feet and socks of three colors. What is the smallest number of socks he must pick from the drawer to be sure of having three that match in color? *(Seven. If six socks did not have a matching set of three, it would have two of each color, and the seventh sock would form a set.)*

Summary

This chapter has given a sampling of arithmetic ideas that have intrigued men for ages. It has described the kinds of real numbers, introduced imaginary numbers, and given special attention to the history and uses of zero. The history and importance of the decimal system and the workings of place value were also considered.

Among intriguing ideas that children can explore in our number system are the concepts of and properties of odd and even numbers, prime numbers, perfect numbers, and friendly numbers. Ramsey theory is also mentioned here as an example of mental games that people have long enjoyed.

Students today should also have mind-expanding experiences as they study arithmetic. Arithmetic need not be dull. It should be more than drill and memory; it should include meaning at all levels, and sometimes some brain teasers and puzzles and a sprinkling of the history of mathematics.

12. Principles of Teaching

Using Achievement Test Results

If your child has taken an achievement test recently, study the arithmetic results closely. A section usually labeled "Computation" contains subtopics of multiplication, division, decimals, estimation, and so forth. From studying these subscores you can sometimes find an area to spend more time on this year in an effort to catch it up with the others.

Also, notice carefully the other large categories. Sometimes there is one other with a name like "Understanding" or "Concepts." And sometimes there is a third, "Applications."

If the Understanding score lags behind Computation, work all year on teaching the *why's* along with the *how's* of each procedure, using manipulative materials often. Spend time on ideas like place value, rounding numbers, and the meaning of fractions. And do problem solving all year long. It is not easy to see daily growth in Understanding, but consistent attention to this over a period of months will pay off, and in your child's next achievement test you will see results.

The score in "Applications" is improved by giving more attention to story problems, real-life problems, elementary geometry, graphs, and the use of various units of measure. Include your children as you study achievement test scores. Help them to understand the profile or the scores as well as they can (an arithmetic application!) and jointly set some goals for this year. It works much better when you and the child are on the same team than when you are the stern "teacher" holding the answer book and the red pencil.

More information about the meaning of the statistical scores themselves is given in the reading section. The best general advice about tests is to not be driven either by current test scores or by ambition concerning the next test. You should allow the scores to be guides where you want guidance, but should not allow them to dominate the goals of your teaching.

Anyway, fear of the tests is usually counterproductive. Inexperienced teachers sometimes stick very close to textbooks, because they think what's in the books must be what's on the tests, and they obtain unremarkable results or even less. But those who teach for meaning (while not neglecting computation) and who emphasize problem solving do achieve remarkable results.

A school district in Indiana reported that their math scores "soared" after they implemented a program with the following four goals. ("Educational Leadership," p.52 Jan 1984.)

1. Meaning and understanding
2. Problem solving
3. Mastery of basic facts and computational methods
4. Studying all prescribed units at each grade

The priority of each goal was about in the order listed. Goals 3 and 4 are closely related, because the textbook units contained facts and computational methods. The teachers implementing this program stated that a major weakness of their textbooks was that problems are classified by types. After a lesson on multiplying, for instance, the following story problems would all involve multiplication. Another weakness of the books was their rule orientation—rules for adding numbers, rules for finding percents, rules for finding area, rules for this and rules for that throughout the program, so that they felt they were teaching isolated bits of knowledge instead of interrelated concepts and thinking skills.

Notice the way that goal 4 is worded. These teachers concerned about weaknesses in the textbooks did not have a goal of slavishly following the textbook units. Instead, they only planned to include all unit topics, presumably being free to decide how much emphasis their students needed on each and being free to adjust and to supplement with more problem solving or meaning-building activities.

These teachers emphasized problem solving all year long, and also made problem solving the first unit of each year. Thus children obtained their customary review of facts and methods in the context of problems. The Indiana teachers found this was highly motivating for children, as well as being efficient and effective for their general arithmetic learning.

What were the tested results of this change in emphasis? Soaring scores. Before the problem-solving program, percentile ranks for grades 2 through 6 ranged mostly in the 30's and 40's with the highest score being 50 (exactly average) and the lowest a very low 8. After the program, the scores ranged mostly in the 70's and 80's, with the lowest being 67—all significantly above average.[1] If your children already score above average, any possible gains in percentile rank would not appear quite so dramatic, but if they are below average, you might achieve dramatic gains too. In either case, you should major on problem solving. This approach has power for all children.

Other Tests

In home tutoring, the testing needs are quite different from classrooms. One mother in the middle of summer admitted that her boy hadn't taken his last arithmetic test yet. "I don't feel like we need it," she said. "I know what he can do." The boy didn't need the test, the mother didn't need it, but they were in a correspondence school and the school was waiting for the test results. The following year that family did not enroll in a school and were free to make their own decisions about tests and assignments.

Elaborate testing structure has grown up in schools to fit their particular needs. Teachers of lower grades may have 30 children and math teachers of upper grades may have 150 students to keep track of. A few test scores jotted in grade books help in several ways with that massive job. One is diagnostic. By tests, teachers can determine whether their classes are ready to move to the next topic, or if they might need reteaching and more time on something important. Another use is grading. For better or for worse, schools use competitive grading systems and teachers need scores on which to base these grades.

Correspondence schools at the lower grades usually have more elaborate testing than classrooms. By tests, they can better "manage" a child through his books. An adequate score on a test shows them that a child has finished a book or unit and is ready for the next. It provides them with a way to grade, too.

If you aren't in a school, you don't need grades. At secondary level, grades can be one item to show at college entrance time, but at elementary level, grades are primarily for teachers to report to parents. When you are the teacher and the parent, that need disappears.

When you are tutoring, the diagnostic need for tests disappears too. You are in daily or almost daily touch with a child's work, so you know whether he is ready to move on to the next unit or topic. Even the children know. In one family, they changed arithmetic books and a boy saw that his started with fractions. "Mother," he said, "if we're going into fractions, I'll have to review multiplication first."

When this happens, the management need for tests disappears too. And you are a very fortunate and good teacher if children in your family react like that. A system of frequent testing says to children, "I'll tell you what to learn and I'll tell you when you've learned it. You don't have to worry, just leave everything to me." But children should take responsibility for their learning. That should be a major goal of education.

One remaining use for tests is motivation. Children can study something, see if they can pass a test on it, and then confidently say to you, "See, I know it." In less ideal cases, you may have to hold out a test as motivation. "You can't _____ until you know these well enough to pass the test." Fill in the blank with "watch TV," "visit your friend," or whatever works in your family. When children have inner discipline, let them use it. When they don't, impose discipline for them. As they mature more of the learning responsibility should fall on them instead of on you.

There is no need to follow school practices in testing. Do some fresh thinking about this matter, and use tests only when they are truly helpful for you and your children.

Three Modes of Thinking

Three modes important to arithmetic are: 1) manipulative, 2) mental-image, and 3) abstract. Some books call these "stages" of thinking, but I am calling them modes to help us avoid a major mistake in using them. We Americans, whenever we hear of stages or steps, think primarily of moving our children up the steps as far and as fast as possible. But in the case of these modes of arithmetic thinking, that is exactly the wrong thing to do. We must make the best use we can of all the modes.

Manipulative Mode. This is the mode that we use when we have to see and feel something in order to understand it. If numbers on a page—of forces, and energy and pistons and other parts—don't clarify for us how an engine works, watching a model or the real thing could be just the learning experience that we need. An architect or a student working out a new structure may sometimes need a model to figure out details that can't be visualized well enough in the mind.

Our generation seems to think that Jean Piaget discovered the manipulative mode, but Comenius in the 1600s used this mode to "give meaning to words by associating them with objects that are familiar to the learner." Pestalozzi in the 1800s rejected the teaching of mere words and facts—the verbalizing common in his day—and used physical objects to improve "perceptions," which he believed were the basis of all knowledge (the same as Piaget's theory). Marie Montessori popularized the manipulative mode for the teaching of young children. Early nineteenth century leaders of manual training in the United States insisted that they were using concrete methods to help students visualize abstract ideas. One professor asked his engineering students to build models to help them understand, and he found they lacked the necessary manual skills. So he set up a workshop where they could develop some skill in using tools. While the manual skills might turn out to be useful in later life, the main idea was to develop the mind. Somewhere along the line, much of our manual training evolved into teaching skills mainly, and the intellectual aspect was forgotten.

The manipulative mode, then, is not only for young children at the stage of counting blocks and cutting apples or cakes into fractional parts. It is for all of us in some facets of our work or thinking. But it is especially important for young children up to the age of about 6 or 7 because their other modes of thinking are not as well developed as ours.

And for children of fourth grade and up it is still a very important mode. You have read here about the effectiveness of "teaching for meaning" and of "problem solving," and now this secret of using the manipulative mode gives you the most powerful tool for doing that. Any time something isn't clear to a child, try to arrange a way for him to work through the process with checkers or rods or coins or other objects. Sometimes you could give teacher demonstrations. The child can in turn try to show and explain to you what you just showed him. If the matter is complex it may take more than one kind of material or demonstration. It may take repeated demonstrations over several days.

If your children in their preschool and primary years have had a good foundation of manipulative thinking, you will find it paying off now in better understanding during the middle and upper grades. If they haven't had it, but are just following procedures with little understanding of why they work, it is not too late to enrich their understanding by manipulatives. At all ages, children differ in their styles of thinking and some children need this more than others.

Mental-Image Mode. A major purpose of using manipulatives is to help children build images in their heads. With images in our heads, we can solve problems without resorting to exterior models. We have interior models to think with.

Thus we should never push children to drop the use of manipulatives, because they will drop them themselves as soon as their mental images are good enough. For instance, when you introduce multiplication, your children can use checkers or some kind of counters while they are working a page of multiplication problems. They can make 4 piles of 6 and see what 4 × 6 is. But this is a slow way to work problems, so children will not persist in this when they can do the problems faster in their heads.

Some old and bad advice said, "Don't let your children count on their fingers." If children count on their fingers, it is a signal that they do not yet have sufficient mental images of the number system. And you cannot force mental images by forcing them to stop using fingers. Better to work at building mental images of the number system. The hundred chart and the number line are two excellent ways to do this. These are explained in a following section.

An alternative to manipulating objects is to draw. A good procedure for children to use sometimes when solving a problem is to draw a picture or diagram of what happens in the problem, to help them image it. Drawing can be considered a transition, being part way between the use of actual objects and the use of mental images.

Another important way to build mental images is verbalizing. There is good verbalizing and bad verbalizing. When people disparage this, maybe even using the term "mere verbalizing," they mean the practice of having children parrot back to you rules or principles which they do not understand.

Good verbalizing is different. This is the practice of having children put into words what happens either in their mental images or in demonstrations with actual objects. Doing this is really quite simple, because you don't need to always be analyzing children's minds and thinking about whether they are imaging and what they are imaging. All you need to do is give them plenty of opportunity to explain things to you. As they work at verbalizing difficult concepts, they will form strong mental images and clarify fuzzy ones.

Most daily verbalizing is oral, but at times try writing, too. To choose words and write down thoughts requires more precision than speaking them. Many people say, "Writing IS thinking." Writing rules or generalizations is especially difficult thinking. Try, for instance, using the hundred chart to help children get a new insight into adding. It might be adding 6 to any number that ends with 8. Point to 8, 18, 28, 78, 48, and other numbers in the "8 family" and have a child count up six squares and tell the total. When he can do this so rapidly that you know he has figured out a "rule" and is no longer counting, ask him to write the rule. Other writing assignments can be to write explanations of how to carry, how to reduce fractions, and other procedures. Children should write every day, anyway, so let the writing do double duty as in these examples.

For children of middle and upper grades, the mental-image mode of thinking is dominant. You will be an excellent arithmetic teacher if you strengthen their mental images. Two teaching processes help you accomplish this: 1) use manipulative objects as often as necessary to explain things the children don't understand, and 2) use the good kind of verbalizing, both oral and written.

Abstract Mode. At about ages 12 and 13, children are able to do more abstract thinking. The numerals and the signs used in arithmetic are abstract, but we almost forget that because we begin teaching them to children at such a young age. Once children write signs and read them and say the words, we think they "know" them. Some educators are now asking the question, "Do we teach these too soon?" They are not suggesting that we wait until age twelve to teach the simplest arithmetic signs, but they are suggesting that more learning with objects and images should precede the abstractions and that we should wait longer than we do now.

Let's see what it would be like in an everyday act to teach its abstractions first. Say that a physics teacher explained to you about the law of gravity and the rate of acceleration in the speed of falling matter, so that falling matter hits a closer object with less force than a further object, all according to a mathematical formula which you must learn. Also, if you hold a pitcher of water in its liquid form, and tip the pitcher, the shape of the water will change and its center of gravity move, so that the surface of the water remains level with the surface of the earth. This shape-changing is easier to calculate if the pitcher is strictly cylindrical, but as the pitcher shape is more complex so is the mathematics required to figure out when the water surface will come to the level at which it will spill out the lip in just the amount and rate you have determined to pour. As a challenge for advanced students, there is one shape of pitcher in which the center of gravity of the water does not move at all, but finding that is an "extra" not required for pouring the water.

Now, when you have everything figured out, you can pour the water according to the laws of physics.

Since we haven't made physics a nursery school subject, we let children in real life learn the "feel" of water in pitchers and falling through the air. They see what happens when they tip a pitcher, better with see-through pitchers than with opaque ones. They use trial and error methods. And somehow or other they all learn to pour water. If we bombard students with abstractions at all, we wait at least until a high school physics course.

More of that order of thinking should happen in arithmetic. Too often, our books lead us to give the children an abstraction, then we must spend great energy and creativity trying to explain the meaning of the abstraction. If we persevere long enough and if the child's mind is mature enough for the abstraction, we can succeed in this, but how much better it would be if children arrive at meaning with the raw materials of arithmetic, with objects and number lines and Cuisenaire rods, with checkers and game scores and batting averages. When enough meaning is built, an abstraction can follow.

Children should feel and see and experience numbers in all sorts of ways in order to build the foundation and the capacity for handling abstractions. The same is true of geometric shapes both plane and solid. Years of art and construction and playing around with shapes will make eighth grade geometry under-standable.

When children can think abstractly about some matters, that does not mean they have moved up the steps and left behind the other modes of thinking. It means that they now have three modes of thinking to use instead of only two. The modes are additive.

Teaching for Meaning

Arithmetic processes are part of a beautiful, orderly system. Everything is related and integrated. "Teaching for meaning" means to help children see some of the patterns and laws at work in this fascinating number system.

Each time your children gain a new insight into the system, they have more potential for further learning. And their thinking about numbers is raised to a higher level. There is power in this kind of learning. By contrast, if their arithmetic study focuses on mechanical skills, children's thinking is at the lower level of memory and habit. And their potential for learning the next skill is not increased as much. Each skill becomes an isolated bit of learning, not part of the beautiful pattern.

It may be that your own arithmetic learning emphasized *how* to do the processes and not enough attention was given to understanding *why* the processes work as they do. If that is the case, and if you want to teach your children more meaning in arithmetic, you probably will find helpful information in the next two chapters on the four basic processes of arithmetic—addition, subtraction, multiplication and division. These give a teacher point of view. If you, the teacher, have a better picture of the system, you can pass some of it along to your children.

A hundred chart and a number line are two simple and powerful aids for helping children at the ages where they think largely in the mental-image mode. Many commercial aids are very good too, but these described below are aids you can easily make at home.

Hundred Chart. A hundred chart looks deceptively

simple, but complex understandings can be developed by using one. On it children can learn to count, and to consider prime numbers, and everything in between. Use the chart often enough that children will carry its image in their minds for years—for as long as they need it, which may be a lifetime or at least until they are so far into abstract thinking that they don't need the image anymore.

Hundred Chart

1	2	3	4	5	6	7	8	9	10
11	12	13	14	15	16	17	18	19	20
21	22	23	24	25	26	27	28	29	30
31	32	33	34	35	36	37	38	39	40
41	42	43	44	45	46	47	48	49	50
51	52	53	54	55	56	57	58	59	60
61	62	63	64	65	66	67	68	69	70
71	72	73	74	75	76	77	78	79	80
81	82	83	84	85	86	87	88	89	90
91	92	93	94	95	96	97	98	99	100

The following activities will give you an idea of the wide range of learnings that can be advanced on this chart. Once you and your children become comfortable with it, you will find more uses in your day-by-day arithmetic lessons.

1. Learn your way around the hundred chart by counting. Begin anywhere and count up to 50 or up to 100. Begin at your age and count to your mother's age. Count by 5's. Count by 2's. Count by 10's. Count by any other grouping that you can.
2. Count by 10's, but start on 2. Count by 10's, starting on 6. On 7. On 1. Start on any number in the first row and count by 10's.
3. Start on 8 and add 4 by counting up 4 squares. Start on 18 and add 4. Start on 28 and add 4. You are bridging from one row (one decade) to the next. Can you add 4 to any number that ends with 8?
4. Start on 7 and add 6 by counting up 6 squares. Start on 17 and add 6. You are bridging again. Start on any number that ends with 7 and add 6.
5. Start on 2 and count by 2's. Those numbers are called the even numbers. Start on 1 and count by 2's. Those numbers are called the odd numbers.
6. Now try everything backward. Start on 50 and count down to 1. Start on 100 and count down to 50 or to 1. Begin anywhere you want and count down to 1.
7. Start on 20 and count backward by 2's. Start on 50 and count backward by 5's. Start on 100 and count backward by 10's. Start on 99 and count backward by 10's. Start on 96 and count backward by 10's. Start anywhere and count backward by any number you can.
8. Start on 12 and subtract 4 by counting backward 4 squares. Start on 22 and subtract 4. Start on 32 and subtract 4. Can you subtract 4 from any number that ends with 2?
9. Start on 13 and subtract 6 by counting backward 6 squares. Start on 23 and subtract 6. Start on any number that ends with 3 and subtract 6.
10. Start on any number and add 10. Start on another number and add 10. Do this until it gets easy for you. Try to write a rule for adding 10 to a number.

11. Start on 9 and count forward 9 more. Start on 19 and count forward 9 more. Start on 29 and count forward 9 more. Start on any number you want and count 9 more. After this gets easy for you, see if you can write a rule for adding 9 to a number.

12. Start on any number and add 11. Can you write a rule for adding 11 to a number?

13. Make up a problem for a friend to do on the hundred chart. Ask your friend to make up a problem for you.

14. Find a page of addition or subtraction problems in your arithmetic book and work them by using the hundred chart instead of by your usual method.

15. Which way do you count when you want to add? Which way do you count when you want to subtract? Try explaining to one of your parents what the hundred chart shows about adding and subtracting.

16. Show a younger brother or sister how to make a hundred chart. Make up some problems for the brother or sister to do by counting forward or backward.

17. Make a quick, disposable hundred chart, or tape a piece of see-through tissue or plastic over your chart. Begin this exercise on prime numbers by crossing off the 1. Next, look at the 2. Don't cross it off, but cross off every number that you could get if you multiplied something by 2. That means you cross off every multiple of 2, every even number. Look at the next open number, which is 3. Don't cross it off, but cross off every number left that is a multiple of 3. Your next open number is 5. Cross off every multiple of 5. What is your next open number? Cross off every multiple of that. Keep going that way until you can't do any more. If you didn't make any mistakes, the numbers left open are prime numbers. They cannot be divided by any number except 1 and themselves.

Number Lines. The hundred chart described in the preceding section is a special form of number line in which the line is cut into strips of 10 and the strips laid one under the other to show patterns that cannot be seen as easily on a straight line. But a straight line gives its own unique image of our number system, and thus can be used in addition to the hundred chart.

You can make a simple number line by writing numbers on a roll of calculator paper or on any suitable material you have access to. A line from 1 to 100 will do a lot of teaching. For special purposes you may wish to make shorter or longer lines.

Major understandings your children should gain from a number line are that counting forward is adding numbers and counting backward is subtracting numbers. To develop an adequate image of this, children need varying amounts of practice on a number line.

For some children, a number line should be left on a wall for months, and almost daily they should be asked to point out on the line how to work two or three problems from their textbook. Use it with addition and subtraction drill problems and use it with story problems. If your children did not use a number line sufficiently while in primary grades, use one quite a lot in fourth grade and continue occasional use in fifth grade. For children who have difficulty in arithmetic, use the number line even more than with other children.

When your children come to the study of decimal fractions, which may be about sixth or seventh grade, a special number line built for that purpose is a powerful learning tool for them. This line is best made from units of some kind that can be cut into halves or thirds. Large wooden nursery school beads in a sort-of-oval shape work perfectly. Get 50 beads of one color and 50 of a second color. String 10 red, 10 yellow, 10 red, and so forth up to 100. If you string these along a wire you may manage a somewhat rigid line that only needs to be nailed up at each end and perhaps in the center. If you use flexible cord and your line drapes between the nails, it doesn't matter.

Begin by having your child show you 1/2 of the string of beads, which is 50 beads or 50 percent (50 per 100). Proceed to 1/4, 1/10, 2/10, and other such fractions of the string. Have the child learn both the common fraction and the decimal fraction way to say each one. For instance, 1/4 (of the 100 beads) is 25 beads. Thus 1/4 is equal to 25 per hundred, or 25%. One-tenth is equal to 10%, 2/10 is 20%, 3/4 is 75%, and so on. Practice on simple fractions such as these until your child has a good feel for fractional parts of the string of beads.

Then cut the 13th bead into halves so that it can be spread apart to show 12½% or ⅛ of the string. Cut the first ⅓ of the 34th bead and the last third of the 67th bead, so they can be spread apart to show ⅓ and ⅔ of the string. Cut others, as your child figures out where they need to be cut to show eighths. Now, your child can work out many problems in converting fractions to percent and vice versa. And he can develop in his head a good image and understanding of what percents are all about. As long as your child is studying a unit on percentage, have him work at least one or two problems per day using the string of beads. Choose problems from his arithmetic book, if you wish. One problem on the beads is worth ten problems on a workbook page.

Major Goals for Mathematics

In 1980 the National Council of Teachers of Mathematics recommended some priorities for curriculum. In the years since then, other groups have agreed with these and worked in various ways to implement the recommendations. Among them are these which may be of interest to parents.

1. Problem solving must be the focus of mathematics instruction. (First in importance, as well as first in order, on their list.)

2. We must redefine what we mean by basic arithmetic skills, so as to include more than just being able to compute.

3. Courses must take full advantage of the power of calculators and computers at all grade levels. (The idea is not to replace learning of traditional skills, as some fear, but to enable students to advance farther in math than they could without these.)

4. More mathematics should be required of all students, and there should be more flexibility to accommodate the needs of all kinds of students. (Because of our technological and scientific society, all citizens need more math than before.)

Problem Solving

You may wish to make their number 1 recommendation part of your math teaching also. If so, you could do as the Indiana teachers did and begin each year with problem solving as a way to review skills the children have already learned. You could also try to use most of the story problem pages in your textbook even if you have to skip some of the drill pages to do it.

Using Story Problems. Here are techniques that help to develop good problem solvers.

1. Talk through a problem. What information is given? What must be found? Break larger concepts down into smaller steps.

2. When a child seems stumped, ask, "What can you do to get started?"

3. Use a simple problem of the same type as the hard one to develop the proper line of thought. This system is said to have been invented by Hippocrates, but many a

school child has reinvented it out of necessity. Other children appreciate the hint being passed on to them.

4. Draw a diagram or picture, when possible, to clarify what is happening in the problem.

5. Sometimes have problems without numbers, where children decide what to do without actually computing. Sometimes have problems without enough information or with too much information, or incomplete problems where children must recognize that they are incomplete and unworkable, or where they obtain the missing information and then solve the problem.

6. Estimate answers before working them out. Or after working them, ask, "Is my answer reasonable?"

Calculators have made estimating even more important than before. Children must learn not to blindly depend on answers they get from calculators, because they may have entered a wrong number, missed a decimal point, or even done the wrong operation.

To be a good estimator requires a good understanding of place value and the number system in general, as well as a good mental image of what happens in a particular problem. It is a high-level mental activity. So at all ages and in all kinds of problems children should practice estimating.

Real-Life Problems. You might enjoy experimenting with real-life problems. This is easier to do at home than in classrooms. For instance, in taking out insurance or buying a car on time and other such family situations, a lot of arithmetic is involved in deciding the best course to take, and these situations make good problems.

Don't be afraid of real-life problems; you don't have to write them out to look like textbook story problems where the necessary information is neatly given and the question is carefully asked. The whole point of real-life problems is that they are not like that. Children may have to search out and collect information. They may have to think about what the real question is: should we buy car A or car B; should we choose the rebate or the lower interest; how long would it take to save up money and buy with cash; and so on. They have to decide what information is needed and what is irrelevant for answering the question. They may find they don't know enough about the situation or about math (and that's not bad; that, too, is real life).

A sixth grade teacher who tries to bring real-life problems into the classroom says it's "dangerous" because it demands so much of everybody both emotionally and intellectually; it draws on skills that may not be in their current unit; it puts them on unsure ground—they may not be able to reach a solution; the questions become increasingly difficult and everybody realizes they have a long way to go to get educated. So why does she do it? Because it is exciting, it stimulates intellectual growth, it has high impact on her students immediately, and has long-term effects too.

Another area for real-life problems is nutrition. Counting calories, counting grams of fat and translating them into calories, balancing proteins, carbohydrates and fats, comparing nutritional merits of various brands and foods, figuring out vitamin and fiber intake—these and anything else you happen to be interested in can make good problems.

Meal planning: Plan a menu; shop for the food, staying within a specified budget; cook, following recipes and measuring ingredients; serve and explain to the family how well your plan went or what problems you had with the meal.

Home-improvement projects: How much cement should we order for the patio? What size boards and what length do we need for the bookshelves? What will the cost be?

Children's projects: How much plastic do we need to line the fish pond? What is the most cost-effective way to buy that size? How can we make the treehouse stronger? How many rows should we lay out in our garden? How can we get them straight?

How can I make my collection good enough to win an award?

Family business: Keep books; pay bills; buy supplies; figure profit or loss; learn about taxes, rent, insurance and other costs.

Even very young children can learn arithmetic from family businesses. A math teacher perhaps got her start in her father's print shop when she was five years old. She had the job of walking around a table picking up pages to collate. The page numbers had to be in order, her mother told her, or the book wouldn't come out right.

Real-life problems do more for thinking skills than manufactured, look-alike story problems. Children brought up on these have a head start when they meet their own adult problems later in life.

In this chapter we have considered teaching for meaning, using your children's mental-image mode of thinking, using a hundred chart and other aids, solving problems, using real-life problems and providing practice in estimating. These principles and ideas, when taken all at once, may make arithmetic teaching seem a formidable activity. But fortunately, you have plenty of time to grow as a teacher while your children are growing as students. If you want to change things this year, all you need to do now is make one decision: "I will have my child make a hundred chart and we will learn to use it," or "I will try to take time each day to listen to my child talk through a couple of problems from his arithmetic assignment." After one new procedure is rolling along enriching your arithmetic course, you can add another new idea. From here to competence in arithmetic is a long road for your children. You get there one step at a time.

13. Addition and Subtraction

Our four operations of arithmetic are: addition, subtraction, multiplication, and division. There haven't always been four operations. Among the ancient Hindus, some mathematicians named as many as twenty operations, including squaring, cubing, progressions, and finding roots. Other Hindus combined and simplified until they had only six or eight operations. In the Middle Ages, two operations were doubling and halving, but we include those in multiplication and division without making separate categories for the twos.

In this chapter we will look at two of the four operations—addition and subtraction—along with some hints for teaching them

Adding

Adding is combining, or putting numbers together. It may also be thought of as counting, and it can be visualized as counting forward on a number line. Suggestions for making and using number lines are given in the preceding chapter. The numbers to be added are called **addends** and the answer is called the **sum.**

Memorizing Basic Facts. Although you must continually emphasize understanding, there comes a time for memory. Every child should memorize all the addition facts shown on the chart. On this chart you can find the sum of any two single-digit numbers. For instance, the sum of 4 and 6 is given where row 4 crosses column 6.

Chart of Addition and Subtraction Facts

	1	2	3	4	5	6	7	8	9
1	2	3	4	5	6	7	8	9	10
2	3	4	5	6	7	8	9	10	11
3	4	5	6	7	8	9	10	11	12
4	5	6	7	8	9	10	11	12	13
5	6	7	8	9	10	11	12	13	14
6	7	8	9	10	11	12	13	14	15
7	8	9	10	11	12	13	14	15	16
8	9	10	11	12	13	14	15	16	17
9	10	11	12	13	14	15	16	17	18

On the chart there appear to be 81 addition combinations, but if you count 4 + 6 and 6 + 4 as the same combination, and other reversals likewise, you can reduce the total to 45 addition facts your children must memorize.

Of the 45, 9 are super easy because they add 1 to each number. Nine more are almost as easy because they add 2 to each number. Most children think the doubles are easy, too—3 + 3, 4 + 4, and so on. If your children don't know the doubles, some practice in counting by twos will help. With the ones and twos and doubles learned, there are only 21 facts left to master.

Your children may have some techniques for remembering the other 21. Ask them. If they need more learning techniques, try these.

1. The nines are almost as easy as tens. A rule for adding a number to 9 is: Use 1 of the number to reach 10, and use the rest to add to the 10. For instance, in 9 + 6 the idea is to start with 9 and count 6 more. After 1 count you reach 10, and you have 5 left to count, which brings you to 15.

   Teach these first on a hundred chart and then practice without the chart. Mix them in various orders, and repeat until your child masters them.

$$9 + 3$$
$$9 + 4$$
$$9 + 5$$
$$9 + 6$$
$$9 + 7$$
$$9 + 8$$

2. Use the same procedure with eights. Count up 2 to reach 10, and the remaining numbers tell where in the teens the count will end. Teach these on a number line and then mentally. Use scrambled order.

$$8 + 3$$
$$8 + 4$$
$$8 + 5$$
$$8 + 6$$
$$8 + 7$$

3. Learn the "almost doubles." If $3 + 3 = 6$, then $3 + 4 = 7$. If $4 + 4 = 8$, then $4 + 5 = 9$. Drill on these in scrambled order until your child can give quick answers.

$$2 + 3$$
$$3 + 4$$
$$4 + 5$$
$$5 + 6$$
$$6 + 7$$
$$7 + 8$$
$$8 + 9$$

4. Know thoroughly all the combinations that make 10.

$$9 + 1$$
$$8 + 2$$
$$7 + 3$$
$$6 + 4$$
$$5 + 5$$

Use these combinations whenever they help. For instance, in $7 + 4$ you can see that $7 + 3$ is ten, and 1 more makes 11. In $7 + 5$, you again can see a $7 + 3$, with 2 more to make 12.

5. Use either flash cards or practice sheets for the above drills. A practice sheet is simply a page with the group of problems written in scrambled order two or more times. Since the adding is done mentally, the same sheet can be used repeatedly by working the problems forward or backward, vertically or horizontally, or by starting on different rows. Homemade practice materials are not

only inexpensive; they also give the message that this is a temporary drill—something that the child should master in a few days. Commercial materials may imply a permanence, but they are a time-saver for you.

6. Post difficult facts on a wall and say the answers in rhythm while jumping on a rebounder or jumping a rope. Don't pass too quickly over this jumping idea as though it were only for hyperactive children or for recess time or other less than serious use with your children. There is powerful memory learning in such techniques, and when this memory is added to understanding, you get a winning combination.

Overlearning. After all the thinking aids and memory tricks have helped your children learn the addition facts so that they could pass a test with 100% accuracy, they are not through yet. They must now learn the facts so well they can answer each with ease. Build understanding and accuracy first; then drill until the children answer quickly and easily.

What makes 2 + 2 such an easy addition fact? Partly it is that we all have a good understanding and good mental image of the number 2. And partly it is that we overlearned it by repetition in counting by twos and other activities in our early learning of numbers. Why is 5 + 5 so easy? Again, because of good understanding and overlearning. If you wish your children to be competent in arithmetic, help them learn all the addition facts as well as they know 5 + 5.

Higher-Decade Adding. Addition of numbers in the teens, twenties, thirties, and on up is called addition in the higher decades. This is not very difficult for students who have good mastery of the basic facts in the preceding section. If your children can add 3 + 5, they can add 23 + 5 or 73 + 5. All such 3 + 5 facts can be considered as a family—the 3 + 5 family.

Families such as 3 + 5, where the sum in each column is 9 or less, are easy for most children. The problems look like these.

64	72	4	24	9	35	3	64	81	63
5	6	44	1	20	3	84	4	7	6

5	5	72	54	27	21	34	23	2	16
92	84	5	3	2	6	5	5	37	3

46	63	42	13	8	32	40	25	81	36
3	1	3	3	50	2	7	1	2	3

It is good practice to try saying the answers to rows of problems like these in a steady rhythm. There's no need to go at breakneck speed. Rhythm is more important; it will show which facts you stumble on and should give some attention to. It is best to do a lot of oral practice, but for occasional paper-and-pencil practice, have your child place the edge of a sheet of paper under a row of problems, and write answers on the paper. For the next row, fold back the paper to have a fresh edge.

Bridging. After children do well on the preceding type of problems where there is no carrying or "bridging" to a higher decade, move on to this next kind, where there is bridging. To practice these, say the answers in a steady rhythm as before, sometimes reading from right to left and sometimes from left to right. Do not carry, but think of bridging to the next higher decade. The bridging process is described more fully following the problems.

7	58	39	83	15	36	48	7	63	36
26	6	1	9	7	7	3	55	8	6

28	39	27	86	63	2	24	36	75	38
3	8	5	9	7	29	9	4	9	8

45	28	8	47	72	83	54	49	59	27
6	5	32	3	9	8	6	7	5	4

What is the difference between bridging and "carrying"? They solve the same kinds of problems. On paper they may look exactly alike. But the difference is in the head. It's in the path your thinking takes as it solves a problem. For instance to carry in the first problem of the set above, you would think, "Seven plus 6 is 13; I write down 3 and carry 1; 1 and 2 is 3; I write down 3, and the sum is 33." To bridge in the same problem, you might think, "Twenty-six and 7 is 33." You know that quickly from the first step of the carrying problem—7 plus 6 is 13. Because you know that 7 plus 6 "bridges the tens," you bridge in this case from the twenties to the thirties without the extra step of carrying a 1.

This is a more intelligent approach to adding. If your children can't catch on to this after some explanations and a little practice, then you could assume that they don't yet have a good enough mental image of the numbers from 1 to 100. In such a case, work with the hundred chart for a while longer to build up that image.

To use the hundred chart for working the first problem above, ask your child to point to 26. Then say, "Add 7." The child can count up 7 squares, either with his finger or mentally, and see that he lands on 33. After some practice this way, the child may not need to point but only to look at the chart while working problems. And after some practice that way, he may not need the chart at all, because he has formed one in his head.

Why is this important? Because in column addition, in multiplication, and other processes, children need to do mental bridging. Column addition is not just more and longer than adding two numbers. It is different. It requires mental bridging, maybe several times in a column. In multiplication units, we sometimes pay little attention to children's adding skills, but many a problem is missed because of incorrect addition rather than incorrect multiplication. It pays to be thorough in the early stages of arithmetic.

Carrying. The process of carrying usually requires paper and pencil, because without those it may be too difficult to hold in mind the partial answer under one column while adding another column. Slower-learning children can master carrying more easily than bridging because it proceeds column by column. Once they can add one column they can learn to jot down the carried number and add another column in the same way. Thus this system is viewed as one which all school children can learn, and it is taught thoroughly in all textbooks. This system does at times require mental bridging while adding a column, and some books may not give enough attention to this.

To help all middle grade children better understand the pencil-and-paper, column-by-column system of adding, here are some ways to demonstrate meaning behind it. Expand problems as shown below. Both these expansions help to show that we add units (ones) in their column and tens in their column, and somehow we have to get the total answer together.

$$72 = 70 + 2$$
$$86 = 80 + 6$$
$$150 + 8 = 158$$

$$79$$
$$65$$
$$130 \ (70 + 60)$$
$$14 \ (9 + 5)$$
$$144$$

Understanding Numbers 1 to 100. No good student should have to get out a pencil to add 38 and 5. And your children won't have to, if you see that they master all the higher-decade facts up to sums of 100 just as thoroughly as they earlier mastered sums up to 10.

When your children practice mentally on higher-decade adding, as described in this chapter, they gain several advantages. A first, elusive, advantage is that they build good understanding of numbers up to 100.

A second advantage is that adding of columns and adding of

two-place and three-place numbers will now be easier. Children will use simple adding skills as they solve more complex adding problems.

A third advantage is that children now have a skill they can use in other arithmetic operations. For example, it will help them to "carry" in multiplication. Consider this problem.

$$\begin{array}{r} 45 \\ \times\, 7 \\ \hline 315 \end{array}$$

Work through the problem and you see a point where you use the higher-decade fact of $28 + 3$. We usually leave this step for children to do in their heads, and hardly notice that we are doing so. If a child gets it, we seldom congratulate him for his complex thinking. And if he doesn't get it, we tend to think something is wrong with his multiplying instead of with his adding.

Two Laws of Addition. When children do well on mental higher-decade adding, they are quite good at using two laws of addition that they may never have heard about. These are:

1. The Law of Commutation
2. The Law of Association

Commutation refers to changing with each other, trading places. Children need not understand all about the word. In fact, they need not even know the name of the law. An achievement test will not ask that, and a child's future workplace will never ask that—unless he turns out to be a teacher.

But every student must understand the workings of the law, and that is as simple as knowing that $5 + 8$ is the same as $8 + 5$. The law also works with more than two numbers. No matter in what order you add a set of numbers, you should always get the same total. That's the **Law of Commutation.** So don't scare your students with it; break it to them gently.

The **Law of Association** works when there are more than two numbers to add, but when adding two numbers you can split one of them into two so that you have enough numbers to use this law. For instance, instead of 8 + 5 you can split up the 5 in your head and have 8 + 2 + 3. The Law of Association says that it doesn't matter which number the 2 associates with. It began life associated with 3 to make 5. But if you join it with 8 to make 10, the law will never get you, and for most people it's easier to add 10 and 3 than to add 8 and 5.

With the kind of mental work suggested in these chapters, your child will probably form all kinds of compatible associations. Some children are afraid to tell because they think it's cheating. You can break the news that it's a perfectly lawful activity that will become even more useful in advanced arithmetic and in algebra.

Adding Two-Place Numbers. After learning the basic facts and after learning to bridge, the next step in mental addition is to add two-place numbers. This is good practice for children who are able to do it. It would be good practice for you too, as teacher, to polish up skills that may have become rusty since your school days.

An alternate way of adding, like this, does not confuse children who have a good understanding of the number system. On the contrary, it builds even greater understanding of both the adding process and the number system. It also is stimulating mentally. When your textbook has rows of drill problems for children to work, try letting them do a portion of the problems orally. Since mental arithmetic takes high concentration, keep the practice periods short, but continue for a number of consecutive days until you notice good improvement in a child's ability to do it.

To add mentally, begin at the left. Follow the arrows in the first problem shown below and think, "80, 84, 89." To make it shorter yet, just think, "84, 89." This problem does not involve bridging. That is, you begin in the 80's and stay in the 80's, instead of bridging into the 90's. Problems of this "easy" type are given here for your use in short check-ups with your children and as samples for making longer practice sheets if you need them.

4 4	54	40	13	22	34	60	81	52	44
↓ ↗ ↓	15	17	71	26	62	25	17	31	45
4 5									

33	51	15	61	72	40	54	11	26	32
46	44	84	38	25	38	23	78	61	53

The following problems involve bridging. Follow the arrows and think, "77, 81."

5 7	56	59	18	83	33	47	64	25	78
↓ ↗ ↓	15	41	44	17	39	25	19	57	16
2 4									

19	39	43	24	67	34	55	48	36	26
11	13	39	18	13	27	36	44	36	48

The answers above were less than 100, but the same procedure works for sums greater than 100. Try these rows, and remember to start adding at the left of each problem. The first row of problems requires you to bridge once. For example, in the first problem think, "152, 158." The second row requires you to bridge twice. In its first problem think, "139, 144."

72	52	90	82	31	82	91	83	76	96
86	92	95	43	78	75	83	86	53	30

79	48	65	96	87	76	69	87	97	86
65	92	79	75	33	59	43	49	46	85

Teaching Tips for Basic Arithmetic. It is worthwhile to proceed carefully, even though slowly, through these basic matters, because more advanced arithmetic is built upon them. All future work will be easier for your children if they learn these first topics well.

But an important principle to remember is that real-life teaching is never as easy as it looks when laid out in a book. Though we can lay out addition problems in a careful progression as here, the human mind is very complex, and children's learning does not grow in the same linear progression as the arithmetic problems.

Thus, if you move along through addition for a time and then find it growing too difficult for a child, it may make sense to move on to subtraction for a while. In other words, add small numbers, then subtract small numbers, then switch back to adding and try larger numbers. If it goes well this time, then progress to subtracting larger numbers.

Children's minds need time to consolidate and digest their learning. They need broad experiences. Take time now and then to teach about quarts and gallons, about measuring cups, about rulers, money, fractional parts of things. Take time for story problems. Read graphs and maps.

The idea is always to find something your child can successfully learn. When practice on basic facts or bridging or any other work seems too difficult and progress is bogging down, then do what your intuition tells you to do. Time will usually solve your problem.

Subtracting

Subtraction is the reverse of addition. While addition is counting forward on a number line, subtraction is counting backward. While addition combines groups to find a total, subtraction begins with the total and finds a missing group.

There is no universal procedure for subtracting with pencil and paper. In this section we describe several methods, and you can follow the one used in your textbook or the one you like best.

Some slow students may be better off if you carefully teach one method only, and help them master it. But if your children are good arithmetic students, try telling them about a second way to subtract. As mentioned elsewhere, getting a view from outside a system helps a person understand the system better. Thus your children will better understand their own way of subtracting if they see another way. Even if they don't practice the second way and get good at it, just knowing it is there and trying it out a time or two releases them from the prison of feeling they know all there is to know about subtracting. Their minds are stimulated. Their view of arithmetic is broadened. The whole subject takes on a bit more excitement.

If you haven't thought about subtraction since your own school days, perhaps the "teacher view" given here will stimulate your mind a bit. If it does, your new interest will rub off onto your pupils, and while arithmetic sessions may not become exciting, at least they might go more smoothly and happily.

Memorizing Basic Facts. As with addition, there are 81 basic facts to learn if you don't count those with zero. And the same chart of facts that was given in the addition section can be used to see at a glance what the subtraction facts are. However, you now must read the tables in a reverse order. The sum, which is now called the **minuend**, is found in the body of the chart. The **subtrahend** to subtract from it is found along the left side, and the answer is found at the top. Or if you prefer, subtract a number at the top and find your answer on the left.

As with addition, your children can quite easily master certain groups of these facts, beginning with subtracting 1 from each number in the 1 row and 2 from each number in the 2 row. They should also know two principles about zero: 1) subtracting zero from a number leaves the number unchanged, and 2) subtracting any number from itself results in zero.

The "doubles" may be easy too. These minuends are in a diagonal reaching from upper left to lower right: 2, 4, 6, 8, 10, 12, 14, 16, and 18. In each case, the number to subtract from it and the resulting answer are the same number. Examples: $6 - 3 = 3$ and $14 - 7 = 7$. Children who learned to add doubles can rather easily do these subtractions.

The tens are in the other diagonal, from lower left to upper right. Each one, again, is the reverse of the addition combinations of ten. In addition, children learned that $4 + 6 = 10$. Now they need to learn that either addend subtracted from 10 leaves the other addend: $10 - 4 = 6$ and $10 - 6 = 4$.

After checking out that your children know the easy facts, or after first teaching the easy facts, you may be left with these more difficult ones. They require extra study and practice.

11	13	13	15	17	15	17	14	16	13	14
7	5	9	7	9	9	9	5	9	4	9

13	13	16	11	14	12	12	15	14	12	15
8	7	7	3	6	3	7	6	8	5	8

All 81 subtraction facts, as well as the zero principles, must be overlearned. So use a hundred chart, and number lines and flash cards and practice sheets even beyond the time children first learn the facts. A short number line only up to 20 will suffice for these facts. Practice mentally and orally as much as or more than with paper and pencil.

Make sheets with problems written in vertical form like the two rows just given, or with problems written in sentence form like this.

$$15 - 9 =$$
$$11 - 7 =$$

Your children should become used to seeing problems both ways. The actual form of writing makes less difference to children when they image better the underlying process of subtraction as counting backward on a number line. If different written forms confuse children, do more work on a number line or with objects instead of with abstract symbols and signs.

That's the important principle, again, of letting children think in their strong mental-image and manipulative modes instead of in their weak abstract mode. For this task and for other memorizing tasks, use the method of spaced review. With this method, you review daily for a time, then weekly, then monthly, then annually, possibly at the beginning of each year. Actually, you don't have to slavishly follow a calendar like that, but the general idea is to put more and more space between the reviews. If you follow other suggestions in this book about doing a lot of problem solving, children will get constant review of these and other basic facts while they work problems.

Higher-Decade Subtracting. The basic facts to learn in the decades from 10 on up to 100 are of two kinds as shown in the two rows below. In one kind, a single-digit number is the subtrahend, and in the other a single-digit number is the answer. Both kinds should be done mentally, with no need for pencil and paper.

78	89	26	55	27	63	85	46	19	98
2	4	3	1	2	1	4	2	4	1
76									

73	47	29	74	83	46	58	89	25	66
70	44	26	73	84	42	53	81	24	64
3									

In the examples given above, no bridging is required, but both kinds of problems also include a group of facts which do require bridging. Examples:

43	64	94	73	62	23	93	32	26	75
8	7	8	8	6	4	5	7	7	7

44	62	47	23	83	52	87	20	51	66
36	53	39	16	79	45	78	12	46	59

You can use these rows of problems to provide a little practice for your children or to check out at what level of difficulty it begins to get too hard for them. For practice, a child can read answers from left to right and then from right to left on the same row. If you try these too, you might gain better understanding of the thinking processes your children must do as they work these. For additional practice, make four sheets of problems, one for each of the four kinds. Most children could make these themselves. The sheets are reusable, since all the practice is done mentally and orally. As mentioned in the addition section, rhythm is more important than speed in saying answers to drills such as these. After good rhythm is achieved, greater speed comes easier.

After your children get pretty good at each of these four kinds of problems, you could make a practice sheet on which the kinds are mixed. But this is not necessary if your textbook has numerous story problems with the skills mixed.

Two-Place Numbers. Next in order is the type of problem in which all three numbers have two places. In the first problem below, children should think, "3 from 7 is 4" and "1 from 8 is 7." This is an easy kind of two-place subtracting, and should present no difficulty to anyone who knows the 81 basic facts.

87	39	82	58	67	93	75	38	73	98
13	38	41	21	11	12	52	23	41	84

Moving up in complexity, we come to problems which involve bridging. In an earlier day when students wrote problems on sand boards or slates where it was easy to erase, they often used the method shown below. The 34 which is scratched out here would have been simply erased and replaced with 26. You start at the left in these problems and think, "30 from 64 is 34" and "8 from 34 is 26." This method lends itself better to mental subtracting, but because of scratching out numbers it was not chosen for paper-and-pencil use.

$$
\begin{array}{r}
64 \\
-38 \\
\hline
\not{3}\not{4} \\
26
\end{array}
$$

Try the **scratch method** on these problems. The second thinking step in these requires skill developed in the first of the bridging rows given earlier. So do not rush your children through these difficulty levels. Give them the time they need. Use short intense practice drills on the newest level for each child and short reviews of easier levels. The remainder of an arithmetic period can be used for other activities, such as solving story problems with paper and pencil.

63	41	93	96	30	83	74	98	92	46
19	26	28	67	18	64	16	29	15	28

84	53	85	41	97	81	72	87	50	93
18	36	48	25	59	63	54	58	12	47

A Common Paper-and-Pencil Method. Most textbooks today teach a **regrouping method**, which formerly was called "borrowing." But the word *borrowing* came under criticism because there is nothing that we borrow in any ordinary sense of that word. What really happens here is that we *decompose* a number, or break it into parts. In the following example the problem is at the left and beside it is an expansion which you can use to help explain to students how the method works.

$$
\begin{array}{r}
64 \\
-38 \\
\hline
26
\end{array}
\qquad
\begin{array}{r}
64 = \quad (50 + 14) \\
-38 = -(30 + 8) \\
\hline
20 + 6 = 26
\end{array}
$$

The step of regrouping 60 into 50 and 14, while at first needs much attention, later should become easy for children so that their thinking jumps immediately to 14. Then they should think, "8 from 14 is 6" and "3 from 5 is 2."

This method of subtracting was developed for paper-and-pencil use and does not adapt well to mental arithmetic. As problems become larger it is even harder to do this mentally.

Children who practiced the preceding rows with the mental scratch method should now place the edge of a sheet of paper along the bottom of the first row and write the answers using this regrouping method. This will help them understand that the same problems can be worked either way. After working the first row, fold back the answer paper to form a fresh edge for working the next row. (This folded-paper technique can save time in drills found in your textbook, also.)

Methods of Subtracting. You can subtract by adding. One such way is called the **equal additions method.** If Bobby, at 9, is 3 years older than his sister who is 6, how much older than her will he be 5 years from now? 10 years? 40 years? He will always be 3 years older than his sister because the number of years added to their ages is always equal. That is the principle behind the equal additions method of subtracting.

To subtract 38 from 64 by the equal additions method, you must mentally add 10 to 4 in the top number and add 10 to 3 (30) in the bottom number. Thus, in the top number you add 10 to the ones column, and in the bottom number you add 10 to the tens column. But the result, nevertheless, is that you increase both numbers equally. Now think "8 from 14 is 6" and "4 from 6 is 2."

Some educators consider this to be the most efficient method for children to use and easiest for them to understand. Perhaps a textbook you choose will teach this method.

One more method we will explain here is the **complementary method.** Many bright students enjoy learning this and using it on occasion. It sometimes looks like number magic. First, students must know that a complement of a number is the difference between that number and the next higher power of ten (10, 100, 1000, etc.). For example the complement of 8 is 2 because 2 is the difference between 8 and 10. Now, to add 2 and subtract 10 brings the same result as subtracting 8, and that is the principle by which the complementary method works.

The rule is: add the complement and then subtract the 10 or 100 or whatever power was used. That subtracting is easy because you need only mentally drop the 1 from the beginning of your number.

Thus, instead of subtracting 8 from 14 in the problem above, you add 2, the complement. That gives you 16, but you drop the 1 (subtract 10) and write only the 6. It sounds complex if you have never done it before, but try it a few times and it gets easier.

The fun comes in using certain numbers that are natural for "number magic." A child who knows this system can say, "I'll race you. Write down 94. Now subtract 75 from it." While his opponent is subtracting, he writes 25 and adds instead, remembering to omit the 1 in the hundreds place.

The Law of Association. This law applies in subtraction as well as in addition. Remember that the names and definitions of this, and other laws, are for people who are strong abstract thinkers, and that does not include children of elementary grades. Though you, the teacher, might understand when you read about this law, and you might remember its name for a while, it is not particularly helpful to teach its name and definition to your elementary children. Junior high students could be introduced to this abstraction if it appears in their textbooks. What children need, is a great many experiences seeing this law at work in specific problems. And they need help in understanding that it is a law, that numbers always work this way. That's why you as teacher should try to understand the law. It will help you in many day-by-day explanations and discussions of your children's arithmetic assignments.

Simply defined, the Law of Association is: In subtraction you may take away the sum of two parts or you may take away first one part and then the other. This allows for regrouping in subtraction. To state it with numbers: if you're going to subtract 38, it's all right to subtract first the 30 and then the 8, as you would with the scratch method of subtraction, thus:

$$x - 38 = (x - 30) - 8$$

To show that this works no matter what the numbers are, we substitute symbols for numbers.

$$x - (y + z) = (x - y) - z$$

The Law of Commutation. This law, as mentioned in the addition section, allows for switching the order of operations. In subtraction it works too. Thus in the problem above, it's all right to subtract first the 8 and then the 30, as you would with the decomposition method of regrouping. No matter what order all subtractions and additions happen, the resulting answer will be the same.

The Subtrahend-Remainder Law. According to this law, when either the subtrahend or the remainder is subtracted from the minuend (sum) the resulting answer is the other number. This is easy to see when translated into numbers, as below.

$$\begin{array}{cc} 7 & 7 \\ \underline{-2} & \underline{-5} \\ 5 & 2 \end{array}$$

Two and 5 are like addends and 7 is like the sum of an addition problem. Thus when either addend is subtracted it yields the other addend.

The Rule of Likeness. Just as in addition you cannot add chickens and books, so you cannot subtract chickens from books. The Rule of Likeness applies to both operations.

The Rule of Compensation. This is the rule applied in the equal-additions method of subtracting. When we add the same amount to both the minuend and subtrahend, the answer is not affected. An example given, is that if Bobby is now 3 years older than his sister, the difference in their ages will always be 3 years no matter how old they are when you do the subtracting.

In addition, the rule works this way: the sum is not changed when we increase one of the addends, provided we compensate by decreasing the other addend the same amount.

The two addends of an addition problem turn out to be the subtrahend and the remainder of the related subtraction problem. Or we could say that the sum of an addition problem turns out to be the minuend of the related subtraction problem. A little playing around with objects can help your children see the close relationships between adding and subtracting.

All along the way in subtraction, the efforts you make to help your children understand the processes instead of just memorizing how to do them will contribute to their insight. And this deeper understanding is what they need for advancing further in arithmetic.

14. Multiplication and Division

Multiplication and division are two of our basic four operations in arithmetic. They are related inversely to each other; we multiply to find the product of two factors, and we divide in order to find a missing factor when we already know the product and the other factor.

Each operation also has a close relative in the simpler operations of the preceding chapter, multiplication being especially close to addition and division being close to subtraction.

Multiplying

Multiplication is usually defined for elementary pupils as: a short way to add equal numbers. Instead of adding 4 and 4 and 4, we multiply 3×4. That definition covers multiplying by whole numbers and fractions.

A ratio definition applies more generally, including multiplying negative, irrational and imaginary numbers, all of which elementary textbooks seldom use. By the ratio definition,

239

multiplication is: finding a number that has the same ratio to the multiplicand that the multiplier has to 1. That's not as complex as words make it sound. If your multiplier is 2, it is twice 1, and you must find a number that is twice the multiplicand (top number in a problem). If your multiplier is 3, it is 3 times the size of 1 and you must find a number that is three times the size of the multiplicand. If your multiplier is ½, you must find a number that is ½ the size of the multiplicand.

Terms Used in Multiplication. We have mentioned the **multiplicand.** It is usually a concrete number. That is, it stands for something in the real world—books, children, money, games won, and so forth. This concrete number is multiplied by a **multiplier,** which is a "pure" or "abstract" number. If you take 2 times something or 3 times something, the 2 and 3 do not stand for concrete items in the world. For example: There are 9 players on a team; how many players on 2 teams? The 9 players are concrete, but you do not multiply them by 2 *teams*; you simply multiply them by an abstract 2 and arrive at the answer of 18 *players*. The answer is the same concrete item that the multiplicand is.

For children solving story problems, it is helpful to know that the top number usually represents the concrete items they can visualize and that the answer will be the same items. But the reason we say *usually* is that according to the Law of Commutation we could switch the numbers around if we want to for convenience in multiplying. Also, in squaring units such as feet or inches, it is not strictly true that one factor is abstract and the other concrete.

Both the multiplicand and the multiplier are sometimes called **factors.** When you read of factors in other connections besides a specific multiplication problem they always refer to whole numbers. Thus 2 and 9 are factors of 18. So are 3 and 6. So are 3 and 3 and 2. But 4½ and 4 are not factors in this larger sense, even though their product is 18.

The answer in multiplication is called the **product.** A

product can be referred to as a **multiple** of one of its factors, as long as the factors are whole numbers. Thus 18 is a multiple of 3. Everything on the table of 3's is a multiple of 3. That includes 6, 9, 12, 15, 18, 21, and so forth. Eighteen is also a multiple of 9 and of 6 and of 2. Every even number is a multiple of 2.

These words are a lot for children to learn to use correctly. To help them, you should plan for talking daily about their arithmetic work. If you have no explanations or demonstrations to make or questions to ask, then just have the children explain to you what they are going to do in their textbook assignments. After their first brief explanations, you can draw out more details and more thinking by asking questions. Ask why a procedure works or why they write a number in this position instead of another position. Ask if they know a different way or a shorter way to work a problem.

Sometimes have the children work one or more problems orally for you, before you leave them to finish an assignment on their own. This technique works for other arithmetic, too, not only multiplication. Opportunity to talk about their work greatly strengthens children's learning, and it helps you to see where there might be misunderstandings so you can correct them before they grow into major frustrations.

Besides talking about textbook assignments, you could spend a few minutes working with a hundred chart or other arithmetic aids you may have. Counting on the hundred chart by 3's, 9's or any other number is a way to see the multiplication tables from a different perspective. Sometimes instead of saying, "Count by 3's," say "Show me all the multiples of 3."

The Law of Commutation. This law applies in multiplying just as it does in adding. According to this law, the two factors may be reversed without affecting the answer. Three times 4 is the same as 4×3. Children should not begin by learning the name and defnition of this law; they should begin by understanding how it works.

You can illustrate by a sheet of stamps, any size. Children

can count the stamps in a row and count how many rows there are and write that as a multiplication problem. Whatever the numbers, their problem could be in this form: $a \times b = c$. Then they could count how many stamps in a column and how many columns, and write that problem. It would be in the form $b \times a = c$. Then explain and help them see that either way they write it, it is the same number of stamps.

One demonstration and one explanation is not enough to enable children to understand the abstract concept of commutation. Children need many such experiences over the years—with objects and with mental images—to become able to make good use of a law and to reason from abstract to concrete. During the middle grades they should reason from concrete to abstract many more times than the other way around. Later, when their minds are ready for abstractions, by the time they study algebra, moving the x's and y's around will be no mystery.

The Law of Association. Since multiplication is closely related to addition, it is not surprising that this law also applies here. Just as you can add in any order, you can multiply in any order. Say you have cartons of eggs stacked in 2 piles of 5 each, and want to compute the number of eggs. You can think, "2×5 is 10 cartons, and 10×12 is 120 eggs." Or you can think, "5×12 is 60 eggs in one pile, and 2×60 is 120 eggs."

By this law, you can sometimes work problems mentally that otherwise would take pencil and paper. Try it with your children when you run out of other things to do on a long auto trip. Take the problem 4×36. By pencil and paper you begin, "4×6 is 24. Write down 4 and carry 2 . . ." But mentally, you can use factors of 4. Break 4 into factors 2 and 2. Then you think, "2×36 is 72, and 2×72 is 144." Children can pose problems for each other and see how difficult they can make them and still manage to solve them mentally. Make a rule that the child posing the problem must know at least one way to work it. Other children may not use his particular process, but comparing processes is part of the value of this game.

The Law of Distribution. This is an extra law for multiplication, not needed in addition. By it, multiplication can be "distributed" as to addition. That means you can break any number to be multiplied into parts, multiply each of the distributed parts, and then add. Take the "4 × 36" problem again. You can distribute the 36 into parts 30 and 6. Think, "4 × 30 = 120; 4 × 6 = 24; 120 + 24 = 144."

In algebra, you read $a(b + c) = ab + ac$. Stating it in symbols like this shows that the principle always works, no matter what numbers you use. The distribution in our problem doesn't necessarily have to be (30 + 6). It could be (26 + 10) or (9 + 27) or (10 + 10 + 10 + 6) or numerous other arrangements. Besides that, you could distribute the 4 into parts, as well as the 36, as long as you are careful to do all the necessary multiplying and to add all the resulting products.

In elementary arithmetic, children normally only distribute a number like 36 into its tens and ones—30 and 6. They normally don't learn the abstract law and the symbolic way to state it and numerous applications of the law. They often don't even learn its name. But they should learn to see this law operating in specific instances. The same is true of all the laws.

That's part of what is meant when you are urged to teach arithmetic by meaning and not just memory. You are laying the foundation for abstract understanding that children grow into as their minds mature.

Memorizing Basic Facts. You may be the greatest "meaning" enthusiast on your block, but there are still some things in arithmetic to memorize. Multiplication tables qualify for memorizing if anything does. For centuries there has been more agreement on this than on any other item in curriculum. Our society requires so much computation that the time spent memorizing multiplication facts pays good dividends throughout life.

As with adding and subtracting, there are 81 facts if you don't count the table of zeros. You can teach a zero rule: if zero is one of the factors the product is zero. Thus either way you say the problem, 0×3 or 3×0, the product is 0. That accords with the Law of Commutation; you can reverse the order and still get the same product.

Eighteen of the basic facts can be covered by a rule of ones: if 1 is a factor, the product equals the other factor. Thus 1×6 and 6×1 both result in a product of 6. With 0's and 1's learned, there are 63 facts left.

The 2's are often easy for children, and if they are not, the children should be given more experiences counting by 2's with objects and on a hundred chart. Once they learn the 2's, they can learn the reverse of each fact. If a child knows that $2 \times 8 = 16$, then he should come to understand that $8 \times 2 = 16$.

When children count by 5's, particularly on a hundred chart, they see that every multiple ends either with 0 or 5. With this mental image, they have a fairly easy time learning the table of 5's at least up to 5×6.

Lower numbers in the tables of 3's and 4's are also easy for children to visualize in their heads, and pupils commonly learn these facts in primary grades.

After those easier basic facts are learned, thirty difficult facts remain. Whether multiplication facts are taught by a meaning approach or a memory approach or a combination of the two, these thirty facts stubbbornly remain the hardest to learn. So if you make flashcards or practice sheets or other helps, these thirty facts are probably all you need. Try them yourself, and if you hesitate on a few, you may wish to relearn the ones you have forgotten, and practice until you have them all down pat. After that refresher lesson, you need not feel guilty driving your children to learn them better.

3	8	7	3	8	6	0	7	4	9
9	5	6	8	9	8	4	9	7	6

8	9	6	7	9	7	8	5	7	5
6	7	7	8	5	4	8	8	5	9

4	5	8	7	6	4	9	8	9	8
9	7	4	7	9	8	3	3	8	7

By the time your children reach these difficult facts, you could show them some secrets about the table of 9's. The first secret is that the answer each time is in the decade below the number of 9's. For instance, the answer to 5×9 is in the decade of the 40's; the answer to 7×9 is in the 60's; the answer to 3×9 is in the 20's.

Some children might reason that since 5×10 is 50, 5×9 must be lower than 50. And so it is; it's in the 40's. Now the second secret is that the two digits in the product always total 9. Thus if the answer is in the 40's, you know it is 45. If the answer is in the 20's, you know it is 27, and so forth.

Your children can try to gain a good image of these secrets of the 9's by studying a hundred chart. What pattern becomes obvious when you add 9 to various numbers? If you add 10, you move directly down to the next decade. But if you add 9, you move down and then left one space. Play with these patterns for a while and then see if your child can explain why the two digits in any multiple of 9 add up to 9.

If you started out trying to teach by meaning—counting by 2's and 3's, using the hundred chart, etc.—then you should not have shown children the peculiar chart we call the "multiplication tables." That is not the way to begin; it is the way to end.

In classrooms, I used to let children have plastic "counters" on their desks while working story problems. They could make 4 piles of 8, or whatever was required, and count to find an answer. After a time, some children decided that was too slow. If they wrote $4 \times 8 = 32$, then the next time they needed that fact they could find it more quickly than by counting. "Is that all right?" they asked. "Sure," I answered, "if it helps you."

But listing facts randomly wasn't efficient either, so children quickly discovered ways to write the facts in order. After a few lists, I gave a suggestion. "You don't have to write 4 × 2, 4 × 3, and so on for your list. Look, you can just write numbers from 1 to 9 along the top of a page and that will do for all your lists. Write a 4 over on the left, and put an answer under each of these numbers." After writing the answers for one row, a child could begin a second row, and suddenly it became clear how to do the whole chart. Whoever discovered it first, ran around showing everybody. It was almost as exciting as when our monthly book orders arrived. All the children busily made themselves multiplication tables.

Working problems with charts on their desks was far more efficient than using counters. I began commenting, "You didn't look up that one. You knew it in your head." "Yes," they'd proudly answer. "I know lots of them."

That was the time to suggest that they should learn the rest, too. People can't carry multiplication tables around all their lives. The children now understood what they were to memorize and why they needed to memorize it. The rest was not exactly easy, but at least it was meaningful to the children. Each child knew the extent of his own task and could make flashcards or whatever he wanted for help.

When your children are ready for a complete chart of multiplication facts, you may wish to show them the chart given here. It is a handy reference for looking up answers they are not sure of, for making flashcards, and later for seeing how division relates to multiplication.

After memorizing the tables, use the same overlearning techniques described in the addition section. That is, children don't get to quit the first day they repeat all the answers successfully. Continue the practice for several more days, then

Chart of Multiplication and Division Facts

	1	2	3	4	5	6	7	8	9
1	1	2	3	4	5	6	7	8	9
2	2	4	6	8	10	12	14	16	18
3	3	6	9	12	15	18	21	24	27
4	4	8	12	16	20	24	28	32	36
5	5	10	15	20	25	30	35	40	45
6	6	12	18	24	30	36	42	48	54
7	7	14	21	28	35	42	49	56	63
8	8	16	24	32	40	48	56	64	72
9	9	18	27	36	45	54	63	72	81

review weekly for a while, then monthly for the rest of the year. You obviously can't use this kind of review on everything children learn, but the multiplication tables rate some **extra** attention.

Multiplying by One-Place Numbers. Once we move beyond the 81 facts of the preceding section, we are into the *process* of multiplying. From this point on, we don't expect children to memorize answers, but to solve problems by various processes, using the facts already memorized. Besides the multiplication facts, children need addition facts—both the 81 basic facts and ability to do mental higher-decade addition.

So before moving further than this in multiplication, you may want to check up on your children's addition skills. Review the facts and relearn any that have become rusty. Practice mental higher-decade addition. Then your children can tackle the new process of multiplication without the extra burden of struggling with weak addition skills.

Textbooks usually begin with problems such as this row, in which there is no carrying. Children can practice giving the answers orally, and also practice writing the answers. According to the Rule of Likeness, they have learned to write ones in the ones column and tens and hundreds each in their columns when they add or subtract. It is the same in multiplication. In the first problem here, think, "3×2 is 6." Since it is 2 ones you multiplied, you have 6 ones in your answer, and the 6 must be written in the ones column.

52	61	93	52	81	70	71	43	61	32
3	2	3	2	4	2	6	2	3	4

Next in difficulty are problems which involve carrying. This is not as easy to do mentally as in addition because the carrying is deferred. You have to hold the carried number in your head while you multiply another number. To hold the number, some children jot it down either above or beside their problem, and many teachers allow that for a time.

Children who have good skills and good understanding to this point in their arithmetic may be able to work the following problems mentally, holding the carried number in their heads and reciting the full answers orally. Most children write out their work either by the "long" method shown at the left or the short method shown at the right.

```
        47        47
         6         6
        42       282
        24
       282
```

With the long process, help children understand that in the second step they are multiplying 6 × 40 rather than 6 × 4. Or they can think of it as 6 times 4 tens. That equals 24 tens and must be written starting in the tens column rather than the ones column. Children may practice the following problems either mentally or with pencil. If writing, they need not copy the problems but can use the edge of folded paper under each row. For extra practice over several days, sometimes work the rows from right to left. Sometimes work the bottom row first.

```
67   58   34   37   64   83   86   89   19   40
 9    3    8    7    4    5    6    2    5    9

90   29   44   15   73   38   60   86   43   18
 6    5    3    8    4    5    7    9    8    7

69   89   67   29   34   26   85   29   59   87
 8    4    8    9    9    9    8    8    9    7
```

Multiplying by Two-Place Numbers. At this level of difficulty, all children use paper and pencil to multiply. The almost universal form is shown below. The first partial product is obtained by a process exactly like that with one-place multipliers, multiplying 45 by 9. The second partial product is obtained by multiplying 45 by 60. The 60 is handled as though it were a 6 except that the product is written beginning in the tens column.

$$
\begin{array}{r}
45 \\
\underline{69} \\
405 \\
\underline{270} \\
3105
\end{array}
$$

Here are some problems, again for your convenience in checking on the level where your children should begin work, or for brief practice and review sessions.

12	54	45	67	49	56	97	51	74	29
69	20	35	18	70	45	29	87	16	48

28	36	90	27	39	92	53	14	86	34
25	38	31	17	67	39	17	52	97	49

216	691	352	939	806	568	357	725
36	45	67	29	80	35	87	94

The Scratch Method. As mentioned in the addition and subtraction chapter, it greatly strengthens children's understanding if they can view other systems besides the one they normally use. Here we take space for just one historic method of multiplying that you may explain in case your textbook does not give historic or other ways to multiply. In this method, children can see the same rules and laws operating that operate in their usual method. But the new setting helps them understand those rules and laws better.

The scratch method began in ancient times when people calculated on sand boards and could wipe out numbers as they went along, replacing them with new numbers. This method continued to work well on slates. Although it is clumsy on paper, the method persisted anyway, and people simply crossed out numbers instead of erasing them.

A completed problem would look like this. Steps for working it are listed below the problem.

$$
\begin{array}{c}
5 \\
\cancel{4} \\
2\cancel{1}2 \\
\cancel{3}\cancel{6} \quad \cancel{7}
\end{array}
$$

The steps are:
1. The problem is 7 × 36. Write these numbers.
2. Seven times 3 tens is 21 tens. Cross out 3 and write 21 tens above it.
3. Seven times 6 is 42. Cross out 6. Write 4 at the top of the tens column and 2 at the top of the ones column.
4. Add 4 tens and 1 ten, cross them out, and write 5 at the top of the tens column.
5. Cross out the multiplier 7. Read the answer from the numbers not crossed out in each column—252.

Short Cuts in Multiplying. All bright arithmetic students and many average students should have opportunity to play around with multiplication short cuts. Learning even one or two of these increases students' understanding of numbers. Some seventh and eighth grade students become highly motivated by this work, and they should be allowed time to practice whatever they wish and to show off their "magic" to other family members.

Some arithmetic textbooks have enrichment work of this kind. In library books you can find more help (Dewey numbers 510 to 513). Here we describe some short cuts briefly, without elaboration. To see that these are easier than they appear in condensed form, you should take time, perhaps with one of your children, to try some of them unhurriedly. Or you could ask a child to figure out a method, practice it for a few days, and when he is ready to mystify the family with his new skill he can perform for them. Then he could explain to you and others how it is done. Or maybe he would rather keep his magic a secret.

1. *Multiplying by Convenient Parts of 100.* This short cut works when the multiplier happens to be 50, 25, 33⅓ or other numbers which translate into convenient fractions of 100. The procedure is to multiply by 100 by annexing two zeros, and then to divide by the fractional part. Example: 25 × 48. Annex two zeros (4800), divide by 4 (1200). This short cut works with parts of 10 and 1000 too.

2. *Multiplying Numbers Near 100.* Procedure: Round the number to 100 and multiply, then subtract or add to adjust as needed. Example: 4 × 98. Think, "4 × 100 = 400. Subtract 8 (4 times the 2 difference between 98 and 100). Result, 392." This short cut works with numbers near 10 and 1000 too.

3. *Multiplying Two-Place Numbers by 11.* If the sum of the digits in the number is less than 10, use this procedure: place the sum of the digits between the digits. Example: 11 × 62 = 682 (8, the sum of 6 and 2, is placed between them). If the sum of the digits is 10 or more, use this procedure: sum the digits as above, and carry 1 to the hundreds place. Example: 11 × 57 = 627. The sum of 5 and 7 is 12. Place 2 between the digits, carry 1 and add it to the 5.

4. *Multiplying Larger Numbers by 11.* Procedure: Place the ones digit of the number in the ones position of the answer. Then, working toward the left, add each product to the digit before it. Repeat the last digit. Carry 1 anytime during this procedure that it is necessary. Example with no carrying: 11 × 413 = 4543. Begin at the right with 3, then 4 (1 plus the preceding 3), then 5 (4 plus the preceding 1), then repeat the 4. Example with carrying: 11 × 976 = 10,736. Begin with 6, then 3 (7 + 6 is 13; write 3 and carry 1), then 7 (9 + 7 is 16 and the carried 1 makes 17), then repeat 9 but there is 1 carried so it is 10.

5. *Multiplying by any Number in the Teens.* This works like

the "11 system" just given. Multiply by the second digit in the multiplier, add each product to the digit before it, and repeat the last digit. Example: 13 × 234 = 3042. Three times 4 is 12. Write 2, carry 1. Three times 3 is 9; add the carried 1 and the preceding 4 for a total of 14. Write 4, carry 1. Three times 2 is 6; add the preceding 3 and the carried 1. Write 0, carry 1. Repeat the 2, but there is 1 carried so it is 3.

6. *Multiplying by any Well Known Factors.* If you are good at seeing possible factors in a number, you can mentally work problems in any convenient order. Example: 18 × 45. Factor 18 into 2 and 9 and multiply by each in turn. Two times 45 is 90, and 9 × 90 = 810 (9 × 9 = 81, then annex a zero). Other examples:

88 × 4 = 11 × 8 × 4 = 11 × 32 = 352 (See number 3 above.)
22 × 150 = 11 × 300 = 3300
24 × 50 = 12 × 100 = 1200
16 × 15 = 8 × 2 × 15 = 8 × 30 = 240

7. *Multiplying by 21, 31, and so on to 91.* Procedure: Multiply by the tens digit. Write the product in the tens place under the multiplicand. Add. Example:

31 × 237
711 (result of 3 × 237)
7347 (partial product + multiplicand)

Students who have learned or invented any short cuts should be allowed to use them whenever they can in daily work. Ability to do this is a sign of mental alertness and maturity in arithmetic thinking, and it should be encouraged. Some workbooks or courses ask students to show all their work in writing, and may even insist that the work be written in one particular way. For bright students, that is justifiable only when the page

happens to be teaching a particular method. But after your
children have learned the method, it is better to let them work
intelligently instead of mindlessly following workbook patterns.

Dividing

Dividing is an opposite process to multiplying, so that each
process can check the other. The product of two factors is called
the **dividend** in a division problem. One factor is the **divisor**
and the other is the answer, or **quotient**. Thus you can check a
division problem by multiplying your answer by the divisor
(multiplying the two factors). If the result equals the dividend
(product), you have a check on the accuracy of your computing.
This is easy to see when shown with small numbers, and it is just
as true when the numbers are large.

$$\begin{array}{r} 12 \\ 2{\overline{)24}} \end{array} \qquad \begin{array}{r} 12 \\ \underline{2} \\ 24 \end{array}$$

Two Meanings for Division. This concept of two kinds
of division sometimes receives too little attention in arithmetic
books. For us adults it doesn't matter a great deal. But for
children, whose strong mode of thinking is either manipulative
or mental-image, it is extremely important. If you explain division with one kind of problem today and another kind tomorrow
because you hardly notice that they are different, you unwittingly make it more difficult for your child to create mental
images of the division process.

Two kinds of division come about because the two factors in
a multiplication problem are different. In practical problems,
such as story problems in children's books, one factor is a
concrete number and the other is abstract. (See the multipli-

cation section of this chapter.) Now in division, it makes a difference whether you are dividing by the concrete factor or by the abstract one. That is, it makes a difference in the way children should image in their heads what is going on.

Don't talk to children about concrete and abstract, though. Instead, talk about what is happening with groups of items in the problem.

The easiest kind of problems for children to visualize is called **measurement** division. In these problems, we know the size of the part to begin with, and we "measure off" the parts to find how many of them we get. Using the numbers from the problem above, we could start with a concrete group of 12, a dozen. The problem might say, "Each carton holds a dozen eggs. How many cartons could we fill from 24 eggs?" This is asking how many dozen we could measure off from the total group.

Measuring off parts is another way to say that we subtract parts. We could start with 24 eggs, subtract a dozen then another dozen. Problems of this kind can be demonstrated on a number line. Have your child find the number that tells the size of the total group in a measurement problem, and then measure backward, group by group, to see how many groups he can take from the total.

The second kind of problem children must learn to visualize is called **partitive**. This is where you must divide the large group of items into equal parts. You don't know beforehand what size each part will be.

For instance in the problem above, let's say you have 24 eggs to divide equally between 2 families. How many eggs will each family get? Children should visualize the large group of eggs being divided into 2 equal parts, and this is not usually as easy as imaging the measuring off of one part at a time, especially when the divisor is larger than 2.

In both kinds of division you start with the total (the dividend). Then in one kind of division you are to find the number of groups in the total, and in the other kind you are to find the size of each group.

Rules of Division. The **Rule of Likeness** applies in division the same as elsewhere. The dividend always is the total, and if it stands for concrete items such as eggs, then one factor, either the divisor or the quotient, is also eggs. Which of these factors is concrete depends on the type of division problem. In the problems considered earlier, the total number of eggs is 24 and the size of each group is 12. Both are concrete numbers. The 2 is abstract in this context, even though it is associated with "families" or "cartons." Because the problem is about eggs, the 2 simply refers to the number of groups of eggs.

The **Rule of Compensation** also applies. You can multiply or divide both the divisor and dividend in your problem by equal numbers and it will not affect the answer. This, again, is easy to see if we use small numbers. In the illustration below, both the divisor and dividend of the first problem were divided by 2 to produce the second problem, and the answer in both cases is 23. By this means you can convert many a long division problem into short division. At the very least, you can reduce the numbers to make your division problems easier to solve.

$$
\begin{array}{r}
23 \\
16\overline{)368} \\
32 \\
\overline{48} \\
48
\end{array}
\qquad
\begin{array}{r}
23 \\
8\overline{)184}
\end{array}
$$

Laws of Division. The **Law of Commutation** works in division, following its pattern in multiplication. In multiplication, this law asserts that either factor can be multiplied by the other and the same product will result. In division, the product is the dividend—the total number, which we place in the box.

And the factors are the other two numbers—the divisor and the answer. So it follows that whichever factor is the divisor, the other will be the answer.

$$5\overline{)30}^{\,6} \qquad 6\overline{)30}^{\,5}$$

The **Law of Continuous Division** asserts that you can divide by a factor of the divisor and then by the other factor. For instance, in the second problem above, you can factor 6 into 2 and 3. Then divide 30 by either factor, say 3, and divide that result by 2. This provides another way to reduce large problems down to easily manageable ones, perhaps enabling you to solve some problems mentally that otherwise would take paper and pencil, or a calculator.

The **Law of Distribution** asserts that the dividend can be distributed—split into parts—not factors, as we just did with the divisor, but into addends. For example, in the first problem above, the dividend of 30 can be broken into 10 and 20. Divide 5 into each part and add the resulting quotients.

We use this law constantly when doing long division. We mentally distribute large dividends into parts, beginning at the left with thousands or hundreds or whatever is the largest part of the number. After we divide into that number, we calculate what part of the dividend is left. If that is large, we again divide only into part of it, and we keep going until we reach the ones place of the dividend.

To help children come to understand that our arithmetic processes operate according to laws takes constant attention to meaning. As much as possible, help your children to see *why* things work as they do. There are times when you have to give up and say, "Just do it this way," in order to keep moving forward in their textbooks. At times children have to learn steps to follow in dividing. But learning the steps with as much understanding as you can manage is better than memorizing steps without understanding.

Memorizing Basic Facts. Use the chart of multiplication facts as a reference for the 81 division facts, but read it in reverse order. A dividend is found in the body of the chart. Divide it by the number at the left of its row, and find the answer at the top of the column.

Dividing by 2, 3, and 4 is easy for most children of middle grades. Other facts with small quotients are also easy. Usually about twenty-four of the higher facts are harder to learn, and children must spend extra time studying these which are listed below.

$$8)\overline{72} \quad 9)\overline{45} \quad 6)\overline{36} \quad 9)\overline{63} \quad 8)\overline{48} \quad 5)\overline{45} \quad 7)\overline{35} \quad 6)\overline{42}$$

$$7)\overline{47} \quad 7)\overline{28} \quad 8)\overline{64} \quad 7)\overline{42} \quad 7)\overline{63} \quad 8)\overline{56} \quad 8)\overline{32} \quad 4)\overline{28}$$

$$9)\overline{72} \quad 6)\overline{54} \quad 5)\overline{40} \quad 9)\overline{81} \quad 6)\overline{48} \quad 9)\overline{54} \quad 5)\overline{35} \quad 7)\overline{56}$$

In the facts just given, the dividend is always an even multiple of the divisor. For instance in the first problem, 8 "goes into" 72 exactly 9 times. But if the dividend were a number larger than 72, say 75 or 76, would your children still know that 9 is the number needed?

Dividends are not exact multiples more often than they are, so it is helpful for children to practice problems like these next rows. On each problem, say the quotient and the remainder. If a divisor is larger than the dividend, the quotient is zero and a remainder is left.

$$8)\overline{14} \quad 6)\overline{23} \quad 9)\overline{13} \quad 9)\overline{23} \quad 8)\overline{15} \quad 7)\overline{20} \quad 2)\overline{11} \quad 7)\overline{19}$$

$$6)\overline{38} \quad 9)\overline{28} \quad 7)\overline{22} \quad 3)\overline{29} \quad 4)\overline{25} \quad 6)\overline{34} \quad 6)\overline{5} \quad 7)\overline{18}$$

$$9)\overline{52} \quad 9)\overline{76} \quad 8)\overline{22} \quad 4)\overline{33} \quad 2)\overline{15} \quad 4)\overline{25} \quad 3)\overline{28} \quad 6)\overline{35}$$

If your children cannot do these well, provide more practice over a long enough time to make a difference. This practice eases the way for one of the most difficult steps in all of basic arithmetic—that of estimating quotient figures in larger division problems.

Short and Long Division. When your children begin learning division, and have problems with one-digit divisors, should they do them by short division or long division? It is important to understand that short division is not the easiest method. Short division is more complex because some steps are done mentally instead of in writing.

Older books taught short division first, using problems with only one-digit divisors. Then they moved on to long division and problems with two-digit divisors. Thus children had two methods to learn, and the most difficult was first. Results from this teaching were poor, but this system was used for many years in our schools, and books using the system are still around.

When this curriculum problem was reexamined, research showed that it works much better to teach long division at the start, using one-digit divisors. Then children move on to two-digit divisors and don't have to learn a new method. They use their familiar method of long division, but have larger numbers. This system has brought better results in children's achievement.

Children who learn arithmetic with difficulty should always use the method of long division. But other children, after they have good mastery of long division, can learn short division as a short cut. It resembles the short cuts given in the multiplication section in that it requires more understanding and more mental computing than long division.

So if your textbook uses the old system of beginning with short division, you can adjust to the more successful system by teaching the method of long division right from the start of division units. Then stay with long division through the pages of two-place and even three-place divisors, if you go that far. Then somewhere down the road, maybe next year or later, you can introduce the short cut method of dividing small numbers. With bright arithmetic students, you may not need to wait so long. You can easily judge when to teach short division if you are involved on a regular basis with your children's arithmetic lessons, since you have a good idea of their understanding and skills.

Divide Larger Numbers? By the time children reach division of large numbers, they have learned the basic four operations of arithmetic. If they learned meaning along the way, they have many skills to bring to this task. For one, they can mentally add and subtract, which helps on some steps of division. For another, they understand place value, and that is crucial to any understanding of what happens in the steps of a long division problem. And for a third, their understanding of numbers should make them good estimators, so that they can select good "trial quotients" in a long problem. (Estimating also can obviate the need for working out a long problem. Both in real life and in multiple-choice tests an estimated answer often suffices.)

Unfortunately, many children do not arrive at this point with good understanding, but only with years of practice on mechanical skills. For these children, it is not too late to teach more meaning in arithmetic. It may mean reviewing place value, mental addition and other background helps they need for doing well in division. And it probably will mean skipping the larger-number problems in your book and working on the smaller-number problems with attempts at meaning and not just mechanics.

In our age of calculators and computers, we must question how much time even good students of arithmetic should spend working pages of problems of ever-increasing size. Does this advance their education or is it just drudgery? Could the time be better spent moving forward to decimals, fractions, and geometry, and outward to topics of statistical probabilities, graph construction, and calculators and computers themselves? These questions are being debated today, not very hotly, because the better answers are obvious to most people involved in mathematics. The conferences and curriculum work today center on how to bring children farther in mathematics than we previously have. Our technological and scientific world requires this.

Curriculum improvements come slowly in the school world. But homeschoolers have an advantage. With just a decision of one or two people, you can make any changes you want. Will you skip the pages with three- and four-place divisors and let your children, instead, learn some BASIC computer programming? The choice is up to you.

15. Grade-Level Guidelines

This chapter gives an overview of what has traditionally been taught in each grade. In tutoring individuals, you need not stay rigidly within such guidelines, but should feel free to move as slowly or rapidly as is appropriate for your particular children. Add work with calculators and computors and anything else your family may be interested in.

There is necessarily some repetition of topics and teaching ideas in these grade-level listings that also appear elsewhere in the arithmetic chapters. These guidelines are primarily for reference to help you assess where your children are and to set goals for the next year or month.

Grade Four General Guidelines

Numbers. Read and write large numbers. Some textbooks go to five-digit numbers, and some go on to six- or seven-digit numbers. Help make large numbers meaningful to your children by such projects as studying the heights of mountains or the populations of towns and cities and noticing numbers in the news. Give more experiences with ordinal numbers— twentieth, twenty-first, etc. up to at least thirtieth. Teach more about zero. For instance, zero plus a number equals that number, while zero times a number equals zero. Read and write Roman numbers up to 50 or to 100, knowing I, V, and X for 1, 5, and 10; and L and C for 50 and 100.

Place Value. As your children read and talk about larger numbers, try to extend their understanding of the places, particularly thousands, ten thousands, and hundred thousands. Show how a comma is used in 10,000 and sometimes in 1,000. The comma is only for the purpose of easier reading; it has no mathematical reason to be there.

Addition Much of fourth grade is given to further drill and overlearning of the 81 basic facts and to mastering the process of carrying. You can emphasize mental bridging instead of paper-and-pencil carrying for children who seem able to learn it. In this grade, work is extended to adding four- or five-place numbers and adding longer columns of three-place numbers.

Subtraction. Provide more drill and overlearning of the 81 basic subtraction facts and the process of borrowing. (Many books today use the term *regrouping* for both carrying and borrowing processes.) Fourth graders practice regrouping with three-place and four-place numbers in all kinds of complex situations, for instance:

$$
\begin{array}{r}
1000 \\
-384 \\
\hline
\end{array}
$$

Subtraction is expanded beyond the "take away" idea, to include problems of the four types listed below. Children do not necessarily learn the types, but must meet this variety of subtraction problems.

1. Compare (how much taller or older is Mary than Tom).
2. Find how much is gone (the clerk returned 25¢ of your dollar; what did the item cost).
3. Find how much more (you have saved so much toward the bike you want; how much more do you need).
4. Find the other part (you know the total and one part; what is the other part).

Multiplication. Children review the basic facts learned in third grade (which was about half of the tables up through 9 × 9) and learn the rest of the facts. Use many story problems, but also use drill to master all these facts. Let children develop their own tables, instead of handing them one to memorize. Teach meaning also. For instance, turn a section of a stamp sheet two ways to show that 3 rows of 4 are the same number as 4 rows of 3. And show that 12 + 12 is the same as 2 × 12 to review the principle that multiplying is related to adding. Multiply two-place numbers by one-digit numbers, first without carrying and then with carrying. Some books proceed to problems as large as three-digit numbers multiplied by two-digit numbers.

Division. Keep division in step with multiplication, mastering the basic facts, dividing by one-digit divisors, and learning that division is related to subtraction. Show the subtraction relation sometimes by actually doing it. For instance, if a problem says to divide by 4, subtract 4, then another 4, and another, until no more 4's can be subtracted from the number. Then count how many 4's were subtracted. The answer should be the same as obtained in the division problem.

At first, division problems involve **measuring** off groups of a certain size: how many 6-inch ribbons can be cut from a piece 36 inches long, or how many teams of 5 can be formed in a club of 30 children? This type is easier to demonstrate with concrete materials, and easier for young children to understand. Later the problems include the **partitive** type: we need two teams in our club; how many will be on each team? Toward the end of the year, have a few problems with remainders. Demonstrate with concrete materials that sometimes you can't measure off another full ribbon or another full team, but may have a few inches or a few children remaining.

Fractions. In primary grades the concept of fractional parts of an item was introduced, but now in fourth grade fractions become for the first time a serious topic of study. Review fractional parts with 1 as the numerator: 1/2, 1/3, 1/4, and so on. Extend this now to fractions like 2/4 and 3/4. Cut up fruit or fold paper to demonstrate. Also extend the fraction idea to fractional parts of groups: 1/2 of our family, 1/2 of the stamps in this sheet.

Begin to show equivalency of fractions. For instance if the stamp sheet has 2 rows of 6, one row, or 1/2, can also be called 6/12. Make your own "Cuisennaire rods" by starting with six one-foot strips of paper, each a different color. Leave one whole and mark it 1. Cut one into halves, one into thirds, one into fourths, one into sixths, and one into twelfths. Mark each piece 1/2, 1/3, and so forth. Match lengths to show that 1/2 = 2/4, 3/12 = 1/4, and so on.

Teach the word **numerator** for the top number in a fraction. It tells the number of parts. The bottom number, **denominator,** tells what size the parts are. When the numerator is larger, there are more parts and thus a larger amount. This can be demonstrated with pieces of pie or apple or paper.

Near the end of fourth grade a little work is done with adding and subtracting fractions, using only like denominators. For instance, subtract 1/4 from 3/4. Also, mixed numbers are introduced, using measures such as quarts or hours: three pints equal 1½ quarts, lunchtime comes in 1½ hours.

Measures. Measures in our life are many and complex,

and they must be taught repeatedly throughout the year for children to develop good understanding and good memory of them. The following measures and concepts are usually taught in fourth grade.

Length: yard, foot, inch, half inch, and mile.

Liquid measures: teaspoon, tablespoon, cup (half-pint), pint, quart, gallon (get help with some of your recipes).

Dry measures: pint, quart, peck, and bushel (more meaningful to farm children than city children).

Weights: ounces, pounds, and tons (not learning alternate kinds such as troy ounces or long tons).

Temperature: Older books usually had only Fahrenheit, and newer books give more attention to Celsius. Explain about the freezing point and about above zero and below zero (an introduction to negative numbers). Keep daily records of temperature readings for a week or longer.

Time: seconds, minutes, hours, days, weeks, months, and years; concepts of a.m., p.m., leap year; how to state 6:30 p.m. or a quarter to five. Digital clocks and watches have made it easier for children to read time but more difficult for them to visualize hours and fractional parts thereof, as they could on a clock face. Use both kinds of clocks and repeated short lessons to help your child achieve good mastery of time concepts.

Problem Solving. Children need almost daily contact with problems either in life or in books. See the "Principles" chapter for problem-solving techniques.

Grade Five General Guidelines

For practically all students, fifth grade is the year basic operations must be mastered. If your child has trouble adding, subtracting, multiplying or dividing, spend time beside him while he "talks out" his work, and discover what kinds of mistakes he makes. Then reteach the skills that will keep him from making those mistakes. Repeat this diagnose-and-reteach cycle as many times as needed to achieve competency in the four basic operations.

Fast learners should have access to a variety of books on numbers and arithmetic—history, puzzles, alternate ways to multiply or divide, short cuts, new topics such as probability theory, geometry, algebra, computers.

The following list gives the topics covered in a typical fifth grade course.

Numbers. Read and write numbers as large as nine places—to hundred millions—the main purpose being to increase understanding of our number system. Sometimes work problems with large numbers. Learn to round off numbers to the nearest tens, hundreds, thousands, or any appropriate value. Learn Roman numbers to D (500).

Place Value. This concept must be well understood, then decimal points and places to the right of the point can be introduced. Children have been using decimal fractions with money, so that is one way to introduce the decimal fraction concept. Odometers and gasoline pump gauges can also be used. Relate decimal fractions to common fractions: .3 is the same as 3/10.

Addition and Subtraction. Check to see whether all fourth grade skills are mastered, and review and reteach as much as necessary, giving special attention to regrouping. Provide practice enough that your children can add and subtract quickly and accurately. Toward the end of a textbook, addition problems may involve as many as six three-place numbers. (Many people question the value of spending a great deal of time on problems of larger and larger size in this age of calculators. Children need enough of this work that they understand and do the problems correctly, but beyond that you will have to decide for your family how much time to spend drilling on more and larger problems.) Subtraction problems include all kinds of regrouping complications. Children should learn to look at their answers and decide whether they are "sensible." They should also try estimating answers before working problems. This ability shows a high level of understanding numbers, and fast learners, especially, should practice this skill.

Multiplication. Check to see that children know the basic facts well and can multiply with carrying. Reteach and drill as necessary. Older books used the terms: *multiplier* (bottom number), *multiplicand* (top number), and *product* (answer). But now some books call the two numbers to multiply the *factors*, a term which students need later for algebra. Spend time teaching the meaning behind *partial products*. For instance, the following problem may be written in the second way to show that ten 4's are forty. We could write the zero, but usually don't, just as a shortcut. And it is not 1 times 20, but 10 times 20, which equals 200. That's why the 2 must go in the hundreds place.

$$
\begin{array}{r}
24 \\
\times 12 \\
\hline
48 \\
24 \\
\hline
288
\end{array}
\qquad
\begin{array}{r}
24 \\
\times 12 \\
\hline
48 \\
240 \\
\hline
288
\end{array}
$$

Ask questions and have your child explain partial products to you. For a language assignment, he can write out an explanation that is clear enough to teach a younger child these concepts. Other cases can be analyzed in the same way, for instance: why don't we write a partial product of zeros when we multiply by 30 or 40 or another number that ends in zero?

Three ways of checking can be learned.

1. Check by adding. In the above example, twelve 24's would be added to see if they equal 288.
2. Check by switching the multiplier and the multiplicand. In the above example multiply 12 by 24. Use small numbers to show the rationale behind this (three 4's are the same as four 3's).
3. Check by dividing the product by either factor. Again, use small numbers to show why this works. If five 6's are 30, then 30 divided by 5 should equal 6. Or 30 divided by 6 should equal 5. Use sections of stamp sheets or other manipulative materials to obtain good understanding of these concepts.

Division. Review and reteach the basic facts and the process of dividing by one-digit divisors. Common terms are *dividend* (the number in the box), *divisor* (outside the box), and *quotient* (answer). The dividend is the product and the other two numbers are its factors. Help children see these relationships between multiplying and dividing. Teach long division with two-digit divisors and, if you wish, three-digit divisors. Extend understanding of division as related to subtraction. The following form is very helpful, especially with children who have much difficulty with long division.

$$
\begin{array}{r}
12\overline{)1632} \quad 100 \\
\underline{1200} \\
432 \quad 30 \\
\underline{360} \\
72 \quad 6 \\
\underline{72} \quad \underline{} \\
136
\end{array}
$$

In this problem, the child thinks, "I can take one hundred 12's out of 1632. This leaves 432. Then I can take out thirty 12's. This leaves 72. Then I can take out six 12's." Adding the right-hand column shows that he has taken out 136 12's. This system works even if the child is not so efficient in taking out thirty 12's and six 12's on the first try. If he took out twenty, for instance, he may proceed by taking out ten more. He ends up with a longer column to add, but his final result will be the same. Write the problem in its usual form alongside this, and compare the two forms. Notice that the 100 is indicated only by a 1 in the hundreds place of the quotient, and so forth.

Fractions. Review the words *denominator* (name of the equal parts) and *numerator* (number of such parts). Use these words often. Do the same with all special arithmetic terminology so the words become part of your children's normal speaking vocabulary.

During the year, develop three meanings for fractions. The first is the concept of **fractional parts** of objects and fractional parts of groups. This meaning should be reviewed and reinforced.

The second meaning is **division.** To illustrate, there are 2 candy bars to divide between 3 girls. One bar can be divided into 3 parts and each girl receives a part. Then the other bar is divided into 3 parts and each girl again receives a part. Each girl then has 2 parts, or 2/3 of a candy bar. Thus $2 \div 3$ is the same as 2/3. Fractions express division.

The third meaning of fractions is **ratio** or comparison. If Mary has 2 new books and Tom has 3, the ratio is expressed as 2 to 3, or 2/3. Mary has 2/3 as many books as Tom. This concept is more difficult to understand, so you can introduce it to your child but you need not spend a lot of time on it this year.

Add and subtract unlike fractions and mixed numbers. Teach that the fractions must be made "alike" before adding or subtracting. For instance, to add thirds and sixths, either the thirds must be changed into sixths or the sixths into thirds, or both must be changed into twelfths. If you list fractions in columns as whole numbers usually are, it helps your child to see that the adding and subtracting operations are really the same as with whole numbers. Fractions are a bit less awesome if they do not appear to be a different kind of arithmetic. When listed in columns, the regrouping principles already learned can apply. In a mixed number problem, if there are not enough fourths to subtract from, just get four more from the ones column.

Introduce decimal fractions, dealing mostly with tenths and hundredths, and using the operations of addition and subtraction. This is usually easy for children; the main new rule to learn is that the decimal points must be kept in a straight column. Show that decimal fractions are related to common fractions: 1/2 of a dollar can be thought of as 50/100 or .50 of a dollar. Have the student read decimal fractions aloud and write them from dictation.

Measurement. Children should: 1) gain experience and become more accurate in measuring and estimating, 2) learn more measuring units, 3) learn to convert, such as ounces to pounds, and 4) increase understanding. Teach the standardization concept that a particular measure is the same everywhere and that everyone measuring a particular item should, theoretically, get the same measurement. A fact such as that British gallons and American gallons differ, does not undo the above principles. British gallons are the same everywhere, no matter who measures with them.

These measures are commonly taught or reviewed in fifth grade.

Length: inches, feet, yards, rods, miles. Convert from one to another. Use rulers, yardsticks and carpenters' tapes or seamstresses' tapes. Practice estimating.

Liquid: cup or half pint, pint, quart, and gallon. Home schoolers should add measuring spoons to this and the dry measure list. Convert from one measure to another (know, for instance, that there are 16 tablespoons in 1 cup, and 3 teaspoons in 1 tablespoon). Provide practical experience with all these measures. Try to use differently shaped containers, particularly when teaching about quarts and gallons, so children do not associate the measure always with one kind of container such as a milk carton. Liquids can vary in weight, but for many liquids "A pint's a pound the world around."

Dry: pint, quart, peck, bushel (and measuring spoons and cups). Dry commodities vary considerably in weight.

Weight: ounces, pounds and tons. Good estimating is a sophisticated skill. Do you think this letter will need one stamp, or is it likely to need two? Which family member can find an item that is closest in weight to this pound of margarine?

Temperatures: These days both Fahrenheit and Celsius are taught. Keep records of indoor and outdoor temperatures. Take temperatures of freezing and boiling water. Use a clinical thermometer and take body temperatures. A scale of temperature differs from some measures in that we cannot compare, say 20 and 40, and declare that one temperature is twice as warm or half as warm as the other.

Time: second, minute, hour, day, week, month, year, century. In Bible teaching as well as other history, the millennium (ten centuries, or 1000 years) is a measure home schoolers may wish to add to the usual fifth-grade list. Standardized time and time zones can receive some attention. Teach the meaning of A.D. and B.C. Time concepts are not concrete, and thus are difficult for children to understand. Centuries are not very meaningful to a child who has lived only 10 years. Thinking backward in the B.C. years (year 413 was earlier than year 412) is confusing even for many adults. And time zones involve many complex understandings. So use patience and teach time concepts in bits and pieces whenever you find opportunity in daily life.

Square measures: Begin with examining squares and other rectangles and have your children tell how they differ and how they are alike. Then they may see that a square is a special kind of rectangle. Next, work with perimeter—the distance around. Next, measure areas by using cardboard squares of 1 square foot or 1 square inch in size. After children form mental images of square measures they will not need these visual aids. Work with square inches, square feet, and square yards.

Tables, Graphs, Maps. Help your children become acquainted with these applications of arithmetic. They may learn to read scale drawings of their rooms or house. They can look at graphs found in periodicals, and read TV schedules, tide tables, and other items found in daily life. This kind of work helps children grow in arithmetic understanding and also helps them score higher in "functional reading" on achievement tests.

Problem Solving. Your children gain more when you work with them on some complex and challenging problems than when you just assign a page of story problems to do on their own. Ask questions like: "Now, what is it we need to find?" "How can we start?" "Where do we go from here?" Use the problem-solving techniques listed in the "Principles" chapter. Also discuss whether an answer could have been reached by another route. How many ways can your child find to solve one problem? Children who are strong in arithmetic usually like mental problems. Besides helping them understand the number system and arithmetic better, this skill has practical use on occasion, such as when shopping. Which brand or size of cellophane tape costs the least per inch? (Though stores intend to have this information posted for you, it often is not complete for all the brands.)

Grade Six General Guidelines

By grade six, many children have quite good mastery of the four basic operations with whole numbers, but some still do not. For the former, a quick review is given and then the work proceeds to the major sixth-grade topics of denominate numbers (measurements) and common and decimal fractions. For the other children, more thorough review and reteaching is needed. There is no point in going on to frustrating topics when a student still has trouble with the basics.

The following topic summaries give an overview of a typical sixth-grade course.

Numbers. Review as needed so that the child can read, write, and work with numbers in the billions, or even trillions. Rounding of numbers is an important, though often difficult, concept. Students should use rounded numbers when they ask, "Is my answer reasonable?" or when they estimate an answer before working a problem. They also should notice how rounded numbers are practically always used when large numbers are discussed in the news.

Extend the reading and writing of Roman numbers up to 1000 (M) or to 2000. Review the Roman system and compare with our decimal system. Notice that there is no zero and that "places" are used to add or subtract values. Compare this with the use of place in our system. The main reasons for studying Roman numbers are for historical interest and for developing more appreciation for the features of our own system. So this topic need not be emphasized heavily, particularly with slower students.

Place Value. Develop a good understanding of the values of places to the right of the decimal point—tenths, hundredths, and so on. Some books carry this as far as millionths. Teach these places as thoroughly as the whole number places were taught in earlier grades, and emphasize that decimals are not a different system, but simply an extension of the number system students already know. Talk about reasonableness in rounding decimal fractions. Ask, "What is the purpose of this number?" If it is money someone must pay, there is no point in writing numbers beyond the hundredths place, because we have no coin smaller than a penny. In working a problem, though, you would carry the fraction one additional place so you know whether to round the hundredth place upward or downward.

Addition and Subtraction. A goal in fourth grade was to learn these processes, and in fifth grade the learning was reviewed and reinforced. So at sixth grade, teachers often check to see whether students have missed something or forgotten something. When the checkup shows no weakness, then "enrichment" teaching is used. Some books provide real enrichment topics that extend knowledge and deepen under-standing. Some merely provide experience with larger numbers and longer columns. Adding is often taken up to 8 one-place numbers or 6 three-place numbers, and some books have 4 five-place numbers. If you want more enrichment than your book supplies, try Dewey numbers 510 to 513 at your library. Give attention to estimating. And talk about *when* to subtract in story problems.

Multiplication and Division. In fourth and fifth grades, a goal was to teach these processes thoroughly. Now in sixth grade you can review and reteach whatever your children happen to need. Also, go over the underlying principles that multiplication is repeated addition, that division is repeated subtraction, and that multiplication and division "undo" each other. That is, after dividing you can multiply the divisor and quotient to "get back" to the dividend. Or after multiplying, you can divide the product by either of the factors to get back to the other factor. These "undoing" procedures offer ways to check the answers. Your children will understand these meanings better now than they did at younger ages. They will also be better able to understand the **measurement** and **partitive** kinds of division and to think through story problems and decide what operations to use. So talk with them about these deeper meanings.

Multiplying and dividing with denominate numbers were introduced earlier with the "squaring" concept and must receive more attention this year. Denominate numbers have specific names, such as 2 feet or 1 mile. In most multiplying, only the multiplicand is specific, while the multiplier is an abstract number. For example, the multiplicand might be a number of books or dollars or children and you multiply by 2 to find twice the number of books or dollars or children. The 2 is abstract; it does not stand for books or any concrete items. Your children can increase their understanding of these fundamentals, not simply by rules or definitions, but problem by problem throughout the year as you help them think.

Common Fractions. Review the words *numerator* and *denominator*, and review the three meanings of fractions listed in the fifth grade section. Until this year, only **like fractions** (with common denominators) were used in adding and subtracting, but now you can expand to **unlike fractions**. Most books present these in a carefully planned sequence of difficulty, beginning with problems where one of the denominators can be the common denominator and advancing to where two denominators, and even three, must be changed before adding. They also begin with fractions only, and move on to **mixed numbers**, and begin with problems which require no carrying or borrowing between whole numbers and fractions, and move on to those which do. Included are practically all complexities of finding common denominators, of encountering **improper fractions** and **mixed numbers**, and so forth. All this work becomes a major topic of sixth grade arithmetic.

Multiplying and dividing fractions involve even more complexities, and most children need a lot of concrete examples in drawings, cutouts, and so forth to visualize what happens in those problems. This, too, is a major task in sixth grade. Older books usually gave a rule, such as "Invert the divisor, and multiply," and then drilled children on using it, with little or no attention to understanding. Today's books provide many ideas for making the processes meaningful. After understanding is built up, your children can derive their own rules. This is educating the mind and not just the hand, or memory.

Division of fractions is a topic that has rare application in the life of a sixth grader. When was the last time you had to divide a number by a fraction? Using the "utility" argument, some people would give little attention to this topic. But if you wish to teach arithmetic as a logical science, you have to include it for completeness.

It is easier to understand dividing by fractions if you use the measurement concept of division rather than the partitive concept. When you measure off portions that are larger than 1 you obtain a smaller quotient than dividend. For instance, 50 yards of a football field are measured off into 10-yard lengths, or 5 lengths ($50 \div 10 = 5$). In division problems children have been used to starting with a larger number like 50 and ending up with a smaller number like 5. But now, with fractions, they may be puzzled to find they can end up with a larger number. If the field is measured off into ½ yard lengths there are more than 50. In fact there are 100 lengths, as though you multiplied by 2. Hence the procedure, "Invert the divisor, and multiply." There are several other ways to show meaning behind division of fractions, and the book you use will include at least one of these. But however you approach it, this topic is difficult and for reasons mentioned earlier you ought not to spend an inordinate amount of time on it.

Decimals. Decimals were introduced in fifth grade and

may have been used in connection with money concepts for several years. Now in sixth grade, they become a major topic of study. Students must understand the structure of decimal fractions, as mentioned in the place value section. Adding and subtracting decimals is not particularly difficult for students who can add and subtract whole numbers. But multiplication introduces a new complication of where to put the decimal point in the answer. If you wish to teach for meaning, one approach is to work a few problems by both adding and multiplying. If it is 2.6 miles to the shopping mall, how many miles is the round trip? The problem can be solved in two ways as shown below.

$$
\begin{array}{cc}
2.6 & 2.6 \\
+2.6 & \times 2 \\
\hline
5.2 & 5.2
\end{array}
$$

The sum shows where to put the decimal in the product. Another approach is to estimate. Would the round trip be .52 miles, 5.2 miles, or 52 miles? After a variety of such problems, your children may be able to generalize for themselves that we point off as many places in the product as there are in both the multiplicand and the multiplier.

The same difficulty about where to place the decimal point arises in division problems, and the "sensible answer" approach, as well as several other approaches, can be used to develop understanding of this.

Percent. Since sixth graders have a lot to master in fractions and denominate numbers, many arithmetic programs leave the bulk of percentage work for seventh grade, and only introduce the concept in sixth grade. Children will likely already know the word *per* as being associated with rate in phrases such as miles per hour or price per gallon. Since *cent* means hundred, as in century, the term *percent* means per hundred.

One common method of teaching this idea is to make a hundred board, which is simply a square marked off into ten rows of ten. Then if 6 squares are colored in, they can be said to be colored at the rate of 6 per 100, or 6 percent. After a little work with the board, move on to situations where the total is not 100. For instance, what if your team won 5 out of 10 games? If they continued at that rate, how many games out of 100 would they win? *(Fifty. Thus 5 out of 10 means winning at the rate of 50 percent.)* The main purpose of this teaching is to build understanding, and not skills in working percentage problems. This is a lead-in to seventh grade work on percents.

Measurement. This year build proficiency in **adding, subtracting, multiplying,** and **dividing** measures. These denominate numbers need special attention as mentioned in the multiplication section above, yet if the principles of working with the decimal system are well understood they can be transferred without too much difficulty to working with feet and inches, quarts and gallons, and so forth. If you don't have enough inches to subtract from, you can borrow 12 more (not 10) from the feet. Or if you need more quarts, borrow 4 from the gallons column. Understanding division as either measurement or partition is also a help when working with denominate numbers.

There is more than one way to work most problems. For instance, gallons and quarts can be arranged in columns or in a division box similar to ones and tens in an ordinary problem. Or they can be changed to mixed numbers (1 gallon, 2 quarts = 1½ gallons) before working a problem. A student who understands principles and can visualize what happens in the problems will not have too much difficulty operating with denominate numbers. Students who are weaker in understanding should be given much concrete-level work. Draw diagrams. Measure real lengths or liquids or whatever is needed to see what happens in a problem.

More work with **square measures** is done in sixth grade—

usually square inches, square feet, and square yards. Some books also introduce square rod, acre, section, and square mile.

Finding **volumes** of rectangular solids is introduced in some sixth grade books, but many leave this topic for seventh grade.

Graphs and Tables. If you read graphs and tables almost daily, you may not notice anymore how many bits of skill and knowledge you must put together to do this easily. Children are not very successful at reading graphs and tables until they have had experience constructing some. They should gather data, organize them into tables, and construct bar graphs and line graphs. They should learn to read circle graphs, picture graphs, and dot maps, but not necessarily construct these.

Scale Drawings and Maps. As with graphs, it is important to experience these from the inside—by drawing some. Sixth graders can manage simple scale drawings, such as of a single room. The concept of ratio becomes part of such a project. Model cars, airplanes, or doll houses help to develop the scaling idea.

Proficiency with graphs and maps is a skill measured in the "Applications" portions of arithmetic achievement tests. They also show up in reading and social studies tests and help a child score higher there, particularly on "Functional Reading."

Problem Solving. In sixth grade, the work on problems is largely an extension of the techniques and concepts taught in earlier grades. Some teachers feel that the major purpose of arithmetic study is to be able to solve problems. After all, if children can only do rows of like problems in an arithmetic book, what good will that do them in life? Thus, problem solving should be extended into real life whenever possible; don't stick only with problems in a textbook, but add others that arise in your family or in someone's reading. And have your children contribute problems which they have thought up.

To develop mathematical thinking, you can use an approach that allows your children to form generalizations or rules, rather than the approach in which you or the book give the rule and the children simply follow it. For instance, collect data about speeds, times, and distances or solve several problems of this type, and then see if your child can set up the formula, distance = rate × time.

Algebra may not be mentioned by name in your textbook, but some of its principles should have been there, perhaps even from primary grades, in the "missing number" type of problem. The missing number approach is useful in finding common denominators, reducing fractions, and changing denominate numbers as from gallons to quarts. So, thorough work on these sixth grade topics can continue to build algebra understandings.

Grade Seven General Guidelines

Many schools begin "tracking" during the junior high years—one track called General Math or Business Math for students who still need help with the basics and another track for students who can proceed to higher levels or to new topics. So in these higher grades it is even more difficult than in the lower grades to specify what might be included in a typical course. And you may have to adjust even more than before in order to tailor your goals and your teaching to the needs and interests of your own children.

Number. Review and extend the understandings of how our decimal number system works. The concept of **sets** can be added, particularly for students who are likely to study advanced mathematics. Using **Venn diagrams** to visualize sets, subsets, empty sets, and their equivalency or union or intersection, is good practice in logic even for non-mathematicians. So if these are in your textbook, spend as much time on them as you think appropriate for your particular child.

Basic Operations. Students should be able to add, subtract, multiply and divide whole numbers, common fractions, and decimal fractions. Those who can do so adequately may, nevertheless, need to gain better understanding of the reasoning behind these operations. Advanced mathematics will be difficult or impossible without such understanding. Can your child see adding and subtracting as counting forward or backward along a number line? Can he see why each of these operations undoes the other? Does he see what a close relative multiplication is to addition? And division to subtraction?

Students with good understanding of these interrelationships find great challenge in alternate and shortcut ways to solve problems. Some short cuts are given in the "Multiplication" chapter, and some texts offer supplementary work on short cuts. Students who really become interested in these must check the library or bookstore for more ideas. Or they may invent them.

The **commutative, associative, and distributive laws** should be well understood, not necessarily as abstract laws, but as they operate in problems. Any good text today includes some teaching on these. But relax; no achievement test is going to ask for a statement or explanation of one of these laws. They go after the real thing. Does your child understand, for instance, the statements listed below?

$3 + 5$ is the same as $5 + 3$
$n + 5 = 5 + n$

$(3 + 4) + 5$ is the same as $3 + (4 + 5)$

2×8 is the same as $2 \times (4 + 4)$ or $2(4 + 4)$

The first two are examples of the order changing or commuting. The third shows that the 4 can associate with either number and the sum will still be the same. And the last shows that the product is the same no matter how the rows of stamps are distributed (in 2 rows of 8, or in 2 arrays of 4 rows of 4).

Ratio and Proportion. In arithmetic we often need to compare. Subtraction helps us find how much larger or smaller one number is when compared with another. Its relative, division, helps us find *how many times* larger or smaller. That's what ratio is—comparison by division.

Here is an example. If you are 33 years old and your daughter is 11 years old, you can compare your age with hers in these ways:

$$33 \div 11 \text{ or } 33/11 \text{ or } 3$$

Conversely, you can compare your daughter's age with yours:

$$11 \div 33 \text{ or } 11/33 \text{ or } 1/3$$

Proportion shows the equality of two ratios. For example:

$$11/33 = 1/3$$
$$11:33 :: 1:3$$
11 is to 33 as 1 is to 3

In the second example above, the : is the ratio sign and the :: is the proportion sign. The second example can be read using the words given in the third example.

When one of the numbers is missing in a proportion, students must solve to find the missing number. They may solve these as problems in fractions, which they have had considerable experience with, or they may solve them as equations after they have had some introduction to algebra concepts. The emphasis always is on understanding and thinking through the problems.

Percent. Seventh graders should have considerable experience with percents and common fractions so that they can easily convert from one to the other. A useful teaching aid is the bead number line described in the "Principles of Teaching" chapter. Also, on a sheet with 100 squares, students can cover squares enough to show various percents. Use such visuals often enough that your children develop good understanding of percents and of these common equivalencies.

$$1/2 = 50\%$$
$$1/3 = 33\tfrac{1}{3}\%$$
$$2/3 = 66\tfrac{2}{3}\%$$
$$1/4 = 25\%$$
$$2/4 = 50\%$$
$$3/4 = 75\%$$
$$1/5 = 20\%$$
$$1/8 = 12\tfrac{1}{2}\%$$
$$1/10 = 10\%$$

There are three "cases" of percent problems, and many texts present all three in seventh grade, although some leave the third case for eighth grade. In case 1, the percentage or part (p) is missing. In case 2, the rate (r) is missing. And in case 3, the base or whole (b) is missing. Some few seventh graders can understand the abstract formula $r \times b = p$. Using the numbers below, this reads: 20% of 30 = 6. In each of the three cases a different one of these three numbers is missing.

1. Find a percent of a number. Twenty percent of 30 is
   _____ .

2. Find what percent one number is of another number. Six is _____% of 30.

3. Find the number when a percent of it is given. Six is 20% of _____ .

Measurement. Understanding of denominate numbers (those denoting feet, inches, pounds, and other measures) has been built up in previous years. Now in seventh grade, students should extend their skills in computing with these numbers. Be sure your child understands the principle that only like units can be added or subtracted—only inches added to inches, or feet to feet. Sometimes feet must be changed to inches in order to work out a problem.

Geometry. The approach in seventh grade is *informal*, in that formal mathematical arguments and proofs are not studied. Experience with **lines** includes: bisecting lines, drawing perpendicular lines, and drawing parallel lines. Experience with **angles** includes: measuring with a protractor, constructing any given size of angle, and bisecting an angle. Knowledge of **circles** includes: center, diameter, radius, circumference, arc (part of a circle), and chord (any line across a circle, including the diameter).

Teach that a **triangle** is a closed figure with three angles and three straight lines for sides. Show that triangles are rigid, and help your child notice how this rigidity is used in constructing buildings and bridges. The student should learn about these four kinds of triangles.

Equilateral: three equal angles and three equal sides.
Isosceles: two equal angles and two equal sides.
Scalene: three unequal angles and three unequal sides.
Right: one angle of 90°.

Students learn about **quadrilaterals**, which are closed figures with four straight sides. Here are some kinds.

Rectangle: four equal angles, opposite sides equal.
Square: four equal angles and four equal sides (a type of rectangle).

Parallelogram: opposite sides equal, opposite angles equal.

Rhombus: four equal sides (a type of parallelogram).

Trapezoid: one pair of parallel sides.

After your children can recognize and draw various triangles, quadrilaterals, and circles, they may proceed to the study of measuring and computing lengths, perimeters, square surfaces, and cubic volumes. It is important to use plenty of concrete illustrations and visual aids to develop new understandings.

Problem Solving. This skill must be taught and practiced throughout all other topics; it cannot be gathered into one unit or chapter and taught separately. The way children become better at problem solving is to better understand arithmetic itself. Each new insight children gain opens up a whole category of problems in which they will be more proficient.

For instance, your children should understand that if $2 \times 3 = 6$, then $6 \div 3 = 2$ or $6 \div 2 = 3$. Stated another way, they can divide a product by either of its factors and will obtain the other factor. This principle, when understood, opens up many kinds of problems. You multiply by the rate to compute the amount of interest due, but you divide to find the rate. You multiply by the rate of speed to compute the distance, but you divide to find the rate.

As students plug along day after day on this or that little matter, they tend not to see the progress they are making. Adults are better able to take a long view, so an important part of your teaching job is to recognize what students are learning, point out to them their progress, and keep them encouraged.

Grade Eight General Guidelines

In a former generation, eighth grade arithmetic was thought of as the "terminal" course for many students. Thus it included business applications and had units on insurance, banking, taxes, and such topics that people need in their workaday lives. When most students continued on to high school, some of the business arithmetic was replaced by more geometry, statistics and other topics, and not everyone agreed with the wisdom of this change. Now with the resurgence of home schooling and, with it, home business, many children are again learning business arithmetic—this time "live."

The topics in eighth grade arithmetic programs thus vary widely. Also eighth graders themselves vary widely—more than in any lower grade. This is the natural result of good teaching along the way. While a lot of effort should be put into bringing up the learning level of slower students, a similar effort should be put into helping faster students learn as much as they can. Thus the spread from bottom to top increases every year as students progress through the grades.

For these reasons it is more difficult to list the contents of a typical eighth grade program than it is to list for any lower grade. And as a teaching parent, you should feel even more free to adjust your plans and goals to the needs of your own child. Does he hope to go to college someday? By all means help him on to the more advanced topics. Is he still having difficulty with some of the basics from earlier grades? Then use this year to deepen his understanding and his facility in computing. Is he somewhere between these two examples? Then start where he is and teach him as much as you can this year. In fact, this last advice is good to use with any grade and all students.

Use this eighth grade list, then, as flexibly as you need to, even going outside the list for other topics if that seems right for your child. Some elementary teachers keep high school math books available in their rooms for browsing. Nothing need be off limits if your child has interest and ability to study it.

The Number System. This topic has been included in every grade, but must be included again, because we cannot assume that every child has sufficient understanding of this "language" which is so essential to our lives. Review and reteach as much as you need to. Extend understandings as much as you can. Eighth grade programs often give more practice in rounding off numbers meaningfully. Many add an introduction to exponents, such as 10^2 and 10^3, which equal 100 and 1000 respectively. Students do not usually work problems with exponents, but just begin by understanding what they are. Many texts do additional work with number bases other than base 10, the purpose being to extend understanding of the base 10 system.

The Four Operations. As with the number system, we cannot assume that all students by this time have sufficiently mastered the operations of addition, subtraction, multiplication, and division. Thus most texts begin with a rapid review. If your student has trouble with fractions, or works carelessly, or lacks confidence, or exhibits any other problem, you should find the cause and help him conquer the problem.

Decimal Fractions and Percent. Many students, particularly those who have been taught by rules instead of by understanding, are confused about percents, and percents are important for our lives today. So go over any of the seventh grade teaching that your child needs to review. Emphasize that *percent* means *per hundred*. The list of fraction equivalents given in the seventh grade section should be thoroughly mastered. Sixths may now be added. Use many story problems and real-life problems, including all three cases of percent problems (see seventh grade section). Many business concepts are learned in units on percent: interest, discount, overhead, profit margin, and so forth.

Measurement. Metric measures are often studied in eighth grade, particularly lengths and weights. Students gain experience in computing within the metric system and have opportunity to see how easy it is with a system based on tens. They need a little work on converting measures to gain an idea of how a kilometer compares with a mile or how a meter compares with a yard, but extensive work in converting is not needed, since life problems seldom call for this skill.

Geometry. Some eighth grade texts devote as much as 20% of their space to geometry. They include further work with lines, angles, plane and solid figures. As in seventh grade, these books don't go into *formal* proofs, but present what is called *informal* geometry.

Graphs. Practically all types of graphs are studied at this level and books usually give data for students to make graphs from. Many teachers, though, prefer that students go through the decisions involved in gathering their own data and deciding how they best can be presented in graph form. Graphs are important in modern life since information is often presented in this form.

Algebra. Simple equations, in which the unknown is limited to whole numbers, are presented. The purposes are to introduce some of the symbols and vocabulary of algebra and to provide experience in algebraic thinking.

Statistics and Probability. Some of this work is introduced at earlier grades in simple forms. For instance: There are three marbles in this container—red, blue, and yellow. What is the probability that you will draw the red one? Averages, frequency distributions, and variances are computed and graphed. It is sometimes difficult to find topics for these problems that are of interest to young students. Sports are often used. Knowledge of these topics is important in today's society just to understand much of the information that comes to us daily.

Part IV:
Beyond the Three R's

16. History and Social Studies

What Are the Social Studies?

The term "social studies" is often misunderstood. Even President Hoover, who majored in social sciences himself, on at least one occasion misinterpreted the term. A school girl wrote to the President and complained about social studies. "Do you think they should make me do those in school?" she asked. "No," he answered. The schools were doing all kinds of things "these days" that were none of their business. The girl should work hard in important subjects like arithmetic and spelling. And if children want to learn dancing and such things they can do it after school.

But that, of course, was a misunderstanding. Under the "social studies" umbrella are five major areas: history, geography, economics, political science, and social psychology. Among these, history is the one elementary children spend the most time on. Other names for parts of these studies are: government, civics (citizenship), political and economic geography, anthropology, law, and more. All studies having to do with man and his societies are included. Other subjects are partly social: philosophy, religion, education, medicine, linguistics, and more. So there is nothing frivolous about having social studies in the curriculum.

Why, then, is there always so much controversy over social studies? One reason is that there is no agreement on the content, points of view, and attitudes that should be taught. And a second reason is that there is no agreement on the way to organize these subjects for the best learning. It is safe to predict that general agreement will never be reached on either problem. In fact, as mankind's knowledge continues to expand and ever more specialized branches of scholarship continue to emerge, the problems will only become more complex.

Children with Christian upbringing develop views that they would not get in establishment schools. For instance in the social psychology area, if they understand about mankind's fall into sin and of the major war in this world between evil and righteousness, they better understand political tyrants, crime, wars and other social topics. If they have much missionary education, they learn something about other cultures and develop a deeper understanding of other religions.

In the areas of government and citizenship, many of today's homeschooled children are learning a lot because of being involved along with their parents in studying local laws pertaining to schooling and in helping to change laws. Children have written letters to legislators, observed and even spoken at legislative hearings, attended rallies and lobbying efforts, and, have seen courts rule on homeschooling cases. Children who aren't personally active in these matters, should at least learn of what others are doing. They are part of an important movement in the history of our country, and it is an ideal vehicle for many learnings. Through their involvement in this, children can learn much about government and citizenship. They can learn that it takes constant vigil to preserve our freedoms. They also will have a basis for better understanding other movements and changes and social problems that they read about in history. Textbook learning can never match this real-life learning.

Textbooks and Workbooks

In no area of curriculum is there more disenchantment with textbooks than in history and the social studies. Disenchanted people include not only certain segments of our population who disagree with points of view in the books, but they include, also, educators who are concerned with their effectiveness for teaching. We will comment here on the effectiveness question.

A recent study of ten major textbook series showed, as studies so often do, what ordinary teachers already knew to be true. It showed scandalous weakness hidden between beautiful full-color photographs, maps, and charts and behind high quality design and layout of the books.

The most obvious weakness is the superficial treatment of most topics. Publishers try to get in everything that states and school districts want included, so their scope and sequence charts look as impressive as their art. But in the study, some topics were found to be only mentioned and not developed at all. They were even mentioned, in out-of-context positions, wherever the writers could manage to fit them in.

Children know this weakness even if they cannot analyze or explain it to you. If your children love to read *The Monitor and the Merrimac* or books about pyramids or knights or explorers or about any of the topics of the social studies but do not love to read their textbooks, they are expressing this discernment.

Some children are articulate when questioned about their books. Here are a couple of comments. "Sometimes they just mention a person's name and then don't talk about them anymore in the whole book." "They should talk more about each topic. For the War of 1812 there should be more information about the fighters and the treaties. What did the Treaty of Ghent contain? Who wrote it?"

The children are right. What is the point of knowing that a war was fought in 1812 and that a treaty was signed? Is this education? Does this help children understand man's problems and follies in this world? Does it help them think? Does it make them better citizens and decision makers today?

This problem of superficiality was found in every series from the ten major publishers. "Christian" series were not included in the study, but they have not escaped the problem either. Many of them are reprints or slightly revised versions of older editions of one or the other of these series. And others are patterned after them in their writing style. These books do have some advantage in content for their users, in that feminism and other views that Christian users may object to are not in the books. But the superficiality problem is exactly the same.

There is no one place to lay the blame for textbook problems. Bureaucracy and state approval systems surely share a large part of the blame. Salesmanship shares its part. Good teachers have always worked their way around the superficiality problem by not depending exclusively on their textbooks. You can do this too.

Another major problem of textbook series is that, for all their publicity about building concepts, skills and generalizations from grade to grade, this is not done. The books are collections of separate, unrelated topics that, as the children perceived, may contain only dates, events, and brief vignettes. And for all their talk about integrating skills with the content, most publishers had separate chapters on map reading skills, and few other skills besides map were included. Any thinking skills beyond finding and memorizing facts were few and far between, so that children have no opportunity to consistently use and practice them.

Another problem for independent thinkers like homeschoolers is the "establishment" view the books have. You probably won't detect this by finding objectionable content in the books, because it is more a problem of omission. If you think, for instance, that students should learn of the rise in power of the international banking families and their plans for one-worldism, you will have to obtain materials other than textbooks for that. And such materials are not easy to find. Books like Cleon Skousen's *The Naked Capitalist* usually are self-published and don't get reviewed in the establishment press. Moreover, they are written on adult level. Views of communism in textbooks seem more designed to foster peaceful international relations than to teach children the ugly truth of what communist governments have done in our modern world. If you want your children to learn of the "New Age" movement, the homeschool movement, the missionary movement, or other topics not handled in textbooks, you will need to search out materials yourself. Networks of homeschoolers and support groups might share this kind of information.

Some educators question whether textbooks, even at their best, could ever do the job. The very nature of textbooks is to present information that is "predigested, prethought, preanalyzed, and presynthesized," says a school learning specialist. A steady diet of such books deprives children of the joy of original thought. It turns them off to learning. They have no opportunity to catch from teachers and other children a spirit of active inquiry, no chance to build a lifelong love for learning.

We tend to view the *structure* of textbooks and workbook courses as their strength, but weakness lies there, too. Answering questions, getting scores, taking tests, making grades—these become the game that children play. They win scorecards; we check off requirements: this is "done," that is "done." Instead of opening minds, we close them.

If and when the publishers develop improved social studies textbooks, it is highly likely that important values in them will not be to your liking. If your children are growing up now, you don't have time to wait for the future, anyway. So your best recourse is to learn how teachers get along without depending on textbooks. It is not as difficult as it sounds.

Learning Beyond the Textbooks

Kindergarten and primary children begin learning history as "story"—stories of "long ago" or "once upon a time." Through stories, children catch on to the idea that people lived in the world before they were born and that their times and doings were in some ways different from ours. They also come to understand that we can learn about the past from books, and from film and other media. At about fourth grade level, most children have reached the information stage of reading, having mastered the mechanics and having built fluency. At this point we become more earnest about history teaching.

Since there is no widespread agreement on what should be taught in each grade, you you can be assured that you will do no damage to your own curriculum by making adjustments that fit your situation. If you are teaching children of several ages, it is perfectly all right to have all of them studying Columbus and the explorers at the same time. Or all can study ancient Greece at the same time. Younger children can read easier books, help make posters or scrapbooks, or take part in skits. They can enter into discussions or sharing times where family members contribute information from their reading or, better yet, raise questions they would like to find answers for.

If you happen to have an eighth grader, then in deciding what topics your children will study together you could choose eighth grade topics. After that, you might be able to work your way downward—seventh grade topics the next year, sixth the next, and so on. For an eighth grade topic "Problems of the New Nation," even primary children can learn about the flag, Indians, George Washington, and other items on their level.

During Civil War studies, they can learn about Abraham Lincoln, Harriet Tubman (underground railroad). In history there is practically always a way to study the same time period on an advanced level or a primary level.

Let's say that this year you are following the fifth grade curriculum or textbook. Next in your book comes the period of exploration of the Americas. You don't have to be any kind of expert on this period to plan a unit for your children. You may be more of an expert when you finish the unit, but that is one of the hazards (or pleasures) of teaching. You must now barge ahead in some way.

A simple start is to have your children look through the unit in the textbook and list people and events that are included. Then take a family trip to the library or send your older children. Get a variety of children's books on Drake, Balboa, DeSoto, and others in the list, being sure to include some easy books for your youngest children. Then everyone starts reading.

After a time, have a sharing and planning meeting. This meeting can be as individualistic as your family is. Ten families would have ten different outcomes from such a meeting. Children could begin by reporting to each other what they learned from reading. Help them proceed to making plans. How will they reinforce their learning? That is, what can they do to remember more of what they are now reading? They might decide to collaborate on a map or timeline or chart, or they might decide to make separate maps or reports or whatever. They could plan a skit or other presentation for the next meeting of your local homeschooling group. The first child to read a book could write questions for the others to answer if they read it.

A technique to use often is to help children write questions they want to find answers for. Who really did reach the Mississippi first; was it the man our textbook says or the man this other book says? Who is the explorer to be admired the most? What sort of end did each cruel gold-seeker come to? Who profited from their searches? Who were the Aztecs, and where did they come from? Save the questions and write each answer as it is found or agreed upon. Some questions may be unanswerable or at least unanswerable in the time you allot for the unit. You can decide whether those are worth pursuing or whether they should be laid aside for now. Children who learn to ask questions are far ahead educationally from when they had experience only in answering questions, particularly in the fields of history and other social studies.

While group study has advantages, in that enthusiasm spreads from one child to another, most of the preceding ideas can also be used if you are tutoring only one child. You and the child can sit down together and plan in ways similar to the group suggestions.

A good way to shop for family books on history is through the Barnes and Noble catalog. After you order, you will receive a monthly catalog for ever and ever. Their address is: 126 Fifth Avenue, New York, New York 10011. I say "family books," because they do not specialize in children's books, but once your family gets hooked on history, you will find some books each month that you want to order—probably more than you can afford or find time to read. Among numerous good history selections, Barnes has an "Everyday Life" series: *Everyday Life of the North American Indians*, *Everyday Life in Ancient Egypt*, and others.

A useful reading plan for some students—and adults—is to have a reading hobby centered on a favorite subject. In history that would be a particular time period or topic or area of the world. A professor once said, "I figure that if I keep reading on the history of education, the day will come when I know more than anybody alive about the history of education." Whether you carry your hobby that far or not, there are great benefits from pursuing one subject in depth. If students have oppor-tunity to do this, then at a planning meeting for a new subject they have many ideas. They now know what it is to know a subject more than just superficially. They now think better and can better take charge of their own learning. It's all right to change reading hobbies from time to time, just as we change other interests in life. Children should do this. And some people can handle one or two secondary reading hobbies alongside the main one.

If someone in the family has a serious reading hobby, perusing book catalogs becomes a hobby in itself. Some of these are almost as interesting to read as the books they tell about. People often quote the first portion of Francis Bacon's famous saying: "Some books are to be tasted, others to be swallowed, and some few to be chewed and digested." But they forget the last part: "Some books also may be read by deputy, and extracts made of them by others." Book reviews, good ones, do this deputy work for us; and book catalogs do a bit of it too. I think Francis Bacon would love today's book catalogs. In them we can read about many books while deciding not to chew or digest them. In a hobby area of reading, though, particularly if it's a specialty without wide popularity, we should take opportunities to add to our collection, because such books often have no second printing. If a hobbyist through the years buys a shelf full of books on his favorite topic, he has a collection that no library can duplicate.

The first reading hobby of many children is dinosaurs, and, unfortunately, that becomes their introduction to evolution. If you want to avoid that, buy your dinosaur books only from Master Books, P.O. Box 1606, El Cajon, California 92022.

Other excellent materials are from God's World Publications (Box 2330, Asheville, North Carolina 28802). They have newspapers on various grade levels, reporting current events and commenting on them from a biblical point of view.

If your children only know the workbook question-and-answer system of studying history, your first attempt to break out and use other activities and other kinds of thinking may not be an experience to brag about to your neighbor. But don't quit after one try. If you saw any glimmer of new excitement about history, aim for another glimmer or two on your next unit.

Timelines

History timelines are extremely popular with teachers and parents because they promise to provide continuity and unity for mankind's story that is bulky and unmanageable otherwise. Do we expect too much from timelines?

A man in my family was in his 90's when he died about the time of our nation's bicentennial celebration. Claude used to say, "I have seen half of our country's history." If you know a Claude, and he and your ten-year-old daughter talked about history, what would they each think when they use the word *century*? The old man who lived almost a century and the young girl to whom ten years is a lifetime would have strikingly different concepts.

Starting out in fifth grade is like committing yourself to being a fifth grader for all the forseeable future; the prospect stretches out endlessly before you. Can you remember what it was like? Children sometimes say, "when I'm in high school" or "when I'm grown up," but that's a lifetime away for them, not the few short years it is for you.

Children's understanding of time is only beginning to develop. History teachers who have been on the job very long know that this is so. In their own style, researchers tell us this too. A college professor says, "I think 26 is the age to begin a serious study of history." Another still-working professor, who is well past retirement age, says, "Do you notice that there are no brilliant young historians making a mark in the world? In mathematics and in science, people can do something when they're young, but history is for old men." This latter professor has in mind not only time, but other understandings too, that contribute to the wisdom of the old.

Young teaching parents are often over the age of 26, and at least one professor would like to have them in his class. Their sense of historical time is now developed enough that they can see more meaning and continuity in history. The bits and pieces they remember from schoolbooks, reading and TV now come together better than ever. If they first meet timelines at this point in their lives, or if someone shows them a beautifully designed commercial timeline, they are likely to get very excited. History is unified, after all. "Now I see how it fits together. Why didn't someone show me this when I was in school?" they have been heard to ask.

So they buy the timelines and hope that history will become as meaningful to their children as it is to them. Unfortunately it won't. The best ingredient in this sequence is the excitement of the parents. That, at least, is sure to have a lasting effect on children's interest in history.

While timelines will not magically mature your children's minds into adult minds, there are ways to profitably use them. First, you must reverse the thinking implied in the preceding paragraphs. For children, timelines are not for pulling together the scattered pieces of knowledge, as they do so well for adults; children haven't yet collected enough pieces to pull together. What timelines can do for children is to provide a framework into which they can put pieces of knowledge as they learn them. For this framework purpose, timelines should be very simple— so simple that children can memorize them.

American History Timeline. Make a timeline with major divisions as shown in the textbook, if you are using one. If you need a suggested list, one is given below. Since American history is getting longer for each generation to study, many curriculums do not expect elementary grade children to study much in the last two periods of the list, but when memorizing a timeline, children should have a complete a list anyway. The timeline can be simple printed titles placed horizontally along a wall under which children can place lists of events or people or drawings or anything they produce during their studies. Or the timeline itself can be a work of art, with illustrations along with titles, that children produce while studying American history. The line could be horizontal or vertical and designed in any arrangement you wish. There is no "right" way to make these.

Exploration and Discovery
Colonizing
Revolutionary Period
Young Republic and Westward Expansion
Civil War and Reconstruction
The Rise of Industrial America
Two World Wars
Modern America

World History Timeline. Keeping this timeline simple requires large time periods and it requires following specifically the roots of our Western civilization. A simple list might look like this.

Preflood Civilization
Early Postflood Civilizations (where secular books begin)
Ancient Empires
Middle Ages
Renaissance and Reformation
Rise of European Nations
Discovery and Colonization of the New World
America and the Modern World

You need not be tied to any particular timelines, but can develop others as the need arises. Sometimes a timeline within a timeline is helpful. For instance, while studying American history, you may want to have a project of making a more detailed timeline of the colonial period or of the Revolutionary War or of anything else you need.

Thus there are two major purposes for timelines, as summarized below.

1. Overall framework for organizing history chronology. For this purpose, timelines should be super-simple, and children should memorize them. These have two uses. One is learning the framework first and keeping it in mind while studying various parts of history. The other is to learn it later for pulling together and organizing what one already knows of history.

2. Children's study project. This use is when children develop and make timelines, either simple or detailed, while they are studying history. It takes its place along with notebooks, skits, murals, field trips, and all other kinds of activities by which children learn.

Problems and Errors in Timelines. When you and your children develop your own timelines for the early periods of history, everybody gets an education in the difficulties and uncertainties. One book gives one date for the Bronze Age, for instance, and another book gives a different date, so you all have to puzzle about what to put on your chart. (Actually Bronze Age timing does vary according to locality; it is an activity, not a date.) But when you buy prepared timelines, children tend to think that history is as precise as the chart, and to think that the chart, because it is in print, is right.

On one commercial chart, a Bronze Age date is given before the Flood and then other developments follow after it, just as though the Flood did nothing to disrupt man's ongoing activities. Other charts have other glaring errors. So you need to realize, just as with books, that not everything in print is true.

Types of Curriculum Plans

The social studies field is so massive that curriculum planners must select only parts of the total content. Then they must decide how to organize so as to fit in all their selections. In this section we describe various attempts at solving these problems.

Posthole Curriculum. Almost everyone agrees that history should be the core of social studies for elementary grades. But even when that is agreed upon, we are left with the question, What history? Shall it be of rulers and wars and treaties? Shall it be of movements among common people, such as the rise of the church or of organized labor? Shall it be of science and inventions that changed people's lives? Shall it concern economic philosophies such as capitalism and communism?

Since every idea from every historic period can't be included, the "posthole" arrangement for curriculum was invented. Postholes reach down through all the historic periods and regions studied, and provide a continuity for students. By this system, children should develop a fair understanding at least of the four posts. And if they don't study thoroughly every period of history and every region of the world while in school or while in elementary grades, these posts provide them with the tools and thinking skills needed for any future history and social studies they wish to undertake.

So the four posts are intended to be a broad and comprehensive look at any society. You might find them useful for evaluating history textbooks or as guidelines for adding extra enrichment material to your children's courses. This combination of posts is a good one now coming into popularity.

1. *Political science:* the traditional "rulers and wars" view of history, power struggles, political parties, etc.
2. *Economics:* agrarian society, nomadic society,

feudalism, industrialism, capitalism, socialism, economic causes of war or of nations' downfall, etc.

3. *Culture:* religion, literature, art, philosophy, education, science, way of life of a people.

4. *International relations:* how tribes, city-states, nations and empires got along or didn't get along with others; successes, failures, principles to be learned from the past.

Framework. Frameworks are not exactly new; any overall curriculum plan can be called a framework within which the semesters and units and daily lessons are supposed to fit. But a recent California state framework made a bold effort to break the mold. The California committee wanted history to be as a story well told—an "exciting and dramatic series of events that helped to shape the present." It should be "rich with controversies and forceful personalities." (Sounds like the way history is presented in the Bible, doesn't it?) Teachers and students should have time enough on each topic to think and to savor it in rich detail. Often throughout this framework, specific books are suggested for reading—biographies of famous people and of immigrants, literature of the times and countries under study, fiction portraying life of other times.

By now, textbooks have been produced for the California view of teaching history. And by now, various groups have already objected to the way they are portrayed in the textbooks. So we may well ask whether this project, too, is on its way toward becoming just another dull textbook series.

But you can go beyond the textbooks, or bypass them altogether and use just the framework if you wish. It is item number 0-8011-0712-1 from the California State Department of Education, Publication Sales, PO Box 271, Sacramento, California 95802-0271.

In their framework, California allots the whole year of fourth grade to study of state history and fifth grade to the study of American history up to 1830. Then they begin a unique three-year chronological study of world history which continues through sixth, seventh and eighth grades. Sixth graders begin at the beginning and study to the fall of Rome. Seventh graders study medieval and early modern times up to the discovery of the New World. And eighth graders study American history.

This three-year chronology is broad-ranging, putting more time on more parts of the world than has usually been done in elementary grades. But the committee has carefully planned so that studies of India and China, for instance, are related to happenings in Western civilizations. They also have made more use of Bible history than is usually done in secular contexts. At several points throughout the plan, specific suggestions are made for relating the Bible to the topics under study, and such relationships would greatly strengthen the learning for children who are brought up on the Bible.

Here are some quotes from the framework that give a flavor of its attitude toward Christianity. United States history is "one of the most remarkable stories in history: the creation of a new nation, peopled by immigrants from all parts of the globe and governed by institutions founded on the Judeo-Christian heritage, the ideals of the Enlightenment, and English traditions of self-government." "One reason for settling California was to bring Christianity to the native peoples."

This framework recognizes the roots of Western civilization in the Hebrews as well as in the Greeks. This point is ignored in some curriculum plans. It suggests learning many Old Testament stories and selections from Psalms and Proverbs so as to understand the literary heritage and ethical teachings we have from the Bible and to know the Hebrew people's concepts of wisdom, righteousness, law, and justice. It suggests using the Sermon on the Mount and some of the parables so that children will understand the teachings of Jesus. For the beginning of mankind, though, they do not give the biblical view, and Christians using this framework would have to adjust on units about beginnings, just as with any secular curriculum plan. As suggested elsewhere in this book, most evidences of early man probably come from after the Flood. For preflood history you must go to the Bible, which this framework does not suggest. It is possible that some fossils may someday be shown to belong to preflood times. Present dating systems are not as certain as books usually imply, and you may well question the great ages they give for mankind. Though a high civilization probably existed before the Flood, afterward people had to start from scratch. After the dispersion from Babel many would also have to start from scratch, starting first with crops, then with homes, and so forth. And in their "confounded" languages some of their former intelligence was lost. So these may be the periods that secular historians think is the beginning of civilized man.

Regional. As mentioned, one common curriculum plan is based on regions. History and geography, as well as the culture of peoples and other social studies topics are all supposed to be included. But since regions are the center of the plan, rather than history chronology, people have criticized this plan as being weak on history. It is usually organized like this.

Grade Four: The world
Grade Five: The United States (more emphasis on early history)
Grade Six: Latin America and Canada
Grade Seven: The Eastern Hemisphere
Grade Eight: The American Heritage (more emphasis on government and modern times).

A Traditional Curriculum

An older plan than the regional is popular with back-to-basics people who want strong history teaching, and we treat it here in more detail than the plans mentioned above. Specific grade-level topics vary among published series or state curriculum guidelines, so we give here a "typical" plan of this type. Although these plans proceed chronologically much of the time, they also have "spiral" features, by which older children return to something they studied earlier, studying it in greater depth the second time. Here is a grade-by-grade listing of such a curriculum.

Fourth Grade. This first year of serious history, is best treated as the beginning of a transition from the story stage. Don't emphasize too many dates and fact details. Don't expect children to understand much about political hassles and other adult motivations in history. And don't expect much understanding of historical time. This year is used to build a background of stories about ancient history and American beginnings. A typical course includes stories of people and events centered around these topics:

The First Americans—Indians. Read about several particular tribes, their clothing, homes, weapons, customs, how they raised crops and hunted game. Learn that some Indians now live on land reserved for them, and some live in cities and towns along with other people.

Local History. Who first settled in your area? This information is easy to come by in some areas and more difficult in others. Local libraries and historical societies can help. Visit historical landmarks and find out the stories behind them. Broaden to statewide information. Who first settled in your state? Why? How did it become a part of the United States?

Heroes. If you live near the homes of heroes like Lincoln, Washington, Jefferson, or near the trail of Lewis and Clark, or otherwise can connect national heroes with local history, do so. Acquaint your child with local heroes; some national heroes, particularly from our early history; and a few great ancient leaders. Ancients can include Hebrews (such as Moses and David), Greeks (Alexander the Great or Pericles), Romans (Julius Caesar, Cicero), and English (Alfred, William the Conqueror). Stories about cherry trees and splitting rail fences help children remember a person, but try also to teach, on a level your child can understand, why these people are great. Good books will do much of this teaching for you, and some conversation now and then about the books will increase your children's learning.

The Times of the European Discovery of America. Read about Marco Polo's travels, Magellan's voyages and others, to learn of trade with the East and motivations for crossing the oceans. (Geography knowledge must keep pace with history.) Read some stories of inventions that helped—the magnetic compass, gunpowder. Read about the printing press, too. (It contributed to the Reformation and many other movements besides the explorations that led to America.) Read about Columbus.

Fifth Grade. In this grade, it is traditional to take up American history in a sequential fashion. Remember that fifth graders still have little understanding of historical time and adult motivations. They still need the story approach as much as possible. Good teachers supplement the bare-bones recital of facts in a history text with reading of real books.

Esther Forbes' classic *Johnny Tremain* has given millions of children—and adults—an understanding of Revolutionary times in Boston in a way that no history text can match, even though it is classified as fiction—a historical novel. A different class of books is narrative history, which are not novels, not fiction, but narrative, nevertheless. Fletcher Pratt's *The Monitor and the Merrimac* is a good example of this kind. Many fifth grade boys love this exciting account of the first naval battle involving an ironclad ship. It is a Civil War story. When your children get hooked on books like these they will begin teaching you history. They will say, "Here Mom, you should read this book."

A bare-bones list of traditional content for fifth grade early American history follows.

> *Exploration and Discovery.* Review Columbus. Read of the Cabots, Drake, Raleigh, Balboa, De Soto, Champlain, Hudson, and others. Where did they go? Why? What land did they claim, and for whom? Mark maps, perhaps a different one for each explorer, to show the routes that they took and to color land that they claimed. (Scholars in this century have uncovered considerable evidence of pre-Columbian voyages to the New World, including Phoenicians, possibly Solomon's ships, and others, crossing both oceans. While such history is fascinating, it is not part of the thread connecting our Western civilization with its roots, so it is not included in elementary school textbooks. Often Vikings are mentioned, not because they are more important than the others but, possibly, because more was known about them when the textbook industry was developing. The main use you should make of this knowledge is to help your children realize that this period of history is when the Europeans discovered and made claims in the New World; it is not the first time that earthlings set foot on it. If this had been better understood, a book proposing that chariots of gods from outer space came to our hemisphere would never have made the best seller list.)
>
> *Colonizing.* Read about the beginnings of several indi-

vidual colonies. If you wish to emphasize religious beginnings of the United States, you can spend more time on William Bradford and the Pilgrims in Plymouth, John Winthrop and the Puritans in Massachusetts Bay, William Penn and the Quakers in Pennsylvania, Roger Williams and the Rhode Island Baptist story. Read about some Spanish and French settlements. Make maps. Write.

Revolutionary Period and Beyond. Some school districts save most of this for seventh grade, believing that it is too much content to cover in fifth grade and that the political ideas involved in topics such as the Articles of Confederation and the Constitutional Convention are not understandable to such young children. But other districts take fifth graders through this period of American history, and through some westward expansion across the Alleghenies up to about 1830, or on through the Civil War.

Sixth Grade. Traditionally, sixth grade has been the time for study of world history. Books typically begin with guesses about how man became man, how he gradually developed language, discovered fire, and so forth. Bible believing families should compare the content of these books with the story of man's beginnings as found in the Bible. Adam had language as a gift from God in the very beginning. A high civilization could have existed before the Great Flood, and it was rapidly rebuilding after the Flood, with people knowing more about some topics than we do today. Because of the misuse of knowledge, God intervened and "confounded" the languages, which surely affected thought and knowledge too. As mentioned in the framework section, evidences cited in history books about the beginnings of civilization in the Fertile Crescent, formed of the Nile valley and the Tigris and Euphrates valley, can probably be placed mostly in the period immediately following the scattering of peoples from Babel.

With this view of early history, people may indeed have begun in a new location with stone tools. But as soon as they had food to eat they could spend time developing mines and moving into the Bronze Age or the Iron Age in less time than the guessers like to give them, because they or their fathers had memory of these industries from before the dispersion. They, no doubt, also knew the history of pre-flood achievements of man.

When early history is given briefly, as in children's text-books, little or nothing is said about the problems in dating and developing a chronology of these early times. But there are numerous problems. Recently, carbon-14 dates all over Europe were revised by comparison with tree ring dating, and suddenly the sons of Japheth could be seen as settling Europe at the same time the sons of Shem and Ham were settling the Middle East, instead of later, as previously thought. Children who are not brainwashed by evolutionary books, but who are led to see that there are different viewpoints may be the very historians who will solve some of the problems concerning this very early period of history.

What is called "historic times," after written records are found, is not problem-free either. For the ancient empires of Sumer, Babylonia and others, much dating is done by what we think we know of Egyptian history. If a king had a war with such-and-such a Pharoah, then he is dated as being contemporary with that Pharaoh, and this leads through a complex network of intertwined bits of information to dating many other people and events. But historian Immanuel Velikovsky recently proposed cutting out several hundred years from the usual Egyptian chronology. If this Pharaoh and this Pharaoh are really one man instead of two, he says in a series of books, then we find many enigmas of history can be solved after all. Needless to say, his theory is controversial, because it conflicts with long-standing theories in many other books.

Most sixth graders cannot read adult books on these

debates, but they at least should not be shut out of future participation in them by textbooks that give answers only, possibly wrong ones, instead of teaching that there are yet many questions for future historians to solve. If yours is a Bible-believing family, one good way to handle such history books is to have family discussions comparing what they teach with what you know of early history from the Bible. Whether you actually solve problems or answer questions does not matter. What matters is that questions are raised and thought about and puzzled over. A generation of historians brought up with this kind of education will make significant progress in our knowledge of early times.

Traditional world history topics for sixth graders include the following:

Man's Beginnings. Topics such as hunting and agriculture, early art, early religious beliefs, the rise of cities and communal life.

Early Civilizations. Old books usually began with Egypt and its contemporary, Babylonia. But during this century more has become known about Sumer and Akkadia, and textbooks began including them. Sumer is treated as a culture and civilization, and Akkadia as the first true empire in which one king ruled over a group of cities.

Ancient Empires. Egypt, Babylonia, Phoenicia, the Hebrews, Persia, Greece, Rome. Some attention is given to China, India, Asia and other empires around the world, but most emphasis is on the roots of our own civilization. The beginnings and spread of Christianity.

The Middle Ages. This period, from the fall of the Roman Empire to about the fourteenth century, formerly was called the Dark Ages, but historians have changed our picture of this time. Topics of this time include: Charlemagne's empire, the Crusades, importance of the Church, feudal life.

The Renaissance and Reformation in Europe. The label
   Renaissance came from fifteenth century Italian
   intellectuals—the same who coined the term "Dark
   Ages." They were describing their own times in glowing
   terms as being superior to those which preceded. The
   label has stuck and is found in most history books. Some
   Christian textbooks give more attention to issues
   involved in the Reformation than to the art and
   humanism implied in the Renaissance label.
The Rise of European Nations. Emphasis is on the Europe
   that found America—France, England, the Dutch
   Republic and Spain. Some topics are: trade routes,
   scientific discoveries and inventions. Catholicism,
   Lutheranism and Calvinism are interconnected with the
   rise and fall of rulers and nations.

Seventh Grade. By seventh grade, the political and
economic motivations of adults become more understandable
and more interesting to students. But this is not true to the
extent that many curriculum planners in the past have assumed.
Brain research showing a spurt of brain growth about this time
in children's lives has caused some educators to jump to a
conclusion that this is the time to pile more advanced kinds of
thinking upon students. But this doesn't seem to work very well.
We might better draw a conclusion that this growth spurt is
when we should let up pressure on students and allow them
time for consolidation and for experimenting with advanced
thinking. This is what we do during spurts of physical growth;
we realize there may be a time of awkwardness and getting used
to the body's new size, shape, deeper voice, and so on.

So while some history texts include complex topics of the
Constitution, political philosophies, taxation, trade and others,
you must be guided by what your children seem able to comprehend. Realize that if your textbooks seem too difficult, you must
bend the books and not the students.

Nevertheless, by seventh and eighth grades history becomes a deeper study with much thinking and logic and relating. If students have read a lot and learned a lot of information in the earlier years, they can now use that information to consider and analyze problems of American life. Seventh grade typically has one general theme.

American History from the Revolution to the Present. This is a spiral returning to the fifth grade topic of American history. Revolutionary times are studied in more depth than before, and the period covered is longer than in fifth grade. Early in our century it was easier to cover all periods up to the students' time, but by now American history is almost twice as long and few courses do very much with recent history, leaving that for high school. So textbooks or frameworks may stop at the Civil War or one of the World Wars.

Eighth Grade. As in seventh grade, students should be challenged to think about problems of mankind. Young teenagers tend to be idealistic and see easy, "fair" solutions to social problems, and a better view of complexities develops slowly with growing up. During this time, discussing history lessons with adults helps to mature their thinking.

Eighth grade curriculum often is divided into two separate semester topics.

State History. A unit from a few weeks in length to a semester in length is devoted to study of students' own local and state history.

American Government. Studies of the Constitution, political parties, foreign affairs, domestic affairs, democratic principles contrasted with communism or other systems.

Can You Do It All? These grade-level listings comprise a very heavy schedule of learning. One way to help meet it is to integrate other studies with history. Have your students write often on history topics and call it language study. Read literature of the times and peoples studied and call it reading or literature. Study their music and arts and call it arts. Learn about their inventions and scientific discoveries and call it science. Identify some of the new words you encounter and call it vocabulary and spelling. Such integration strengthens both the history learning and the other integrated subjects as well.

And when it comes to hard choices about whether to omit some topics on your original plan, remember that many thinkers have stated that it is better to study less and learn it well than to study more and learn only superficially.

Objectives of Civics Study

The National Assessment of Educational Progress is informally called "the nation's report card." This is government funded research which continues across the years so that it can provide information on changes in students' performance over time. Periodically, a civics test is given nationally as part of this assessment.

Before anyone can write questions for this test, the assessors get input from a broad spectrum of American educators and the public. Just what is it they want to assess? What should children learn in civics? From that effort they developed a list of objectives under four categories, which are listed below. The objectives include more than any one curriculum can offer, so don't feel overwhelmed that you can't do it all. And they include all ages, through high school, so only part of this learning can realistically be done by eighth grade. But reading these objectives gives a picture of what a good many people think civics education should be. As you look at them you might see how you can accomplish a lot of these objectives by reading and discussing selected current events—Supreme

Court appointments, presidential elections, local sewer or road problems, and so forth.

1. **Democratic Principles and the Purpose of Government.** In this group are objectives such as "Understanding the basic principles and ideas expressed or implied in the Declaration of Independence, The United States Constitution, court decisions, and laws." These principles include representative government based on the consent of the governed, basic rights such as freedom of expression and belief, freedom from arbitrary governmental actions, equality of opportunity, the rule of law, limited government, federalism, and understanding how our system developed through Greek and Roman laws and English common law. (Hebrew law and ethics should be added to these "roots" of our system.)

2. **Structure and Function of Political Institutions.** This category includes knowing basic differences between our political system and those in nondemocratic nations; knowing the organization and institutions of our government; understanding the system of checks and balances among the legislative, executive, and judicial branches of government; understanding how state and local governments relate to each other and to the federal government.

3. **Political Processes.** This includes understanding the range and importance of decisions by branches of government and by regulating agencies (laws by Congress, approval by President, decisions by courts, regulations by IRS and other agencies); understanding the limits of governmental decision-making power (due process, constitutional constraints, public opinion, interest groups, cost and time); understanding influences on governmental decision-making (political bargaining, law suits, the media, others); understanding the role and structure of political parties, Political Action Committees

(PACS), and public opinion polls; and understanding about initiative, referendum and recall.

4. Rights, Responsibilities, and the Law. This includes understanding specific rights and liberties guaranteed by the United States Constitution, the Bill of Rights, and state constitutions (citizenship, due process, equal protection, the right to bear arms, free speech, freedom of the press, and exercise of religion); recognizing the constitutional provision for national defense; knowing the duties and responsibilities of judges and juries; understanding that sometimes rights may conflict, such as freedom of the press versus the right to a fair trial; understanding the purposes of law to protect, provide safety and order, provide ways to resolve conflicts, and others; recognize citizens' responsibility to respect legitimate authority and to comply with laws such as those related to taxes, licensing, and driving; recognizing legitimate ways to dissent from wrongful laws and arbitrary authority; exercising responsibility to be well-informed and to participate in community, state, and national affairs.

17. Science and Health

Science: How Do Children Learn?

In an interesting research, the National Science Teachers Association chose schools which scored high on science achievement tests and had reputations for outstanding science programs. Then they inquired of these schools what texts they used and found that none had *a book* for the curriculum. Teachers quipped, "We supplement our curriculum with textbooks," or "We use all we can find."

Some schools have students work in groups of four. Each student in a group reads about a topic in a different textbook and finds additional information, as well. Then the group must reconcile the differences they found. These students learn far more than the science in any one book, and on examinations they can explain various points of view. Many students in these programs use textbooks only as references for their projects and researches. The schools studied were high school level, but these ideas work in elementary grades too.

Is this approach only for science professionals, or can a

more ordinary person teach this way too? One example of a more ordinary person was a third grade teacher who said to the good readers in her class, "I want each of you to choose a topic and read at least three books on it. When you finish, you can tell the rest of us what you learned." The topics were duly registered; some were on science, some on history, literature, and other fields.

Imperceptibly at first, and then visibly, that class was carried along on the power of children's natural desire to learn. Each report or display sparked interest in several other children, and learning built upon learning until the teacher could hardly shut it off if she had wanted to. There was no count of the books the class read that year, but at testing time a number of children had to be given junior high achievement tests to obtain their scores, which in some cases reached into high school levels in reading ability and knowledge of science.

An important point in this story is that the teacher did not know all the science the children studied. She learned a lot that year along with her pupils. This was also true of teachers in the excellent science programs mentioned above.

Why does it work this way? Why, when young children select their own topics and when older students don't stick to the textbooks, do they score so high on tests? It is easy to think, especially if we have a back-to-basics turn of mind, that if children read and study and test their way through a textbook they will learn what they're supposed to at their grade level and that they will score well at achievement test time. But there are two major fallacies with this thinking.

One fallacy concerns the nature of achievement tests themselves. It is important to understand that they do not test fourth grade learnings, fifth grade learnings, and so on in a ladder to see how far up children can go. Tests work, instead, according to sampling theory, the same way popularity polls work. That is, the test items are a sampling of a large number of possible items. If a child can answer 45% of the sample items, the theory predicts that he could answer about 45% of the possible items. A child, then, who studies a fourth grade textbook all year is not necessarily learning the content that is in the test. And a child who studies his own projects of pond life or the solar system or whatever, may get different questions correct on an achievement test than the textbook child, but he could score just as high, or more probably higher, as predicted by the research mentioned above.

This last point is the second fallacy of the "strict textbook" thinking. For high success we must take into account the way people learn. The textbook style of science learning is traditional in our schools, and research is showing that as students progress through the grades they like science less and less, until after grade 12 only 10% still give "attention" to science. The other 90% are considered scientifically illiterate. Research into the causes has shown that students especially in high school, perceive books and teachers as "knowing" science and as "answer givers." This progressively turns off students' own curiosity, motivation, and interest in the subject. When students learn pre-selected information, pass a test, and receive a grade, they tend to feel that they have "finished" a subject. They close the door on that chapter, soon forget a large part of the information, and have no open questions that they intend to search out answers for.

So as teacher, you do not have to be an "answer giver." That should take pressure off practically all of us, since only a few science professionals probably feel qualified to take that role.

Thinking Skills. Raising good questions is one of the most important science thinking skills. At the frontiers of science, people who discover new knowledge do so by pursuing new questions. George Washington Carver read in Genesis that God gave to man every tree yielding seed and said, "To you it shall be for meat." Carver connected that knowledge with his knowledge of Southern farmers whose poor soil could manage to grow peanuts, and he raised the question, "How can we use peanuts as meat, so these farmers will have something useful to sell?" He went on to invent peanut butter and about 300 other products.

While Thomas Edison worked with telegraph, he invented a device to automatically record votes in Congress. While he worked in a brokerage, he invented a stock ticker. He had a habit of always asking how a job might be done more quickly and efficiently (he read voraciously too) and at a young age he became a full-time inventor.

Another science skill is observation—both under natural conditions and under experimental conditions. Louis Pasteur's close observations of fermentation led to his discoveries of bacteria and other small organisms. This led, in turn, to his development of vaccines for several diseases and to pasteurization of milk. Before Pasteur, diseases were treated with ineffective methods based on evolutionary beliefs about life, but Pasteur's work changed that forever.

Besides asking questions and observing, what other thinking skills do scientists use? They measure, organize, classify, interpret. They make judgments based on large amounts of information. They form theories and plan experiments to check them out.

Childhood activities naturally make use of most of these skills. One homeschooler I know spent much of his summer planning and building a fish pond in his backyard. Physics, math, and biology learning proceeded together, and the boy's room was strewn with fish books opened and well marked. Another boy spent his summer learning all he could about dinosaurs from the museum where his uncle worked. A third littered his house with astronomy books and kept the family up late to look through their telescope. All that those families need for good science learning is for the summer activities to spill over into the school year.

Science: What Should Children Learn?

At this writing (1993) we see the greatest effort ever toward reaching a national consensus on what children should learn in school science. This effort is coordinated by the National Research Council (NRC), an arm of the National Academies of Science and of Engineering. Over 100 science, technology and education organizations are participating, and wide input was obtained from science educators and the general public both before the work was begun and during the process. They aim to obtain consensus through a series of reports, feedback critiques and revisions. The final draft is scheduled for Fall of 1994.

The NRC intends to issue curriculum standards in a narrative form which will describe a broad range of what is possible for each age grouping and for each topic they address. They stress that they will not prescribe curriculum, they will not define a specific course of study, they will not make checklists. Their standards will provide a vision of excellence for science education.

Here, in brief, is an outline of the framework within which they are working. Three broad categories make up the knowledge base for school science: 1) science disciplines, 2) philosophy of science, and 3) history and sociology of science.

1. Science Disciplines. In this category are three subdivisions: 1) life sciences, 2) physical sciences, and 3) earth and space sciences.

Life sciences include learning about organisms—living things—and learning about the ecology or interdependency of all these. Also, evolution is listed as a topic within the life sciences. Whether or not the final draft mentions learning about problems in evolutionary theory, creationists could certainly include that and thereby have a stronger education on this topic than those who do not.

Physical sciences include matter, forces, motion and

energy—the traditional topics of physics. Earth and space sciences complete the triad. This last is another area where the evolutionary and creationist viewpoints become important.

Those three disciplines make up the body of scientific knowledge. As with other recent projects in science curriculum, this committee, too, stresses that this rich body of content should not lead to a large collection of facts and information, but to a limited number of fundamental ideas. Teachers should teach less in order to teach it better. This will lead to more meaningful learning.

This "less is better" theme appears repeatedly in various science curriculum projects. Everyone seems to agree that textbooks today are overstuffed and undernourished, and the problem now is not to add but to eliminate. This principle, they admit, may be difficult to sell through the textbook bureaucracy. Homeschools may be the arena where this very sensible suggestion can be successfully used.

2. Philosophy of Science. In this category of learning, there are again three subdivisions: 1) modes of inquiry, 2) habits of mind, and 3) attitudes and dispositions.

"Modes of inquiry" refers to the thinking skills mentioned earlier. Before high school, this is not very formal. Children simply need to get acquainted with things, observe them, collect them, handle them, describe them, become puzzled by them, ask questions about them, and try to find answers.

Some habits of mind that children need include skepticism and tolerance of ambiguity. These characteristics of science thinking are different from thinking in some school subjects, and they are different from the traditional school idea that the textbook and the teacher have "right" answers. But in science, they should hold answers or opinions tentatively, sometimes skeptically. New ideas and knowledge may change these views. This is true in small matters such as wondering whether the child's experimental results are accurate or flawed for some reason and in large matters such as wondering about population growth and other topics that scientists bring to the world's attention. Living with such ambiguity is important for science thinking.

Attitudes and dispositions to encourage in your children include curiosity; reflection or careful consideration of science topics and problems; and pleasure in understanding.

3. History and Sociology of Science. Studying about people and events of the past will show how science has developed and how it has affected civilization. Often this is motivating, as when students see how a Louis Pasteur has helped mankind. Study of events and issues today may be similarly motivating as students catch a vision of what might be accomplished.

Sociology is a word with broad meaning that here includes the entire context of science in our civilization. Thus it includes study of how science relates to math, politics, economics, culture, and to technology.

Science in its social context becomes mixed together with technology. The National Science Foundation illustrates this with the topic of a community traffic control system. For the community to solve this problem, it must use three levels of technology, several sciences, and factors in society itself. All these interface with each other. The lights, timing mechanisms, and machines that stripe the roads and make signs and surface the roads are called "hard" technologies. "Soft" technologies are used for the system that controls the traffic—its timing plans, maintenance schedules, procedures for evaluating, and even the laws. Work such as changing the burned-out lights and striping the roads is low-level technology. Science and social areas in this illustration include energy, population, human engineering, environmental quality, and use of natural resources.

Thus we have a whole—the traffic system—with three

aspects or sides to it: 1) science, 2) technology, and 3) society. When organized this way, need for the old-style chemistry course could be questioned. Your children would learn chemistry as they study nutrition and diseases or as they study agriculture and soils. Learning would begin with more meaningful wholes, and specialization be left for later years. Curriculum would not be arranged as diluted bits from university courses, all intended to lead eventually to university study, but turning off 90% of students on the way.

It has been recommended that this science/technology/society triad be one of the broad areas of higher study, taking its place with the areas of life sciences, physical sciences, and earth and space sciences. So alongside the physics building on campuses, they could build new STS buildings. In the NRC project, STS is not part of the content but part of the context of science, in this category called "history and sociology."

Testing of Science. A lively debate is now in progress on evaluation and testing of children's learning. This NRC project will address those issues, too, and major changes may be taking place in the next few years.

In the meantime, homeschoolers usually must live with the traditional style achievement tests and adaptations of them. So it is helpful to know that for elementary grades about half the questions are in the two fields of life sciences and the earth and space sciences. Physical sciences are left largely for the high school years. The other half of the questions include the history, sociology and philosophy of science as described above, as well as elementary questions on physics.

To do well on these tests, a student must be able to read and understand in these various fields. And reading space science, for instance, is quite different from reading about plants, mainly because the vocabulary is not the same. Thus your family may want to read and talk and study about a variety of science topics. Discussion, especially with adults, is the best known way for children to raise their level of thinking, which raises their test scores.

Science: Why Should Children Learn It?

It may be well to beef up our science education. But on the other hand not everyone agrees with the governors in the United States who set a national goal to be "first in the world in mathematics and science achievement." Many are alive today who remember 1957 when the Soviet Union launched Sputnik I, the world's first space satellite. Americans were shocked. Most blamed the schools, rather than political leaders, for failing to make us first in space. In reaction to Sputnik, the government led and financed crash efforts to produce new science curriculums, more high school students signed up for advanced courses, and school science achievement was raised.

For us who remember, history seems to be repeating itself today, but at a less panicked pace. For what purpose? We must ask important underlying questions. Is it science that will improve the lot of mankind? Will science literacy for all citizens lead to better decisions?

Many thinkers today, even among humanists, are sadly disillusioned at what science achievements have produced in our world. Novelist Kurt Vonnegut, recipient of the "Humanist of the Year" award, said in his acceptance speech, "The fruits of science so far, put into the hands of governments, have turned out to be cruelties and stupidities exceeding by far those of the Spanish Inquisition and Genghis Khan and Ivan the Terrible and most of the demented Roman emperors. . . . science is yet another human-made God."

Science is a god in that people look to it for truth and for solutions to human problems. It is the Messiah that can save us from evils in the world. The underlying humanist belief is that our human intellect is the source of these good results.

We Christian educators should make curriculum decisions with full awareness of the foundational differences between us and humanists. The world may need better scientists and a nation may need citizens who are scientifically literate, but far more do we need leaders and citizens in the moral and religious realms. With that we would make better use of our science knowledge.

Creation Science

Everybody agrees that science influences our society. Science affects the way we live, and we affect the way science progresses. Society and science interface in both directions.

For this reason, it is extremely important that we be on the right side of the creation-evolution issue. This is not a minor issue that we can ignore in order to avoid controversy. The way mankind deals with this question determines in large measure the path mankind takes in society.

If people believe that humans evolved from animals and are a species of animal, then society becomes more animal-like. People kill babies, the elderly and other weak persons. In many ways, humans trample on humans as they move in directions they call progress. Marxism, humanism, and atheism are all natural results of evolutionary beliefs.

Perhaps no issue in education is more important than this. Some of the societal reasons and religious reasons for its importance are mentioned in the history and Bible chapters. Here we will just say that it is simply good science to investigate thoroughly what all the controversy these days is about. For that, you can't depend on reports in the establishment press and TV. Those usually are slanted to make Bible believers appear to be ignorant or intolerant or something else that really is not the case.

To learn more of what the creation scientists themselves are teaching and discovering, you need their own publications.

Your local Bible bookstore probably has some good books. Good mail order sources are Master Books and the Bible Science Association (addresses given at the end of the Bible chapter). These carry both adult and children's books on a variety of topics, and new ones are constantly appearing. Do your children's textbooks give an outdated version of how coal is formed? Do they tell about studies of the depletion of earth's magnetic current and how old the earth is shown to be when dated by these results? Do they tell any of the numerous problems with evolutionary theory? The creation scientists write about these and numerous other interesting matters. Like the excellent science teachers mentioned earlier, you may use all the books you can find.

Big Ideas. When students have some understanding of the big ideas of **evolutionism** and **creationism** they can correctly interpret much that is going on in the world around them. They can read more discriminatingly in almost every field. Students in schools which teach only one view—evolutionism—are cheated out of a real education. Students who learn both views are ahead. They not only know two views, but they understand even the evolutionary view better than their cousins who have only one window on the world.

Connected with evolutionism, is the big idea of **uniformitarianism.** That word means that processes now observable in the world have always happened in the same way and at the same rate as today. For instance, if you could have watched the Colorado River eroding its banks as water made its way toward the ocean, before all the dams were built, then that process would tell you how the Grand Canyon was formed— little by little, year after year. You would do your arithmetic and figure just how many millions of years it was.

But creationists allow for **catastrophism** at some points in the world's history. They can consider whether the Grand Canyon might have been formed at some time after the Flood when water trapped in the Great Basin of the West finally broke loose and surged toward the ocean, cutting a deep canyon at a time when the sediments and other materials were softer than now. Evolutionists, who don't like to include catastrophes, must nevertheless say that there must have been a small catastrophe here and another small one there, and there, and all over the globe, in order to explain how fossils were deposited in those places. Creationists can consider whether the great catastrophe of the Flood might account for a good portion of all fossils.

And so it goes. When they try to explain the polar ice caps, the enormous organic deposits of oil, the continental shelves, and other features of our world, the evolutionist tries to find uniformitarian explanations and the creationist is free to also include catastrophic explanations if those fit the facts better. So your children need a good understanding of these two big ideas—uniformitariansm and catastrophism.

Another big idea is **entropy**, the energy that can't be used in a system. In physics, students learn of the second law of thermodynamics, which states how it is impossible to use all the energy in a system; energy is wasted through friction or other means. Perpetual motion machines, then, are impossible. They eventually run out of energy, and stop.

The world as it now stands, under the curse of death, is not a perpetual motion machine either. It is decaying and running down. Many observable and measureable phenomena—the facts of science—fit that view of the world. Evolutionists have to believe the opposite, that things are not running down but are evolving into better forms and better systems. If they could observe and measure such a thing happening, they would have evidence tending to support evolutionism.

These are major big ideas in science for students to be acquainted with and to use in their thinking. Learning big ideas like these is not accomplished by simple vocabulary lessons of memorizing definitions and writing a sentence for each word.

Probably the best learning activity is conversation. Talk about these ideas with your children. Then have them read more in science books, and talk again. Continue this "read and talk" plan with occasional writing assignments added. Children can write paragraphs explaining in their own words things they have read about—how the water cycle works, how it might have worked differently before the Flood, how dinosaurs came to be mostly extinct or how they might have some small-sized descendants yet today.

Balance this "book learning" with some hands-on science of collecting, observing, experimenting and so forth, and you will have as strong a science program as anybody could desire.

Health and Safety

Health and safety are taught far better in the home and family than in the classroom. As a parent you have advantages in most subjects, but in health more than any other. We judge classroom programs to be successful when students learn to eat well, to use seat belts, not to smoke, and so forth. Good habits, attitudes, and behavior in health and safety matters are the objectives, the end result that schools aim for. But in the home, you often have attained those objectives before you start thinking about what to teach in health.

If you ever have to fill out a form where school officials ask how you teach about alcohol or drug abuse or other matters of this kind, you might try saying that you use "total immersion" teaching. This is a technique some educators write about, and, of course, the home is the only place where it can really be done. I don't know how officials would perceive this kind of answer, but I know that homeschooling parents all over the country have clear goals and superb success in teaching many of the health topics that our education bureaucracy is so concerned about today.

To achieve these goals is the reason many parents have decided to homeschool. It seemed foolish to them to send their children into a drug and sex infested atmosphere and then hope that health courses could undo the damage. If education leaders wish to do a better job in health education, they should study the success of homeschoolers, particularly Christian families.

A national task force published their recommendations for state policy makers, and they consist of ten content areas, which together make a comprehensive health education plan. As you look over the topics, you are likely to find that you have already taught well in some of these areas without even thinking of "school" health lessons. The other topics can provide guidelines for future health teaching.

If yours is a structured school, one lesson per week on health is usual, and even that can be skipped when Christmas or other activities become too numerous, because forty periods per year are considered sufficient. The periods range from about thirty minutes for fourth graders to fifty minutes for eighth graders. Instead of one period per week, you could plan a couple of health units during the year between science units. Looking into possible careers in health could be added to several of the topics listed, particularly nutrition, environmental sciences, and research on diseases.

Up-to-date materials for most health topics are available from the Cancer Society, your local hospital or health plan, government publications, magazine articles, and so forth. We are fortunate to be surrounded with encouragement to live a healthy lifestyle. Here are the ten areas to consider teaching.

1. Accident Prevention and Safety. Accidents are the leading cause of death in the school-age population, so children must learn about prevention. They should learn about safety in biking, swimming, hiking, boating and other sports. They should learn about electricity, poisons, knives, fire and all home hazards. They should learn to use seat belts, obey traffic lights and other safety laws. They should learn first aid for bleeding, and older children can learn CPR, and the Heimlich maneuver for choking victims. They should be aware of the symptoms of choking because this can happen to anyone anywhere. They should know how to use emergency phone numbers, and the home should have plans for what to do in case of fire, heart attack and other emergencies. Children who babysit could develop a manual in which they collect all the safety information they may need on a job. It is not too early to teach road courtesy and other attitudes that make driving safer. And, very important, is to develop a general attitude of safety consciousness and avoidance of foolish risk taking.

2. Community Health. Know about local hospitals, clinics, community help for the aged or handicapped or poor. Learn about government health workers, disease prevention efforts, and community health issues. Know of some private organizations like the American Heart Association, the Muscular Dystrophy Association, and local volunteer agencies. The report suggests that students should know where to go when they need help. You may wish to add the other side—that students sometimes should volunteer time or contribute money to a health organization. Older students can investigate career possibilities in community health work.

3. Consumer Health. Recognize advertisers' false claims or appeals to emotions and values in promoting diet aids, skin care and other health products. Identify their techniques in promoting tobacco and alcohol. Become aware of questionable health practices and quackery. Understand about over-the-counter drugs and prescription drugs.

4. Environmental Health. Study pollution, radiation, waste disposal. The recommendations add overpopulation, but some people believe that if we properly take care of God's world it will properly take care of all the people God allows to be born. The problems of crowded populations remain, though, whatever your views on this question. Learn not to litter. Learn how your community ensures safe water supplies and sanitary trash and sewage disposal, how it controls noise pollution. Older children may study what can be done about environmental carcinogens.

5. Family Life Education. On this topic, you probably need no help from the recommendations. What they suggest is investigating the different kinds of "personal life styles individuals may choose," and beginning sex education early. Abortion, birth control, dating, divorce, and other such topics are listed.

6. Mental and Emotional Health. This includes learning to deal with life problems of stress, depression, fatigue, violence, and even suicide. Again, homeschoolers have the best answers. Family environment, especially when schooling is relaxed and informal, is the ideal place for growing children. And the spiritual dimension that homeschoolers can legally include is important for mental and emotional health. You probably already use total immersion teaching for these health matters.

7. Nutrition. The end result desired here is positive nutritional habits and attitudes, but knowledge is necessary, too—knowledge of proteins, carbohydrates, fats, calories, fiber, cholesterol; need of protein to rebuild cells; dangers of too much sugar, salt and fat; ideal weight; effect of diet on teeth, heart attack, cancer and general health. Good information from reliable sources is readily available in our health-conscious society.

8. Personal Health. Learn the structure of the body and

the functions of its parts. Learn that the heart muscle is strengthened by exercise, know the benefits of aerobic and anaerobic exercise, of rest, and of good nutrition. Learn how to care for teeth, skin, hair, eyes, ears. Learn how to avoid obesity, lower back problems and high blood pressure, which are major problems in our society. Each family should add special study of problems of their own—allergy control, blood sugar control, or whatever they might be. Learn about the effects of puberty on development.

9. Disease Prevention and Control. Learn about communicable and noncommunicable diseases, of man's past achievements in conquering some of these by immunizations, pasteurization of milk, improved sanitation, chlorinization of water supply, and antibiotics. Learn that good diet, exercise and not smoking prevents much cancer and heart disease, the greatest killers in our time. Learn of some present-day efforts to conquer disease. In public education, much emphasis is on sexually transmitted diseases of AIDS and others, but families who teach the sure prevention method of sexual abstinence until a person is ready for a faithful, monogamous marriage usually prefer to spend less time thinking about these diseases. It is another of the reasons that people have decided to homeschool.

10. Substance Use and Abuse. These recommendations say "there is a fine line between use and abuse," and "abuse is the escalation of use to the point that the drug interferes with one's economic, social, psychological, or physical well-being." This is another reason for homeschooling; public schools don't teach total abstinence from non-medical drugs and from alcohol and tobacco. Homeschoolers who desire this teach it best by the total immersion method of rearing children in a family with that kind of lifestyle.

18. Music and Art

In curriculum, "the arts" includes music, art, theatre, and dance. The first two—music and art—are almost universally included in schools and the last two are widely neglected. Though there sometimes is talk of dropping the "frills" of music and art when the budget is tight, at least 2000 years of public sentiment and education writings support the arts. You could not find a major education writer or thinker from Plato onward who did not emphasize the importance of the arts in our Western education. The ancient Hebrews also supported musicians and artisans in their culture. People are not fully human without art in their lives.

If your children are talented, you should make special effort to encourage and develop that talent. If they are not, your job is probably more difficult, but just as important. All children of elementary grades should have opportunity to learn the arts. When they are older and begin specializing in their studies, some will bypass most of the art and pursue science or something else, but they must have the basic art education so they know what it is they are choosing or not choosing. They also need this basic education for a richer life. They should gain enough knowledge that they will be able to teach themselves later in life and to participate in church or community music or other groups if they wish.

For any of the four arts there is a simple three-part formula you can follow. Briefly stated, it is:

1. Do it
2. Appreciate it
3. Learn about it.

All the parts intertwine. You can't emphasize one of these aspects without the children advancing on the others also. But if you keep in mind the three-pronged approach and avoid spending all your time in one emphasis, you will have a good, balanced art education program.

Churches and the Arts

With Christians, conscience often forbids some of the arts. If that is your case, teach what you do approve of and you will be contributing to raising standards in the arts.

We might wonder whether so many Christians would be against dancing if former generations had taught it with high standards and had not let it degenerate into mostly social dancing or night club dancing with their accompanying evils. What sort of dance did David perform before the Lord as the ark was brought home? What about the dancing women who welcomed victorious David home from the wars? What joyful harvest dances did the farm girls perform from even earlier times? Our culture has lost those, and we have lost any thought of dancing before the Lord (except for some liberal churches).

If we don't strive for high standards in music, we may someday be in the same situation with this art. It will become so degenerate that parents will warn their children against music the way some now warn their children against dancing.

Christians should be the most creative people and lead the way in music, but unfortunately a good many today are imitating instead of leading, so you can hardly tell Christian music from the world's cheap music.

"But isn't it snobbish," some ask, "to think that your kind of music is better than my kind? Who set you as a judge?" When you're thinking straight and not under the brainwashing influence of today's "no value" society, you have to answer that of course some music is better than other music. And who can judge? Those who have education enough in music to be able to judge. Those who know the most can judge the best. What the church badly needs today is a whole generation of people well-educated in music. Tomorrow's performers and listeners and creators all need this education.

Drama in the church could be improved too. Few churches buy plays, so not many publishers and not many good writers are attracted to this work, and most plays now available are mediocre at best. Many a church has performed one of these plays and then decided they would try writing their own for next Easter or next time, whenever that is. This is a healthy reaction to mediocre quality.

It would enrich us all if some of today's students become interested in drama and someday write good plays. While we wait for that, hopefully more churches will become interested so there will be market enough that publishers can afford to put out the new and better plays. Also hopefully church people will become more educated about the ethics of copyright law and realize that they should buy copies enough for the whole cast instead of buying one copy and illegally photocopying the rest. Often those photocopies cost just as much as the printed copies would, and the money has gone to Xerox and Weyerhauser instead of to the Christian publisher and to the writer's royalties. We must pay our playwrights if we hope to have good playwrights. The same is true of our composers and other artists and writers.

Listening to Music

Even if you feel you know nothing about music, you can begin by teaching your children to *listen*. Much of our society seems designed to teach us *not* to listen. Music is in the background while we shop or while we eat. TV sets are on while people talk and go about whatever they do in their homes. TV programs themselves have music behind practically everything. The organ even plays while the pastor prays. Everything conspires to teach us to screen out music sounds. We learn not to listen instead of learning to listen with concentration.

Have you ever attended an amateur travelog where the traveler plays a music tape as background noise for his talk? Most people at such a gathering, having spent their lives learning not to listen to music, would ignore it and listen only to the narration, but one or two music appreciators present (like me) would have a mental battle trying to hear the narration but not being able to ignore the music.

This ignoring of music may be an American peculiarity. I was talking with a friend, a science fiction fan and also a music appreciator, about this matter when suddenly a light went on in his head. "Oh," he said, "that may be why I like watching British science fiction better than things like Star Trek. The British don't have music going on with theirs."

This bombarding of the senses with stimuli was supposed to be a way of speeding up and of strengthening learning. The books say to use the "eye gate" and the "ear gate" as routes to learning, and in our American way we decided more was better. Why not several pictures at once, and why not speech and music at once? We tried to push learning through the gates by complex multi-media presentations. What we forgot was that all gates lead to the brain, and the brain is where learning happens.

Instead of better learning, we accomplished "sensory overload." And people cope as best they can by practicing a technique of screening out the excess stimuli. Homeschooling families have a unique opportunity to raise children in a quiet, unstressful atmosphere in which they can develop powers of intense concentration—powers that many students seldom or never experience.

For music, you can begin by helping children listen to music you especially enjoy. That way you can point out to them certain features that attracted you to the music—the rhythm, the busy violins, the high or low singing voices, the melody, and so forth. By listening repeatedly to certain pieces of music, children develop skill in hearing more than at first. They learn to find not only the melody, but various other things going on with non-melody parts. They learn to recognize different kinds of instrument sounds, identify whether a bass or tenor is singing, whether a solo instrument or a whole orchestra section is playing a particular part, and so on.

This is part 2 of the formula given earlier—appreciating music. The more children know about the music they listen to, the more interesting it becomes. Over the months and years, as they proceed with part 3, learning about music, they can begin to use technical language in telling what they hear or what they like in various pieces of music. They may talk about the crescendos or the tempos, and later on, even things like the rondo section, or the minor mode.

If you're a music appreciator yourself, you can just continue teaching the children what you know. But if your own music education has been neglected and you want your children to have better, then you can branch out from the familiar music. Try a piano concerto, a symphony, symphonies by different composers. Try folk music, Negro spirituals, Spanish music, Irish songs, marching band music. Children can't learn everything, but they should become able to identify some types and some historic period music.

You can intersperse music through a day by playing it as accompaniment for jumping rope or other aerobic exercises.

These are types of "dancing" that no one seems to object to, and they do not interfere with listening to music, as the eye and ear problems mentioned earlier. On the contrary, they enhance it, since children actively interpret the rhythm and other features as they listen. It is toe tapping extended to more of the body. After children learn some basic aerobic movements, they can create patterns of movements to go with certain pieces of music. A bonus of one or more short aerobic periods in the day is that children can return to arithmetic or science with invigorated brains.

Making Music

Singing. By fourth grade, children should be able to sing in tune. If yours cannot do so yet, this is the first skill to develop. Give them practice in listening to single tones and to short phrases and matching them. See that they learn from memory several simple songs and can carry the tunes all the way through. When children cannot do this, it may be that they cannot yet match the pitches well or it may be simply that they have not learned a particular tune and are making up their own. In both cases they need practice. Some children enjoy learning to whistle. The beginning stages of whistling are difficult and require much concentration and listening to pitches.

Choirs and singing groups for children should be run with the philosophy that the children's music education has first priority and their performances have second priority. In other words, the choirs should not be primarily for performing at church or parents' meetings or in contests or anyplace. Every meeting and practice of the groups should have some time allotted to teaching children how to use their voices and how to read music. Then the choirs can spend the remaining time practicing these skills as they prepare music for performance.

It is necessary, then, to buy music for children's singing

groups. You cannot just hand them photocopied words, have them memorize the tunes, and then perform the music thus learned. Too many of our children grow up in Sunday schools and youth groups doing just that, and they miss all those years of music reading practice.

Maybe homeschooling families can join together occasionally and sing, from books. The ones among you who know the most about music can teach bits of music reading and some ear training, to learn how to jump from do to mi, for instance. There is no quick route to reading music, just as there was no quick route to reading words. It grows bit by bit with practice. At first children can learn that when the notes are higher on the staff they sing higher tones; and when the notes go down they go down. Gradually they can refine their knowledge and skill. If you need a mother who knows more than you do about all this, find one and talk her into joining your group. You probably have a skill you can offer her in return. You need no piano or other accompaniment in these groups, because you're going to learn to read music, not to follow a piano. Children should use their light singing voices and not be urged to shout "louder," as enthusiastic song leaders sometimes do. Balance the hard work of figuring out new songs with the enjoyment of familiar songs. Families may sometimes share solos or duets they have prepared, and keep the meeting time short—certainly under the fifty minute period that eighth graders would have in school. Regular group singing like this, or regular family singing, will grow a generation comfortable with music and able to take advanced training or sing difficult music in the choirs they may later wish to join.

Recorders. Beginning at about fourth grade, children can learn to play musical instruments. For family use, the inexpensive beginner instruments can be a lot of fun. Most commonly used today are recorders, wind instruments which require players to blow air through an end mouthpiece and to cover holes with their fingers. These come in different sizes—soprano, alto, tenor and bass. Inexpensive plastic recorders cost less than $10, at this writing, and wooden ones cost somewhat more. Children are generally happy with the plastic recorders, but adults notice the mellower tone of wooden ones and prefer to use those.

Wooden recorders are not toy instruments, but genuine flute instruments with a history that reaches back for many centuries. In the Middle Ages these end-blown instruments were called "flutes," but in fourteenth century England they came to be called "recorders" and were very popular. They went out of fashion when the side-blown flute was invented, but our century has brought them back into fashion again. Some musicians form ensembles of recorders, harpsichords and other old instruments, to play music from the Middle Ages, folk music, and other compositions that particularly fit these instruments. Schools use them by the thousands as pre-band training for children. It is easy to switch from recorders to flutes, piccolos, clarinets, oboes and bassoons.

When you purchase recorders you will probably get instruction booklets with them, or at least you can obtain beginner books from the music store. By following the instructions carefully, you could be playing simple songs by about the second day.

As you learn songs, you are learning to read music, too. If you get an instrument for each family member or at least for a couple of your children and a couple of neighbor children, you can have a recorder choir. This is not for only musically talented children, but is something that practically every fourth grader and older child can do. At the beginning of a school year you can visit a music store, look at catalogs, find out prices, decide on instruments, and earn money. Sometime in October you can get the instruments and begin learning together. And by Christmas the choir can play in a program, playing both alto and soprano parts of Christmas carols. Parents can be in the ensemble along with the children.

If you know very little about music yourself, you should use only soprano recorders so everyone in your group is playing the same notes the same way. Adding alto and other size recorders involves transposing to prepare music that everyone can play together. If you understand music well enough to do that, then you could help other families by preparing such a book of hymns and other songs. Advertise your book in parent magazines or homeschooling magazines, and you may soon have a sideline business for your family.

With soprano recorders, spend a lot of time at first playing songs only in the key of C—with no sharps or flats. "Joy to the World" usually is written in D, with two sharps, but someone in the family may be able to rewrite it in the key of C by making every note just one position lower. If you're afraid of this job, try asking a musical friend to do it or to show you or one of your children how to do it. This is wonderful note-reading practice for whoever does the writing.

Try humming the first line of that carol: "Joy to the world! the Lord is come." Did you notice that it simply runs down the scale? It begins on a high C and note-by-note steps down the scale until it reaches middle C. The rest of the melody also proceeds mostly in scalewise steps either up or down, with very few jumps between notes. Thus as soon as your choir members can play a C scale they can tackle this melody. Later, the more advanced note readers can try playing the alto part.

"The First Noel" has a similar melody, moving up and down in scalewise steps. It too may have to be transposed from the key of D into C for your beginner choir.

Next in difficulty could be "While Shepherds Watched Their Flocks." This also must be transposed from D to C. While its melody contains many scalewise steps, it has more jumps than the other two carols, and it adds a new note because it reaches above the high C in two places.

"Silent Night" can often be found in the key of C. Its melody has both steps and jumps, and it adds three new notes above the high C.

Once your choir is this far along, they can probably play many songs in the key of C, each song being easier to learn than the one before. After a time they should try songs with one sharp (key of G) and one flat (key of F). And if they keep playing all year they can add more sharps and flats. But take it slowly enough that the children don't get confused.

Chording Instruments.   When children's hands are not yet large enough for guitars, try the ukulele. The ukulele has only four strings, instead of six as on a guitar. Somebody in the family will have to be able to tune the ukulele for children who are just starting to learn. A beginning instruction book will tell you what note each string should match, and you can tighten each string until it matches that note on a piano or recorder or pitch pipe.

With only one finger of the left hand on a string, a child can play a D chord, and with only two fingers he can play a G chord. An instruction book will show diagrams of exactly where to place the fingers. The right hand strums across the strings. The child should practice four strums on G, then four on D, four on G, and so on. When he is able to change chords smoothly, without losing a beat, he can begin chording for the song "Nothing But the Blood" while he sings or other family members join in singing.

G
What can wash away my sin?

                 D G
Nothing but the blood of Je-sus;

What can make me whole again?

                 D G
Nothing but the blood of Je-sus.

Oh, precious is the flow

D   G
That makes me white as snow;

No other fount I know,

                          D G
Nothing but the blood of Je-sus.

Children who play melody instruments can learn this song and play along with the ukulele, to form an ensemble with both melody and chords. Though the song has one sharp (F#), this note never appears in the melody line, so beginners who have not yet learned any sharps can play this.

Some children may be able to learn the C chord next, and with the three chords G, C, and D they will be able to play many songs written in the key of G (those with one sharp). But the C chord is more difficult than the other two. So another next move could be to learn the A chord. With chords D, G, and A they could play many songs written in the key of D (those with two sharps).

An instruction book should help children move along slowly like this. The idea is to be able to play many songs and not have to learn too many chords while they are young. If you wish the children to play hymns, you can write chord names above the words in a hymn book. Or if you can't do this yet, ask a musical friend to write them for you. Songs with repetitious phrases will be the easiest for children to learn.

An alternate to the regular ukulele for beginners is a baritone ukulele. It has four strings which are the same tones as the four highest pitched strings of a guitar, so transfering to a guitar later will be simpler. If your family owns a guitar, a beginner may start by just playing on the four highest-pitched strings. In this case, play "Nothing But the Blood" in the key of C. Change each G in the song above to C and each D to G. The song will be pitched several notes lower and be easier for many people to sing.

Creating Music. Young children and older children often make up songs of their own. If this happens in your house, don't be like the teacher who said, "Okay. Now we're going to sing some real songs." What song could be more real than the one a child just made up? Be an audience when children want one. Help them write their songs, so as to keep from losing or forgetting them.

Children should be encouraged not only to try totally new songs, but also variations of songs they know. One idea is to ask children to play "Twinkle, Twinkle Little Star," making it sound as happy as they can. Then see what other ways they can play it. Sad? Sleepy? For marching? After having fun with this, they can listen to the second movement of Haydn's "Surprise Symphony."

Learning About Music

There is logic behind the system of scales and chords in music, and you may know more of this than you realize. If you have taken piano lessons or studied music in other ways, you know plenty of music theory to teach your children who are starting out. Begin by teaching them what you know.

For some reason in our society we have perceived music and art to be mystical areas that only certain priests who are initiated into the elect inner circles can teach the rest of us. And we have thought that music must be learned by individual tutoring (music lessons), whereas practically everything else can be learned in groups or from books or by other means.

But it doesn't. Once you decide that your family can learn music just as well as anything else they want to learn, you are over the first hurdle. Proceed with singing and playing simple songs and clear as many more hurdles as your time and interest take you.

While following instruction books and playing songs, children will be learning to read music, bit-by-bit as they go along. It is after they have experience with making music that you will have the most success teaching how scales and chords are built. Have a child play "Joy to the world! the Lord is come" on his recorder and then show on a piano how the same tune can be played by going down the scale from C to C. This gives the child a better picture of a scale, and it's far more effective than if you had tried to teach scales and note reading and other theory before you let him play songs.

A preacher and evangelist friend of mine played guitar and sang solos for many years, and was considered by many to be a professional musician. One day he asked me questions about music, so we sat for a few moments at a piano and I showed him there what was happening with the chords he played on the guitar, how they were arranged logically and mathematically. He said, "You know, I have learned more about music in these five minutes than I have in all my years of guitar playing."

That, of course, wasn't strictly true, but concerning the logical arrangement of chords it may have been. You can learn this in a few moments too. And then you can teach your children, not in five minutes, but as they are able to understand. And it is much easier to understand if they already play an instrument, as my preacher friend did.

Scales. A piano keyboard with its white and black keys is the best place to get a visual image of scales and chords. So sit at a piano and find C. If you don't know even that much then it will take you a few more than five minutes, but ask somebody where C is. It's the white note just below the two black notes. Play the C. The next higher white note is D, the next E, then F, then G. Play them from C to G. That's as far in the alphabet as music goes. The next note is A, then B, then you reach another C. Play all the way from C to C. It should sound like do, re, mi, fa, sol, la, ti, do. That is the C scale.

Now compare the first four notes and the last four notes.

Both sets have the same pattern, which is: whole step, whole step, half step. That is, C and D have a whole step between them, D and E have a whole step between them, but E and F have only a half step. This is quite obvious on the keyboard because there is no black note between E and F, while there are black notes between the others. When you sing "do, re, mi, fa," you just naturally make a half step between mi and fa. It wouldn't sound right if you sang it any other way.

Start with G and play the upper four notes of the scale and notice the same pattern of whole step, whole step, half step. When you sing the scale, you also naturally make a half step between ti and do.

Thus in a full scale, you make half steps after mi and ti. To explain this with numbers, we could say that there are half steps after the third and the seventh notes of the scale. You can think with numbers or with do, re, mi syllables, whichever you feel most comfortable with. Just get the picture of where the half steps are. Try to see two groups of four notes with the same pattern of steps in each group. There is a whole step, also, between the two groups.

That's all you need to know about what is called a major scale. With that picture of the C scale, you can figure out any other major scale that you want to.

For example, start on G and play four notes: do, re, mi, fa. So far, so good. The whole steps and half steps fell in the right places as long as you stayed on the white notes. Now move on to sol, la, ti, do and you find a problem with ti, or the note of F. To get a half step between F and G, you have to sharp the F. That is, you have to play the black note above it. Once you get the scale figured out, play it all from G to G remembering to sharp the F. See if it sounds right.

After you have figured out that the G scale has an F sharp in it, you know that the "key of G" has an F sharp (F#). If your young ukulele player has learned to play in the key of G, then he can look through song books for songs that have only one sharp shown at the beginning of the staff. It will be F# and it will indicate that the song is in the key of G.

All the other scales can be figured out in the same way. Sometimes to get the whole steps and half steps to come out right you have to flat a note. That is, you have to play the black note just *below* a white note. (Try making a scale from F to F.)

At first it's hard to remember what sharps and flats are found in each scale, but in this lesson you can learn that each scale is arranged in the same pattern as described above. And as you practice songs written in more of the scales, you gradually get used to them.

Chords. As with the scales, it is easy to begin with C, and it is easy to see the patterns if you use a piano keyboard. Look at the scale from C to C. Play it.

Now, the most important chords begin on notes 1, 4, and 5 of the scale. Or if you think syllables, they begin on do, fa, and sol. In this scale, those notes are C, F, and G.

Play the C chord first. Place your thumb on C, your middle finger two notes up, and your little finger two notes up from that. In other words, you play alternate notes—every other note. To make it sound like a chord, play all three notes at once.

Now lift up your hand, move to F and play a three-note chord in the same way. Move your hand to G and play a three-note chord there. To sound finished, you can move on up to the higher C and play a chord there.

Done? You have played the chords in the key of C. That's all there is to it. The only thing to remember is that you start the chords on notes 1, 4, and 5 of the scale. With that pattern in mind, you can figure out the chords in any other key.

In the key of G, for instance, you might first play the scale to get the picture of that key again, remembering to sharp the F. Now figure out which are the first, fourth, and fifth notes of the scale and that is where you build the three chords. In one of the chords you will come to F and must remember to sharp it.

In these sections we have looked at these basic patterns of scales and chords.

Scale: made of two sets of four notes, each set with the pattern of whole step, whole step, half step.
Chords: built on notes 1, 4, and 5 of each scale.

This basic information can take your children a long way in music. A lot of other information that they find in music books should fall into place in this framework. For instance, if a book explains about the "key signature" at the beginning of each song, they can see that it is telling how many sharps or flats are in the scale used for that song. They can learn little memory tricks along the way; they will learn to play better in some keys than in others; they will learn more complicated information about chords; but it is all mathematical and logical. This framework helps them start.

I worry that some people at this point will have children memorize the above definitions or patterns of scales and chords and then figure the job is done, but that's not what I'm getting at here. To really learn chords, students need to spend time playing around with them, getting used to their feel and their sounds. One of my sons, experimented with rhythmic patterns as he played chords. He liked the sounds, so the experiments expanded—to more complex rhythms, to both hands, all over the piano, louder and louder. The rest of us thought we should put up with it because it was so "creative." Later he began singing his own melodies and words to the accompaniments of either guitar or piano, his practiced ear helping him choose chords to fit. This home-learned music carried him to quite advanced levels of composing and theory, and in college he could skip beginning theory and take an advanced class—once he convinced skeptical professors he could do it.

Every child, of course, will not carry an elementary music education that far (some may go farther and make music a life work), but all children ought to have as many opportunities presented to them as can be managed in the few short years we have them in our homes. And you never can be sure which of the opportunities a particular child will run away with. One girl's parents took her to a neighborhood park and introduced her to tennis, which was about all they could do as their own tennis was quite unskilled. But that girl went on to win championships. A boy was allowed to sketch horses by the thousands, and he became one of the West's great artists.

Every child should experience the arts enough that they enter into the kind of thinking that only the arts provide. So avoid turning your arts teaching into simple verbalizing of things like what a chord is.

Appreciating Art

This aspect of children's education not only means learning to view Renaissance paintings; it enters daily life. How we decorate our homes, where we plant flowers, what color clothing we wear, and other daily decisions all involve awareness of art principles. Your children will learn much just from hearing you try to decide about new curtains or paint color. In one family a member drew an outline of the exterior of their house, they made numerous photocopies, and then everyone experimented with coloring them. They judged and discussed among themselves, hung favorite colorings on the wall and lived with them awhile, then talked some more. At last they agreed on what colors to paint the exterior of the house, and they were happy for many years with their decision.

But art appreciation usually conjures up visions of setting before children some of the great paintings and sculptures of the past. Is this necessary? Practically anyone who thinks about this at all agrees that, yes, it is necessary. Children must have some exposure to this record of our human past. It is at least as important as learning about kings and kingdoms of the past. Great paintings, like great music, are part of our common culture. They are part of the core that educated people enjoy and share and through which we all gain deeper understanding of human possibilities in this world.

Considerable experimenting is now going on in schools as art educators search for ways to help children "see" art. This is similar to the listening problem discussed in an earlier section on music. If people glance at a painting and dismiss it as bad art or as not delivering immediate satisfaction, these educators say that shallow looking may be to blame.

One teacher held up a print of a painting called "The Giant" by N. C. Wyeth in which children are playing on the beach at the feet of a cloud giant. "I see a man," said one of the children. "What made you look up there?" asked the teacher. And they all examined the way the artist used lines to draw his viewers' eyes up to the cloud.

A print of Winslow Homer's showed children playing Red Rover in front of a mountain schoolhouse. In this painting all the lines seemed to be horizontal—the mountains, the children's outstretched arms—and the lines drew everyone's eyes to the schoolhouse. A child pointed out the shadow lines at the feet of the Red Rover players, and the teacher knew that her children were catching on. They were beginning to see deeply instead of shallowly.

Elements to see, besides line, are: color, value or intensity, shape, texture. Some principles of design to see are: repetition, contrast, rhythm, balance, space, and variations. And of course the main element to see is the subject matter (landscape, battle scene, etc.), and the ideas or sometimes symbolism or allegory portrayed. One of the new experimenting groups has suggested that instead of beginning with standard elements and principles of art, we could try helping children notice "aesthetic effects" that an artist wants to portray: suprise, motion (or lack of it), mood, and personality.

I can remember the mood of a painting that hung at the front of my classroom all through sixth grade. I'm afraid to guess how many hours I looked past the teacher and was lost in the painting instead. We talked about it once, but I have forgotten its name. It was probably a medieval theme of some kind, as it showed nymphs dancing in a forest. I'm sure its mood added to my already strong love for forests. Many a day after school I wandered about in our woods with that picture in my head, and the woods seemed a very romantic place to be.

What the new art education is telling us to do is to help children see deeply the pictures themselves. Memorizing the names of Michelangelo, Rembrandt, and Grandma Moses is not exactly of first importance. What we want is for children to use their minds in a kind of thinking that they don't experience while practicing subtraction or learning the past tense of verbs. Howard Gardner at Harvard says that if we omit the arts from the curriculum "we are in effect shortchanging the mind." Others have commented that arts do more than exercise the hands and heart; they exercise the mind as well. Art is essential for the intellectual development of all children—those who are talented, and those who wander in the woods instead of drawing the woods.

Doing Art

As a young teacher I kept myself busy scrounging through books and teachers' magazines to find art ideas. I thought I had to have something different for children to make in each art class. But one year I discovered a better way. I arranged the system so the children could get out paints and clean up and the housekeeping would flow smoothly enough that I could live with it, and for weeks on end they painted and painted and painted. Instead of tiring of it, they became more interested. They taught themselves a lot and once in a while I taught them something too.

Later in the year we switched to charcoal and worked on still life and trees, and light and shadow, and a few more weeks happily passed. Now I read an art educator saying that children need time to learn to use a material with a sense of control and imagination. In music children wouldn't try the violin one week, drums the second, and clarinet the third, he says. By that method they would never develop any competence or mastery or ability to use the instrument for artistic expression. In art we shouldn't shift material on a weekly basis either.

It's not only the material that shouldn't be shifted, but also the subject matter. The boy who sketched horses in his childhood later drew horses as skeletons, then with muscles and sinews, and in every conceivable position. He learned to see horses possibly better than anyone alive. Most young children start out that way. They learn to draw, say, a house with a tree and a flower beside it and the sun in the sky, and if they have time and materials they will practice these by the dozens.

Older children can learn to build on their drawing hobbies and teach themselves or learn from books or other people how to do something better. A girl who climbed trees a lot, saw in her head trees with every twig attached to a small branch and every small branch attached to a larger branch, and so forth. So the trees in her pictures were drawn that way. Then one day she watched an artist on public television demonstrate how to paint trees. A few deft strokes of his brush, and he had a whole hillside full of trees. Then a bit of brown here and there supplied them with trunks. A teacher showed her that she could try things like that even without paints like the artist had. If she peeled paper off some crayon pieces and drew with their sides instead of their pointed ends, she could have a tree trunk growing with one or two upward strokes of a brown crayon. And the side of a green crayon could be swirled around to make the billowy tops of deciduous trees. Or a little more control with smaller and darker green could make evergreens above the trunks.

In one family the children learned how to set a point beyond the edge of a picture and then draw the two sides of a road or of railroad tracks aiming toward that point. They were delighted with the "perspective" of distance that resulted, and they produced dozens of road pictures while practicing that skill.

Many art books are available which teach such techniques of drawing and painting, as well as crafts. Also, there are beautiful books and print reproductions which teach about great artists and their masterpieces. Home school suppliers and other book catalogs often carry an excellent selection of such materials.

Learning About Art

With both music and art, children should gain some historical view. They should learn to recognize types such as Indian art, ancient Egyptian art, or early Christian art; and they should know some famous artists and their works, particularly in our Western culture. When this study is balanced with children's own experimenting and thinking as they "do" art, they will see more in the historic art. After children have worked on trees, for instance, they will observe more keenly the various ways that artists handle trees. After they have worked on perspective, they will be more aware of this feature and of various techniques by which artists achieve good perspective. Thus, learning about artists and their work can be, and should be, an exercise in thinking, and not only a memory task.

If a student becomes serious about studying art or music of the past, this can become a "posthole" into history. Postholes are explained in the history chapter in connection with economics, culture, and some other broad topics. But a specialized post of just art history, if a student is interested in that, can work well too. Students might learn about the art and pyramids and temples of the ancient empires, architecture of the Greeks and Romans, and some early Christian and Italian

Renaissance paintings, and with these they have a post passing through much of our ancient Western history. Then when they read of Renaissance scientists or Greek philosphers or anything else in those periods of history, they are not so lost in time. They can tie these other learnings to their art post.

And for students not that serious about art history, a taste of it is important anyway. You should include some attention to art in most history units that your family undertakes. Study more than the tyrants and wars of the past. Enjoy the best of civilization. Enjoy music and art.

19. The Bible

The Bible is important in Western civilization and thought. Literature teachers, history teachers, science teachers and others cannot ignore it. Northrup Frye, a great literature professor wrote, "Why does this huge, sprawling, tactless book sit there inscrutably in the middle of our cultural heritage like the 'great Boyg' ... frustrating all our efforts to walk around it?"[1] Your children will be better educated, they will understand their world more fully, if you don't try to walk around the Bible.

The ancient Hebrews used the Bible as the core of their education. The pagan Greeks developed their own core. At first they taught only Homer, Hesiod, Aesop, and popular sayings, because those were the only Greek writings available when, because of their emerging commercial state, the Athenians added reading and writing to the former curriculum, which had produced warriors and worshipers of the Greek gods. Reading and writing, then, were taught through study of Homer and the other poets.

Soon the Greeks realized that their poets provided them

with more than clerks and scribes to keep business records. Since all pupils studied the same content, the Greeks had a "core" curriculum, a body of knowledge common to all educated Greeks. This gave them a foundation for Greek cohesiveness, a consciousness of nationality and community among Greeks. As time went on, the Greeks obtained more kinds of learning from the poets, until they developed a rounded education combining artistic, aesthetic, patriotic, religious, ethical, and intellectual elements.

Educators have been searching for such a core ever since. For a time in America we came close to having it. At least as we nostalgically look backward, we think we did. Our first schools had Christian beginnings where the Bible and biblical values were emphasized, and much of our national history was intertwined with Christianity. National songs and Christian hymns sometimes were indistinguishable from each other. Thus when children studied American history, read from American schoolbooks and early American authors, and learned the Bible, it was one cohesive whole. Furthermore, all students shared that common core of knowledge, so it provided for us the kind of national unity that the Greeks had.

Agreeing on core literature and core history knowledge is more difficult for us than for the Greeks because we have hundreds of thousands more books to choose from. No two people would make the same core list of either literature or historic events, but on more lists than any other would appear the Bible. That huge, sprawling book has influenced Western civilization so profoundly that no Western child can be educated without it.

Christians have religious reasons for teaching the Bible, and those they handle well in their homes and Sunday schools and camps. Jews, too, teach the Bible for religious reasons. These reasons are first in importance for such people. But here we look at other reasons why the Bible should be included in curriculum for all children.

The Bible as Literature

Literature professionals use the word *myth* to mean a traditional story of unknown authorship which explains some phenomenon of nature such as the origin of man. They say myth does not refer to the truth or falsity of a story; it simply refers to the story's content and its old and unknown authorship. The Greeks and other ancients had their myths of how the world and mankind began, and we have ours, they say. And the mythology of a people is central to their education. We ordinary people use another dictionary meaning of *myth*, which is "a fictitious story." So if we believe the Bible story is true, we don't like it being classified as the mythology of our times. We would prefer that evolution be called the mythology of our times.

Why is the mythology of a people, true or not, central in their education? Because it is their beliefs concerning the all-time great questions of man—his origins, his reason for being here, the doings of his gods and heroes. These beliefs affect the literature and the politics and history of a people, and it is folly to study literature or history without the roots which underlie them.

This is the predicament of people who wish to remove the Bible from curriculum. The Bible is not simply the religious book of a minority who call themselves Christians and who should not impose their book on the rest of society. The Bible permeates our greatest literature. If ever there was a ready-made core for literature, this is it.

Northrup Frye said it beautifully, if you can overlook his use of the word *myth*.

The most complete form of this myth is given in the Christian Bible, and so the Bible forms the lowest stratum in the teaching of literature. It should be taught so early and so thoroughly that it sinks straight to the bottom of the mind, where everything that comes along

later can settle on it. That, I am aware, is a highly controversial statement, and can be misunderstood in all kinds
of ways, so please remember that I'm speaking as a
literary critic about the teaching of literature. There are
all sorts of secondary reasons for teaching the Bible as
literature: the fact that it's so endlessly quoted from and
alluded to, the fact that the cadences and phrases of the
King James translation are built into our minds and way
of thought, the fact that it's full of the greatest and best
known stories we have, and so on. There are also the
moral and religious reasons for its importance, which
are different reasons. But in the particular context in
which I'm speaking now, it's the total shape and structure of the Bible which is most important: the fact that
it's a continuous narrative beginning with the creation
and ending with the Last Judgment, and surveying the
whole history of mankind . . . in between."[2]

The Bible is to American education what Homer was to
Athenian education. It is our classic, the core. Scholars, critics,
and teachers of literature—those who spend their lives
immersed in it—see in literature an overriding theme, which is
THE story of mankind. In this theme, man once lived in a
"Golden Age"—in the garden of Eden, or Hesperides, or
Atlantis—but that happy world was lost and man hopes to get it
back again. Within that framework is THE hero who has adventures, dies or disappears, and then is resurrected and/or
married to his waiting bride.

Collectors have found 345 versions of the tale of Cinderella.
People familiar with the Bible can easily see this spiritual
analogy: the bride is clothed in garments not her own and the
king's son comes to claim her for himself. In the Russian version, the family goes off to mass rather than to a ball, thus connecting the story more closely with religious beliefs. In the
German version, doves alight upon the shoulders of Cinderella

and attest that she is the true bride. In the Irish version, the prince must fight and his blood is shed before he wins the bride.

Connecting such tales with the original true story is not a far-out exercise of professors; it is simply common sense. I once had occasion to notice the making of a legend in only seven years' time. In the Alaska Room of the Anchorage library, I read of a missionary who passed through a certain coastal village shortly after the United States bought the territory from the Russians. He told of holding some preaching meetings there. In another document I read of another white man passing through the same village a few years later. He wrote of a strange native legend, in which a man comes down from the sky and captures a bride to take back to the sky with him. Any person who has heard evangelists preach of Christ returning for His "Bride" has no trouble reading between the lines of these two reports.

In the same manner, pagan tales can be seen to have their origins in the early history of our world as told in the Bible. Preflood giants were monstrous figures largely responsible for God's decision to destroy mankind; and their memory could well be preserved in pagan tales of the doings of heroes and gods. Satanic worship flourished in the time of Babel so that God intervened again, this time to confound the language, which is certainly a more traumatic event in the history of man and his thinking than we can imagine. In the degenerated languages, ancient pagan tales survive as a hazy memory of that early world.

Genesis 3:15 is a statement of THE story of mankind that scholars have detected in literature: man's paradise is lost, he now is in conflict with his environment, and he hopes to regain his lost identity. God is talking to Satan:

> And I will put enmity between you and the woman, and between your seed and her seed; it shall bruise your head, and you shall bruise his heel.

In this passage, we are introduced to the main characters—the hero, the antihero, and the woman—all three of whom figure prominently in pagan myths. Achilles, vulnerable only in his heel, is an obvious example.

Children can memorize this story of the world and let it sink to the bottom of their minds along with other Bible stories. Then subsequent learning can settle on top, and both it and the original framework will become more meaningful as years go by.

Within the framework, arise the romance, tragedy, comedy and satire of fiction works throughout history. But in modern literature we seldom find the vision of regaining paradise. Writers are stuck in the conflict portion of the story. Literature books say they write about "the human condition." Man is in a wretched state, at odds with his environment. Sometimes he acts heroically, nevertheless, but often his very existence seems absurd to the non-believer.

This explains why some literature seems depressing to Christians, who, while they know that man is fallen and in a state of sin, live with the hope of regaining paradise. If you and your children choose not to wallow around in the mood portrayed by writers who are stuck in the middle part of man's story, there is no reason why you should, even if one of these selections is in your literature book, and even if the author is a "great" writer. There is plenty of literature to select from, plenty to enrich your children's lives and develop their minds.

Stories. In teaching the Bible as literature, begin by simply teaching the Bible stories. It is important to know the stories of Adam and Eve, Noah, Moses, David, Elijah, Peter and others, and of Jesus. Don't worry about having "scientific" teaching methods. Far too much has been written about the need for visual aids and certain kinds of lesson plans, and most of it is myth, in our everyday meaning of the word.

A function of literature is to develop the imagination, and

constant use of visual aids is a hindrance to this. *Imagination* is another troublesome word because of its multiple meanings. One meaning is "a foolish notion or empty fancy," but that is not what we mean here. Other meanings refer to our God-given power of forming mental images of that which is not present, or of that which we have never experienced (angels, for instance), or of creating new images by combining previous experiences (creativity). Still another meaning refers to the ability to appreciate the creative imaginations of others through their works of art.

The time-honored way to pass on stories is by telling or reading them to children and, after the age of the printing press, giving children storybooks to read. If you enjoy the art of telling flannelgraph stories or of using puppets for stories, by all means use your art and skill. But if that is not your talent, be encouraged by the viewpoint of master storytellers who insist that words are their medium, not pictures. Trust the words, they say. Do not introduce confusion into children's minds by expecting them to watch you, listen to your words, follow the story, and at the same time watch a flannelboard to see what someone else thinks a happening looks like. Any particular picture may be entirely different from the one the child is imaging internally. Pictures are fine in their place, say storytellers, but not while children are caught up in a story experience.

One father, at the dinner table each evening, is going through the Bible with his family. He feels that reading the words directly from an adult Bible might not be meaningful enough for the younger children, so he developed a technique of looking at a passage and telling what happens, in his own words made up on the spot. This is not artistic, not scientific, not anything to write books about, but a natural way for this man to pass on stories to his children. If you could visit and ask the children, "What happened in yesterday's story?" they would give you a perfectly satisfactory answer. They like listening to stories from their father.

A good use for flannelgraph and puppets and the like is to let children use them. They can develop speaking skills and storytelling art by presenting favorite Bible stories with these props. They also may "play" the stories, either for an audience or in the more informal way they played House when they were younger children. They may illustrate stories with their own pictures arranged in picture book form along with their rewriting of a story, or in wall-hanging form for their bedrooms or the family bulletin board. All such activities strengthen children's learning and help them experience the stories more fully.

Epigrams. Besides stories, there are a variety of literary forms and techniques in the Bible which children can begin to learn. One of these is the epigram, or the saying. The early Athenians used sayings, along with Homer, for educating their children. In our society, we use sayings informally in our homes, but we haven't made much use of them formally in our schools. Many of us tell our children "An ounce of prevention is worth a pound of cure," or "Thirty days hath September . . ."

An epigram is a brief poem or terse statement, and usually contains opposites or contrasts. In the above examples, an ounce is contrasted with a pound and the months with thirty days contrasted with those not having thirty days. Jesus used epigrams in His teaching: "Render to Caesar the things that are Caesar's, and to God the things that are God's"; "Freely you have received, freely give"; "It is more blessed to give than to receive." Solomon used epigrams to teach his son—and all of us: "Go to the ant, you sluggard; consider her ways, and be wise"; "A wise son makes a glad father: but a foolish son is the heaviness of his mother."

If you encourage your children to memorize these and other Bible verses, even though all may not be classified as epigrams, and if you refer to the sayings in your daily life, you are using an ancient and proven teaching method. Few but Christians practice this method today and it, no doubt, deserves far more credit for the enduring strength of Christian education than anyone thinks to give it.

Parables. A parable is a short, simple story from which a moral lesson may be drawn. The action in a parable illustrates one abstract idea of a spiritual truth or of good or bad, or wise or foolish behavior. Thus parables are intellectual, aimed at the head instead of the heart. The woman who lost the coin, the man who lost the sheep, the husbandmen and householders of Bible parables are not people like the shepherd boy David, the brave Daniel or other real characters in Bible stories. They are impersonal, and young children do not sympathize or identify with these. Some parables have been rewritten into fine children's stories. For instance, the lost sheep has been written into versions where children can indeed identify with the sheep, feeling sadness at being lost and joy at being found. In this way preschoolers and primary children are introduced in a deeply meaningful way to some of the parables.

By middle grades, children are ready for the intellectual challenge of parables. Some stories, like the good Samaritan, teach how we should behave. Others, like the lost sheep, teach a truth about God or the spiritual kingdom by portraying a commonplace analogy to the spiritual truth. With both kinds of stories, children enjoy trying to figure out the meaning themselves. A group of children can discuss and do this together. If your children have already been taught in Sunday school or somewhere the meanings of most of the Bible parables, they can get this kind of thinking experience from Aesop's fables, also. Children love to read one of these fables to a group, omit the final statement of the moral, and let the other children try to tell its meaning.

A more advanced activity is to choose an epigram and try to compose a parable to illustrate it. This is too difficult an assignment for one child to do alone, but children thinking together, with your help too, can have a stimulating time with this activity.

This task has two main parts: 1) choosing the characters, and 2) devising an action to illustrate the chosen behavior. Sometimes there will be a third part illustrating the consequences of each behavior. Consider illustrating, "It is more blessed to give than to receive." Although it would be possible to have one character who meets a situation two times, it probably makes a better contrast to have two characters, one who gives and one who receives in a similar situation. Your characters could be two sisters or two brothers, perhaps twins. Or you could go Aesop style and make them two monkeys or other animals. This introduces humor and makes it easier to add part three—the reward for giving and disillusionment for wanting to receive. With human characters, the reward is likely to be internal and difficult to show in a story.

Now comes the tough job of inventing the situation. You must think in the pattern of the good Samaritan story where its three characters passed by the same needy man. You probably will recognize it as the pattern of many old tales where suitors vie for the hand of the princess, and the youngest and kindest always wins. Family events that led to choosing a particular saying may help the children to think of situations where the giving behavior or other needed behavior can happen. If the characters are animals, imagination and probably humor can be used more freely.

If your family succeeds in constructing a parable, award yourselves a five-star gold medal and blue ribbon for literary thinking. Invisible rewards will be the growth inside the minds of your children, and in your own minds perhaps some literary growth too, and maybe also an expanded view of educating your children.

Epics. Continuing upward in size from the epigram,

through the parable and larger stories, we come to a literary form called the *epic*. The primary meaning of epic refers to a long narrative poem about a traditional or historical hero, usually a national hero who embodies the qualities admired and emulated by a nation, such as Odysseus for the Greeks and Beowulf for the English. Outside of the dictionary, writers' definitions of an epic vary, and many people would include Job.

Job is a narrative poem, and although its hero is not Jewish, the theme is the common Jewish one of being victimized. This is a difficult book for children of middle grades. They can deal with its story, but for the long, philosophical discourse of Job and his friends they probably should wait until they are teenagers. You may wish to experiment with condensing the discourse. It is a good Bible study, in fact, for older students to select key portions and write out in play form the three rounds of the discourse in Job. With the opening and closing, and with the conversation with God added on, students could end up with a condensed form of the epic of Job, written as a play.

Stephen Mitchell has written a shortened story of Job into English poetry,[3] and its words flow beautifully, giving us some of the feel that it must have in its original language. You may wish to use something like this with older children. A few lines contain explicit language about sex and other private body functions, so you would need to consider how you will handle those, but this is a problem you run into in other parts of the Bible, too, when you study it in detail.

Epic has come to refer also to prose and even to movies or plays that are regarded as having the style, structure, and importance of an epic. King Arthur is an example. The epic of Moses can certainly qualify. To experience this as an epic, children need opportunity to hear or read it in the full power of its story form—from Moses' unusual infancy, his royal education, his choice to stand by his downtrodden people; through his confrontation with Pharoah, leading the people through the

Red Sea, and the wilderness adventures; to his final hours on Mount Pisgah and burial by God. You could read or tell an episode of this story each day until its finale. Or older children in the family may prepare portions and take their turns telling episodes.

Two more good Bible epics are: 1) David, from shepherd boy to great king of Israel, and 2) Joseph, youngest of twelve brothers in Canaan who was sold into slavery, imprisoned, and yet rose to be second highest ruler in Egypt, and whose bones were at last returned to his home. Since Moses carried the bones, these two epics connect and, together, help children understand much of the Hebrews' early history. If you find these epics rewritten into continuous prose story form that you like, you can use those. Otherwise you will need to get the stories directly from the Bible, selecting what applies to the lives of the heroes and omitting other passages.

Poetry. Hebrew poems do not have end rhymes as English poems do, but they have a variety of poetic features. Psalm 34 is an acrostic, having twenty-two verses, one for each letter of the Hebrew alphabet. If someone wrote a similar poem for our alphabet it would be easy to memorize because we could repeat lines in alphabetical order. Each verse of Psalm 34 is also a couplet—two lines for each alphabet letter. Both lines of the couplets repeat the same thought but in different words. Here is how such an ABC arrangement might look in English. The thoughts in these lines come from Psalm 148.

> All the earth will praise its Maker;
> Age and youth will name Him Lord.
>
> Birds will sing and winds will whisper;
> Bells will ring and waves will roar.
>
> Come all nations, join the chorus;
> Carol nature's joyous song.[4]

You could try letting your children look at the above lines and see if they can find what is unusual or poetic about them. The first couplet begins with *A*, the second with *B* and the third with *C*. That is the acrostic feature. There are consonant rhymes: *th* in the first couplet, *w* in the second couplet and *l*, *n*, and *j* in the third couplet, and others. There are vowel rhymes: *a* in *praise* and *name* of the first couplet. The second couplet has the rhyming words *sing* and *ring*. The third couplet has the near rhymes *nations* and *nature's*, as well as *join the* and *joyous*.

All this is too much for children to imitate in their writings, but it is worthwhile to simply raise their awareness that there are many features that make a poem sound like a poem. These features illustrated above are some of those used in Hebrew poems. After a lesson of finding, marking and talking about some of those, read the whole poem aloud again and see if it sounds better to the children now that they understand more about it's form.

One feature that children can easily recognize, and perhaps even write, is the couplet. This is one of the most striking features of Hebrew poetry, and it is not lost in translating into English. In some couplets the second line *repeats* the thought of the first.

I will bless the Lord at all times:
His praise shall continually be in my mouth.

In some couplets the second line *contrasts* with the first.

The young lions do lack, and suffer hunger:
But they that seek the Lord shall not want any good thing.

And in some couplets the second line *completes* an idea or image in the first.

This poor man cried, and the Lord heard him,
And saved him out of all his troubles.

The above couplets are taken from Psalm 34. To learn about couplets, children can copy others from that psalm, or copy the entire psalm with lines arranged as above to look like a poem.

Advanced or older students may try to rearrange the rhythm so it works out better in English. The rhythm feature, as well as the acrostic feature and other alliteration, get lost in translating, so people who translate poetry have an additional job of trying to make a new poem in the new language. Here is one of the couplets rewritten for better rhythm in English. These are not exactly metered lines of poetry, but you could make four slow claps on each line as shown by the capitals.

The YOUNG lions do LACK, and SUFFer HUNGer:
But THEY that seek the LORD shall HAVE no WANT.

An assignment that almost any child can do is to search other psalms for couplets and copy some in pairs to look like stanzas of a poem. Only two days of lessons on the techniques of Hebrew poetry can open a new awareness that leads to a lifetime of greater enjoyment of the psalms and other poetry in the Bible. Children who respond with high interest in poetry should have more than two lessons for exploring the Bible poems.

Metaphor and Analogy. These literary features of the Bible are usually well-taught to children in their Sunday schools and churches, so we will say less about them here. Practically every Sunday school child understands that the sacrificial lamb of the Old Testament is a "type," or picture, of Christ the sacrificial lamb of the New Testament. The story of Ruth and her "kinsman-redeemer" gives another picture of Christ, our brother and redeemer. Many children learn that the curtain in the temple separating the Holy of Holies from the other room was torn from top to bottom when Jesus died, signifying that everyone can now enter into the presence of God. And they learn that as the Temple was a dwelling place of God, so their own bodies, if they are Christians, are dwelling places of God and they should not defile them.

If your pastor preaches on the great analogies and metaphors of the Bible, your children should be there participating in the wonderful literary education.

The Bible as History

Familiarity with the Bible can give children a head start on history. The stories they know of Joseph and Moses and of the Hebrew slaves in Egypt give them a good picture of life in ancient Egypt at the height of her power. Stories of David and Solomon show ancient Israel in her golden age. Stories of Daniel, Nebuchadnezzar and others in Babylon acquaint them with that powerful ancient empire. The story of Esther acquaints them with a Persian king who once fought against the Greeks and lost. A later king, Darius, was overcome by Alexander the Great, and then the Greek empire was dominant during much of the period between the Old and New Testaments. Shortly before the opening of the New Testament, Rome had conquered the Mediterranean world and all the stories of Jesus and the early church happened during the Roman period.

Thus children brought up on the Bible know all the major empires which are roots of our own culture, but few history books help them make connections. In Sunday school they learn of the Hebrew slaves making bricks and in their school books they learn of wealthy Pharoahs building temples and cities and pyramids, and neither learning is allowed to strengthen and add meaning to the other. Any time you can make such connections for your children, they will suddenly be five jumps ahead in their understanding of ancient history.

One reason that connections are usually not made to Bible history is that most courses do not give sufficient attention to the fact that the roots of our own culture go back to the Hebrews, as well as to the Greeks and Romans. Much is made of our roots in pagan Greece and Rome, while the important Hebrew roots are slighted. From the Hebrews, Western civilization obtained its monotheistic religious beliefs; its dominant religion, Christianity, as well as Judaism; its ethics and ideals of justice in law. Much of our greatest literature, art, and music is based on biblical themes. People who know the Bible and can relate it to world history, have a far better understanding of history than those who overlook the importance of the Bible.

History without Bible principles tends to be evolutionary in outlook in almost every endeavor of man. For instance, secular history books often teach that "primitive" religion was polytheistic, and more advanced religions became monotheistic. But from the Bible we know that the reverse is true. At the beginning, people knew and worshiped one true God but people who rejected Him degenerated into their heathen religions.

History without the Bible teaches that the first communication between men consisted of grunts, and gradually languages evolved. Again, from the Bible we know that Adam had language right from the start. Linguistic scholars also cannot find support for the evolutionary view of language. They find, instead, just the opposite—that the so-called primitive languages are very complex, and that passage of time brings with it a simplifying of language instead of an evolving into higher orders of complexity. No one has found a primitive language that is on its way up from cave man talk to civilized talk, either in ancient times or modern times. The findings of linguists do not fit an evolutionary picture of upward ascent of man's intelligence and language ability. They better fit the Bible framework. We could say that there is a "law of degeneracy" in language which began possibly with the curse after original sin or more likely with the "confounding" of languages at Babel. But some history books still teach the grunt theory of language development.

History without the Bible teaches that primitive people were savages, and that savages gradually evolve into civilized human beings. But from the Bible we know of man's sinful nature and that humans without God can act like savages whether they are in a jungle tribe or in a modern "civilized" nation.

Prehistoric times can be especially deformed in history books. More comments on this topic are given in the sixth-grade section of the history chapter. The Bible is now the only reliable source of information about prehistoric times, and its story is brief, taking only the first eleven chapters of Genesis. As with everything else in the Bible, discoveries in archaeology or linguistics or elsewhere tend to uphold the Genesis story rather than contradict it. Some deep studies into Chinese pictograph writing reveal that from about the time of Babel those ancient people knew many details of the Genesis story. And for 1500 years, until the time of Confucious, the Creator God of Genesis was the God known in the great land of China. Civilization meant to those people "the transforming influence of writing."[5] What a contrast to the meaning we tend to attach to the word— that of complex social organization with cities and technology and commerce!

The dispersion from Babel accounts for much else that we learn in the history and sociology of peoples the world over. All have literary traditions of a flood and a Noah figure, of a Creator God, of a lost paradise, and other dim memories of that early time. Heathen religions, too, can be seen as having their roots in Babylon. The many gods of the ancient Greeks, or Norwegians or Germans probably all had their beginnings in the anti-God religious system headed by Nimrod at Babel. Some people, like the ancestors of the Chinese, may have traveled far from Babel, glad to leave that terrible evil, and taking with them stories of the true God. Thus both the true stories and the false stories spread from that same center. While many historians puzzle about whose flood story is the oldest and who copied from whom as it spread all over the world, your children can learn that the Flood really happened so there is no mystery as to why people everywhere have stories about it.

Leaving the early world and moving to later times, the coming of Jesus from heaven to die for mankind is the central event in all of human history. Once sin and death and the curse fell upon mankind and the earth, nothing could restore the original paradise conditions or bring man back to God except the death of Jesus on the cross. That price is paid and the paradise conditions will return, according to God's plan for His creation. The Bible is unique in telling future history before it happens, and students should learn that there is purpose in history. Just as God is the first cause, the Creator of the world, so He is the final cause. History will culminate in the fulfillment of God's purposes.

Learning the Bible as history and as literature is not different from or separate from growing spiritually through the Bible. The predominant attitude today equates spiritual truth with pop psychology, and too many lessons and sermons deal with only this level of Scripture—how it should affect the psychological aspects of our day-to-day living. But the mind and soul need the proteins and vitamins of the Bible along with its psychological sugar.

Bible Timelines. General rationale behind the use of timelines is given in the history chapter. This section supplements that information with some specific Bible timeline ideas.

The simplest, and a commonly used, timeline is to divide all history into B.C. and A.D. Children learning history from the Bible can be taught to make sense from that division of time. Before Christ, were prophets who foretold of His coming. Before Christ, worshipers were still required to make blood sacrifices. After Christ, Paul and other missionaries preached about Christ.

Children who understand this much can then know that Abraham, Elijah and anyone else who built altars of sacrifice must have lived before Christ. Your young children could draw their own first time chart, maybe just a vertical line to divide a piece of paper into two parts. Then you can suggest people or events that they know, and they can decide on which side of the line to write each one. Include some non-Bible names too, such as Columbus. For this first effort, allow young children to simply list or scatter the people and events that they write, requiring only that each item be on the appropriate side of the line.

Here is a more complete timeline which is still simple enough for children to memorize.

Creation
Fall
Flood
Babel
Patriarchs
Egypt & the Wilderness
Conquest
Judges
Kings
Captivity & Return
Jesus
Early Church
Future Events

You or your children can design as simple or as elaborate a chart as you wish, and then refer to it at appropriate times. After

Sunday school all family members can report who or what their Bible lessons were about, and decide where they belong on the chart. What person or event did the pastor use in his sermon? Place it. You can actually write these on or below their divisions of the chart, or you can just talk about where they go, depending on the kind of chart you designed. The same could be done for home Bible lessons or clubs or wherever your children study Bible.

The Bible and Science

An often-quoted cliche says, "The Bible is not a textbook of science." But if we gulp such a saying whole without any chewing time, our brains may suffer from indigestion. I asked, "Why not?" Why shouldn't the Bible be a textbook of science? After all, its author is the One who created all the things we study in science. After thinking about it, I decided the Bible has a far higher standing than a textbook; it is the great source book—the authority by which to test our thinking and hypotheses and conclusions of science. Opponents of Christianity test their hypotheses by evolutionism. We should test ours by the creationism taught in the Bible.

Christians from the earliest days of the church have opposed the same idolotrous views we must oppose today. The early Greeks had false gods of the kind we easily recognize as false—Zeus and others. Later Greeks had more time for education and they were into *philosophy*, which was the word for *science* in those days.

Stoic philosophers said that everything happens spontaneously, that the universe is uncreated and that nature is eternal. No longer was Zeus the lord of the sky who gathered clouds and sent rain and the mighty thunderbolts. Stoics were scientific; they didn't believe the old myths anymore, and since they believed that matter was eternal and uncreated there was no need for any god. Epicureans, likewise (the "eat, drink, and be merry" people), believed that matter is eternal, and the world and all that we see is produced by various motions and forces of the atoms. In biology, Epicurus taught a natural selection (Darwin was not so original as he is given credit for). In psychology, he taught a behaviorism—that there is no soul or mind, but only physical senses which dissolve with the body at death. Thus the "enjoy life" attitude. If there were any gods, they had nothing to do with men.

The Greeks would have been better off with Zeus. It would have been easier to replace Zeus with the true Creator God when someone came to preach creation to them. But their case was less hopeful with their gods of materialism—the physical forces and motions and energy of eternal matter. They were in about the same situation as those who carved themselves idols of wood and then worshiped those gods of their own making. The so-called eternal forces of nature were gods of their own making.

The Apostle Paul said of those Greeks that the preaching of the cross was foolishness to them. The Greeks felt no need for a savior because they had no Creator. So what did Paul preach to them? He preached the Creator God who made the world and all things in it, who gives to all men life and breath and everything else, in whom we live and move and have our being (Acts 17:24-28).

This is the message our society needs today. After people believe in a Creator God, we can talk to them about the Savior. Some students of evangelism have pointed out that response to the preaching of the cross is not what it used to be because today's audiences are like the Greeks. If matter is eternal and spontaneously gave birth to life, and if people are in that evolutionary life chain with no purpose but what they create for themselves, what place is in their thinking for something like the cross? None at all; it is only foolishness. People first need the preaching of the Creator God.

But, sadly, most colleges and seminaries and churches are fence sitting. Most Christians do not seem to understand how fundamental the creation-evolution issue is. They don't see that evolution is the same pagan idea that Christians have stood against for two thousand years.

Evolutionism is no doubt the biggest of the "big ideas" or concepts taught today. You cannot shield your children from evolutionism, because it permeates books, TV programs, and our general culture not only in science but in other areas as well. But you can help your children learn about the opposing big idea—creationism. Understanding the two views and how they differ provides children with a good science education.

The first eleven chapters of Genesis are crucial to such a study. When twelve-year-old children read these chapters, they know what they say. These chapters do not hide secrets that only twentieth century Ph.D's in science can understand. The chapters say that God created the heavens and the earth in six literal days, that He created plants and animals to reproduce after their own kinds (not to evolve into other kinds), and that He created and made Adam in His own image and formed the first woman from Adam's side. Man fell into sin and thus the curse of death came upon mankind and upon the earth itself. After some generations, which are carefully recorded, God intervened in the world's affairs by bringing a great worldwide Flood. After some more generations, God intervened again at Babel, confounding the languages and causing men to begin spreading throughout the earth.[6]

That framework is important for children to know. All the findings of science can fit neatly into it. Most fossils, for instance, can be seen as laid down during the Flood. Scientists who deny a Flood have a difficult time accounting for so many fossils so widely spread, for sedimentary deposits on mountain tops, and so forth. But they keep trying to fit facts into their evolutionary faith.

The Flood year also can account for much of the mountain

building, which otherwise is a mystery and the cause of many unsubstantiated theories. Climatic changes after the cataclysmic flood year brought the ice age upon the earth. Hints of violent storms and of snow and hail as far south as the Mediterranean area are found in the book of Job, which concerns a time not very long after the Flood.

The curse of death, which came upon not only Adam and Eve but upon the whole earth at the time sin entered the world, accounts for the way the world is running down. Evolutionists must believe that the world is growing more orderly—that higher complexity constantly develops from simpler forms. But the natural tendency of things is toward disorder and not toward more order. The facts of science fit the Bible framework better.

When you were in elementary grades there were few books for your teachers to consult even if they had wanted to teach you about the creationist view. But today there are numerous excellent books and periodicals for both you and your children. If you haven't tried these yet, you have ahead of you the greatest intellectual adventure of your life.

[1]*The Educated Imagination* by Northrop Frye. (Indiana U. Press, 1974, p.xviii.)

[2]*Ibid.* p. 110.

[3]*The Book of Job* translated by Stephen Mitchell. (North Point Press, San Francisco, 1987.)

[4]*The Times of the Kings* (children's workbook) by Ruth Beechick. (Accent Publications, Denver, 1977.)

[5]*The Discovery of Genesis* by C. H. Kang and Ethel R. Nelson. (Concordia, St Louis, MO, 1979.)

[6]Unit studies on these eleven chapters of Genesis are given in *GENESIS: Finding Our Roots* by Ruth Beechick, Arrow Press, 1997. This integrates history and other studies with Bible. For older students.

Index